LATE CITY EDITION

LATE

CITY EDITION

by Joseph G. Herzberg

AND MEMBERS OF

THE NEW YORK HERALD TRIBUNE

STAFF

ARCHON BOOKS 1969

REPRINTED 1969 BY ARRANGEMENT WITH
HOLT, RINEHART AND WINSTON, INC.
IN AN UNALTERED AND UNABRIDGED EDITION

SBN: 208 00739 3
LIBRARY OF CONGRESS CATALOG CARD NUMBER: 69-15792
PRINTED IN THE UNITED STATES OF AMERICA

To

OGDEN REID

(1882–1947)

FOREWORD

Late City Edition originally was planned as a new kind of textbook for journalism students. As it took form, however, the book was broadened to make it of interest also to the general reader. It is a book put together by active newspapermen, each writing of a particular field. By far the largest section of *Late City Edition* is devoted to the reporters, because reporting is most vital to a newspaper and represents a paper's essential function. The best reporters make the best newspaper.

How concerned readers may be with the organization and preparation of a newspaper, the editor and contributors to *Late City Edition* make no pretense of knowing. Yet they feel that a presentation of the methods, skills, and problems involved in the daily editing of a newspaper devoted to the best ideals of the press should be important to readers and students. The newspaper is as great a part of American society as the ballot box or the system of free schools. It touches the individual perhaps even more closely. The cheapness and availability of newspapers—the casual reading of them and the preponderance of trivia in their pages—are in themselves a recognition of an accepted tradition in democracy. Much the same way we accept trial by jury or habeas corpus, not as growing out of man's long struggle for freedom, but as things easily come by, like water from a tap.

Late City Edition presents the newspaper as it is. Its intent is to explain what work lies behind the daily front page. There is no attempt to build up newspapers as paragons of journalistic virtue. Neither is there any concerted effort to reply to any of the attacks against newspapers. Those who made this book believe this is no place to labor that question. This is not to say that they see no justification for at least some of the criticism of newspapers. They mean only that implicit in their brief essays about the jobs they do is a belief that they are devoted to achieving the most difficult of all goals—getting at the truth.

Good reporting and editing function with complete freedom from the whim of any publisher. The good publisher gives his reporters and editors such freedom. It is this unfettered reporting, editing and publishing that *Late City Edition* seeks to portray. An honest appraisal would admit that not all publishers fulfill this qualification, but equal honesty must make it clear that there are publishers who value most the objectivity and reliability of the stories their papers use. In organizing this volume, it was felt there was no need for a special chapter on publishing. In a larger sense, publishing the kind of newspaper represented in *Late City Edition* is an end product—a product that results from having everyone, from top editor to newest cub reporter, devoted to getting the facts and printing them that way.

Although throughout the book there are references to the Sunday newspaper, no chapter has been devoted to it specifically. A Sunday paper is little more than a swollen daily and whatever is said about the daily paper is equally true of Sunday special sections.

This book is the work of *The New York Herald Tribune* men and women. There is no particular reason for such exclusiveness except that when the editor conceived *Late City Edition* he assigned various tasks to his friends on the paper. He believed that all knew their jobs well and could best tell about them. The *Herald Tribune* itself has no other connection with the book, although the editor must express his gratitude to the management for its foresight in having on the paper so many helpful people.

Although members of the *Herald Tribune* staff have a monopoly on the contents of *Late City Edition,* their opinions and the incidents they relate are not peculiar to any one paper but are applicable to newspaper work as a whole. It is hoped that the various chapters will be of value both to the student and the general reader. For the student *Late City Edition* seeks to avoid the textbook formula which frightens the hopeful future reporter or editor because such a book teaches reporting and writing by diagnosis. How diagnose a newspaper story when there are a hundred different ways to tell it well and a hundred other ways to tell it badly? For the general reader, the value of *Late City Edition* should lie in having set before him the technique that produces each day a picture of a world of conflicting interests and ideas. These ideas and interests weave a net that draws more and more tightly about us. If we are ever to break through the strands before they crush us, we must be helped by the knowledge offered us in our daily newspaper.

J. G. H.

CONTENTS

ACKNOWLEDGMENTS

Grateful acknowledgment is made to *The New York Times* for permission to quote from the obituary of P. A. S. Franklin, Jr., December 3, 1946; and to *The New York Herald Tribune* for permission to use various quotations throughout this book.

LATE CITY EDITION

[1] THE CITY ROOM

by Joseph G. Herzberg

INTO the city room come the bright and the shoddy, the gay and the sad, the glories of the strong and the despairs of the weak. A modern newspaper is Thucydides sweating to make a deadline. From the Broadway night clubs and from strange places thousands of miles away, the stories come in side by side; the world is measured off once in twenty-four hours, and one who drops a coin on a newsstand and picks up a paper buys a piece of himself each day.

There are many definitions of news but, like the electricity men read by, who knows what it is? The only clew is the one that spreads through newspapers since their beginning in America. In 1690, there appeared the first newspaper in the colonies, *Publick Occurences both Forreign and Domestick;* and its editor, Benjamin Harris, would be a good editor by today's standards. In his paper, suppressed after one day because of something he said about the King of France, Harris had a suicide story, a story about the shortages of husbandmen, a weather story, a piece about an epidemic in Boston, reports of a fire, the war in Canada, escaped prisoners, and ship arrivals. Such events, now as then, are news.

The best editor is the man with an insatiable desire to know the facts of a matter, and an instinctive tendency to be interested in the matters his readers care about. The best reporter is one who lives by this same devouring curiosity. And by indirection, this supplies a definition of news—news is something newspapers are curious about.

Luckier than most of his fellows, the reporter's curiosity is a privileged thing. He can ask questions another man would hesitate to bring up. He can question the suspected embezzler without mercy; ask the bank president if his business is liquid; discuss with the ax murderer the particular technique adopted in delivering the fatal blow. His only touchstone is a simple one—does the reporter himself care to know the answer? If he does, it is news; it is his business to get it.

His curiosity keeps him alert. Asking questions simply as part of a job is an unrewarding pastime, particularly since the person being questioned is usually doing his best to withhold information. But a reporter who is truly curious hears the overtones of the answer, sees the facial expression, notes the giveaways. He phrases his next question a little more deftly than the one that was dodged, for finding out has ceased to be a job and has become a mission.

That is why the good reporter, and the good editor, loves his job. Most of his time he passes doing exactly what he enjoys doing. It keeps him young, which is balance enough for the fact that it also keeps him poor. If he leaves it for a better whack at wealth, he manages at least once a day to say—a trifle wistfully—"I used to be a newspaperman myself."

No two city rooms are alike and in each of them methods of handling copy differ. In general, however, city-room operation follows broadly the system used on *The New York Herald Tribune,* where news is handled by three main desks, as follows:

Local (also called City)—Covers New York State and the entire adjoining states of New Jersey and Connecticut.

Telegraph (also called the National or Domestic)—Handles copy from the Washington bureau of the paper and from all localities in the United States outside the local area.

Foreign (or Cable)—Edits stories from all countries outside the United States.

By far the largest unit in the city room is the city desk, which on a paper the size of the *Herald Tribune* has a staff of sixty reporters and rewrite men and several hundred correspondents within the local area. Overlord of this small army of newsgatherers is the city editor, who fortunately is much too busy to go to the movies. No city editor ever reaches the stage of rudeness considered standard equipment by his Hollywood counterpart. The loudmouthed person imagined by film directors would not last a month on a real newspaper. Any city editor who hopes to do at least a passable job has far too much respect for his reporters to act like a boss stevedore, and without the respect of his reporters no city editor can hope to achieve the kind of news coverage he dreams about.

The modern city desk has available any kind of reporter it needs for the many different types of stories that have to be covered each day. The foundations for good coverage are laid in the staff of district reporters, who never get by-lines or much notice, but who have a lot of friends among the police. They are assigned to particular spots, where they are most likely to hear of anything that might make a story. The nerve center is police headquarters, where men are stationed day and night. When there is any crime or disaster, the police telegraph bureau gets a report from the precinct where the event occurred. The telegraph bureau writes out small slips giving bare details of a crime, which provide enough information for the headquarters man to transmit to his city desk.

If the story is big enough, the desk editor may send out a man from the office to cover the story or, particularly if it is a night story, the editor may use another district reporter to get the details and telephone them to a rewrite man. Often, these night district men hear of things even before the first report is sent to headquarters and some of the more alert operatives arrive at the scene even ahead of the police.

With police news covered by the district men, the city editor must next organize his staff to watch other sources of news. For this he uses "beat" men—reporters assigned regularly to definite spots. The most important "beats" are city hall, the courts, politics, ship news, schools; as news becomes more complex, labor, science, medicine, and aviation require special coverage.

News is so variable that the one thing a newspaperman learns about it is the certainty there always will be something new. For stories that cannot be channeled to his district men or any of the specialists, the city editor uses general-assignment reporters, who cover anything. Where the beat man or the specialist knows the background of any development in his field, the general-assignment reporter begins best when he recognizes that he knows nothing about the story which he has just been handed. Once he picks up a trail the good reporter moves with increasing speed in getting his facts and then making them fit together.

Filling out the staff are the rewrite men, who are most often engaged in taking stories telephoned in by district men and correspondents. From a few notes, a good rewrite man turns out stories of all kinds. Storms, fires, murders are of a piece to a rewrite man with stories about lost children, heroic dogs, trapped cats, and one-paragraph announcements of important dinners. And whenever a big story breaks near deadline, the rewrite staff writes it up.

To tie his organization together the city editor has two sets of assistant editors, one for the day side and one at night. For the day editors, work begins early, between 8:00 and 9:00 A.M., more than twelve hours away from edition time. There is a common phrase, "Nothing is so dead as yesterday's newspaper," but to the man on the day desk yesterday's paper is quite alive. It is the point of departure for him. A well-run paper seeks a continuity in the news and always there are stories from the day before that develop "follows," the newspaper term for stories good enough to produce a second-day story and in many cases for many days thereafter.

Besides the stories which must obviously be watched for further developments the day editors may choose stories from the "futures." These are clippings from earlier papers, announcements sent in by organizations, suggestions and tips from staff members, all of which tell of events scheduled to take place on a particular day. For example, the American Museum of Natural History may be holding a special meeting or there may be a hearing on the budget before the New York City Board of Estimate. In a city as large as New York, hundreds of these events are listed each day and the assignment editor must pick the ones he believes will produce the newsiest stories.

Even as he culls these announcements, fresh things happen in the city. On the *Herald Tribune,* reporters start their day at 1:00 P.M., and let us say that at 11:00 A.M. there comes a flash from police headquarters that a beautiful young woman has been found brutally slain in her apartment in East Fifty-second Street. The district man at headquarters phones in his information and the editor checks in the newspaper library to see if anything has been printed about the victim. He assigns a reporter and also notifies the picture department, which will send out a photographer and check its files and those of picture services to unearth photos of the slain girl.

In covering the story, the experienced reporter goes to the murder scene and familiarizes himself thoroughly with the layout of the apartment. Suppose the husband of the victim has vanished. The reporter talks with their neighbors, searches out their friends, and pokes into their past, seeking the tremendous minutiae that might possibly indicate the reason for the slaying. Always he must be watchful of the police and the district attorney, who question various persons and attempt to keep such information away from newspapermen, sometimes successfully but more often not.

By early evening, the reporter has gathered all the details available up to that time. When he returns to the city room, the night city desk is functioning. The night city editor has the assignment sheet, complete with the names of the reporters and the stories on which they have been working. Where necessary, the day man has added verbally to the bare statement on the assignment sheet, giving any facts which will help the night side in getting the story written properly. Using a day picked at random, an assignment sheet might carry items such as the following:

REPORTERS ASSIGNMENT SCHEDULE—OCT. 19

Arm	Beautiful young woman slain on East Side; cops seek missing husband.
Donovan	Civic groups ask budget cuts; fight brewing over ten-cent fare.
Donovan	Mayor confers on airport as union groups continue jurisdictional fight.
Snyder	Tammany Hall divided by intraparty squabble.
White	Scientists organize to fight for control of atom bomb as tool for peace.

These are a few of the assignments that would show up on such a day. Before the reporter begins to write, he gets a "slug" for the story from the editor. "Slug" is a newspaper synonym for "name." The story of the murder of the young woman probably would be called "Slay." This slug is written across the top of the first page of the story and will be repeated on each page thereafter. Both in the city room and in the composing room, where the type will be set up, this slug is the sole identifying mark for the story. Without the use of such a simple device any newspaper office would be a madhouse.

From the day's stories the night city editor makes up his own schedule, giving the slug, the space allotted, and a brief description, all for the benefit of the make-up man. Still using the slain young woman as an example, the night city editor's schedule would read in this fashion:

SLAY 150 East Side beauty slain, husband sought.

The "150" refers to the length of the story. For a full column of 7½-point type the typewritten equivalent is about eighty-five lines. Knowing the length of the story is important to the make-up man, who must allow sufficient room for it on the page where he wants it to go.

After the night city editor reads the story for errors he sends it to the copy desk, where further corrections are made and the headlines written. From the copy desk the story moves to the night desk, where the night editor or his assistant are quick to catch errors of fact or a misstep in an overplay or underplay of a story. Notice particularly how, throughout the entire movement of a story on its way into type, the perspective changes. First, the reporter is close to the story, and no reporter is worth anything unless he believes that the story he is working on is the best story of the day; next, the city desk, which, although eager for the best play it can get for local news, has at least twenty main stories to handle and must judge each against the others; next, the copy desk, one step removed from the city desk, which is interested only in seeing that the story is accurate and that the best headline is written; then the night desk, which handles copy from all the desks and is able to assay a story, not from the vantage point of any desk—local, telegraph, or foreign—but in the larger pattern of the day's news.

Of final importance to the judgment of a story is the managing editor's conference, where the night city editor, the telegraph editor, and the cable editor list their top stories before a critical group headed by the managing editor. It is at this conference that the leading stories of the day are sifted and the best of them arrayed in the newspaper's showcase—page one.

Work on the telegraph and cable stories also begins early in the day. While the cable and telegraph deskmen actually do not come to work until late in the afternoon, the stories they subsequently will edit are being prepared almost everywhere around the world.

From Washington, the telegraph editor at 6:00 P.M. or so receives a schedule detailing fifteen or twenty stories of major events in the nation's capital. The *Herald Tribune* Washington bureau under a bureau chief has men assigned to the White House, both houses of Congress, the State and War Departments, to labor, and any other government activity that promises to produce important news.

A typical day in Washington might develop a schedule as follows (to cite a few leading stories):

1. Day in Congress (box).
2. Treasury Announcements.
3. War and Navy Dept. Changes.
4. Industry leaders tell Senate portal claims will bankrupt aircraft, injure steel, etc. N.A.M. counsel sees flood of suits equal to portal to portal because of lack of clarification of other phases of Fair Labor Standards Act. Tobenkin 700.
5. Senator Taft attracts record turnout at Press Club luncheon, where he says strikes have done the nation no great harm, despite their number, and should not be banned. Taft may add to his leadership jobs by taking chairmanship of joint economic committee, which can't decide whether to act now on Truman economic message. Twitty 600.
6. Vandenberg says legislation being prepared to give businessmen and farmers more influence in tariff planning after conferring with Clayton; latter, seeing hard fight ahead for reciprocal reduction, turns most of his duties over to assistant to push program among legislators; other angles, with budget request, house investigation of British loan breach. Warner 600.

The telegraph editor will substitute a slug for the number given above. No. 4 becomes "Portal," No. 5 "Taft," and No. 6 "Tariff." The name at the end of each story is that of the reporter and the "600" or "700" gives the wordage.

The telegraph editor also has Associated Press and United Press copy duplicating his bureau file from Washington; and from other cities throughout the country he has stories from the AP and UP and from the paper's own correspondents or special bureau, such as Chicago. Frequently, out-of-town stories are covered by reporters from the local staff, whose copy is telegraphed or telephoned into the city room. Use of the telephone to transmit stories has increased in recent years and the *Herald Tribune* has a special recording room, where the reporter's voice is recorded and then played back for typing.

The telephone, as well as cable and radio, and occasionally air mail, also brings in the stories from correspondents stationed in many countries in Europe, Asia, and South America. These reporters operate under the foreign editor, who is nominally in charge of all news from areas outside the United States. Actually, it never works out this way. The Antarctic, for example, is covered by the Washington bureau because only the United States Navy, with headquarters in Washington, can move copy by radio from Admiral Byrd's expeditions. The moon, curiously, falls to the city desk as a local assignment, because radar signals bounced off the moon are recorded in New York. Even the reporters in Asia and Europe, many thousands of miles nearer the news than the foreign editor, usually advise him of a trip, or a temporary change of assignment, after, rather than before, it happens.

It is still the foreign editor's job to try to make sense out of the coverage of the entire foreign world by a paper's foreign service. Some of the bigger newspapers and news services have established a multitude of bureaus in all the world's major cities; others, and chief among them the *Herald Tribune,* have tried instead to keep a small number of central foreign bureaus and to develop around them roving reporters, specialists in ideas rather than on areas, who can take full advantage of quick and cheap modern transportation.

In either case, it is part of a newspaper's function to keep these far-flung correspondents reasonably in touch with American life and with the interests of its readers, and this is the chief job of a foreign editor. In doing this, he can control to some extent the main pattern of foreign news which reaches his paper, and can make something a little better than a coin-tosser's choice as to what developments in foreign countries will be covered, and what disregarded.

In the case of the *Herald Tribune,* the job is a little more complicated by its publication, in Paris, of a six-days-a-week European edition, which requires frequent synchronization in news and in policy with the New York edition. Almost all papers in the United States which maintain foreign services number several foreign newspapers among their syndicated customers, and this means that the foreign editor of almost every big metropolitan newspaper must also concern himself, as best he can, with the readership habits and tastes of men and women who are far from being his neighbors.

The stream of copy from the local, cable, and telegraph desks begins to flow with mounting speed after 5:00 P.M. and reaches its peak three hours later. Each desk is a dam, designed to hold back the river of words and let through only a relatively small trickle. The art of newspapering is to know what to leave out and to condense what is left.

After the managing editor's conference, the make-up man from the night desk consults the night city, telegraph, and cable editors and gets from them the slug, length, and nature of each "spread" story carrying the largest head. After the managing editor has approved the layout of page one, the make-up man spots his stories and pictures throughout the rest of the paper.

Important as they are, local, telegraph, and foreign news do not make up all the paper. The sports, financial, business news, real estate, fashions, society, amusement, and marine departments all organize their stories, prepare their copy, and make up their pages along the same general lines as do the main news desks. The editorial writers, under the guidance of a chief editorial writer, develop their comments and opinions of the news. The daily features that spice a newspaper—comics, cartoons, columns—are set up in advance by the paper's own syndicate.

Despite the flood of copy from so many departments, the editors, by a system of copy control, know at any time of the night where they stand in relation to the amount of space they have, how much copy has been sent down, and how much "overset" there will be. Overset—stories that are crowded out—is something every good newspaper has. The best paper must be created from a total number of stories which add up to 20 to 35 per cent more copy than can be jammed into the available columns.

The copy-control system divides the newspaper into two main sections—the number of columns for advertising and the number of columns for news. This news space is subdivided into two parts—one part for general news, which comes from the local, telegraph, and foreign desks and the second for reservations, the space required for the other departments and features. Under reservations on the *Herald Tribune* go the number of columns allotted to editorials and letters, sports, financial, business, real estate, radio programs, marine, society, amusements, women's pages, fashions, weather map; also included in this space are such features as Walter Lippmann, Sumner Welles, the Alsops, Mark Sullivan, Elmo Roper, and Lewis Gannett's book review, not all used on the same day but spread out over the week. The reservations also note the space required for any texts the paper is prepared to print.

The copy-control system works in this fashion: If the paper is 40 pages, or 320 columns and there are 155 columns of advertisements, that leaves 165 columns for all the news. From this 100 columns are to be deducted for the reservations, allowing a hole of 65 columns for general news. On an ordinary night, local may take 30 columns, telegraph 20, and foreign 15. These allotments change, of course, as the weight of the news shifts, with one of the three desks getting a lot of space while the other two suffer a cutback.

The night editor always has to cope with overset. Late stories may be better than those sent to the composing room earlier and the new stories must be set, even if the paper has more than enough type to fill. Other stories may be left out because some pages closed early and type destined for those pages cannot find other places in the paper.

As the first edition goes to press, these overset stories are "proofed up." A galley proof is an impression of the type before it is put into the page form. It is called galley proof because the type, as it passes through the various stages in the composing room, is laid in narrow trays, called galleys, which are generally about three inches wide, an inch more than the width of the type. The type is locked in the galley by wedge-shaped pieces of wood called "quoins."

The overset proofs are delivered to the night desk and if the editor there finds stories on these proofs that should be in, he makes the necessary "kills" in the paper, thus allowing room to transfer matter from the overset. He also may have to kill out stories already in the paper to make room for late pictures, or conversely he may have to drop some pictures to gain space for important stories. Between the first and second editions, the night editor has an hour to accomplish all these changes and he needs trained newspaper judgment to help him to decide which story should be in the paper and what can be safely left out. He not only must be sure that the story he picks to print is better than the one left out but in many cases he must keep in mind that opposition papers might give a heavy play to a story he rejects.

Papers are torn apart each edition on the night desk as late stories develop. The city desk may have a late fire or homicide, a terrible quake may have killed thousands abroad, or an important man may die at any hour. So highly skilled is the organization and so dovetailed the work of the separate desks that these late stories get in, although they may require many changes in the make-up of the paper. Stories are shifted from page to page, new pictures constantly arrive, space must be made for late theater or music reviews. The presses roll through the night and when they stop another twenty-four hours of world history has been set down.

[2] THE CUB

by Thomas P. O'Hara

HOW sad it must be for the new clerk to walk into a bank and report for the first day's work. Or how fearful the new curate, ringing the rectory doorbell and asking for the choleric old pastor. Again, how corroded and woefully burdened the new lawyer feels as he begins the slow climb upward in a great law firm, suspecting that years may pass before he hears the thump of a jurist's gavel.

These young gentlemen have nothing on the cub reporter.

Bravely, the new reporter steps into a chattering, chaotic city room. Not until he semaphores from here to Philadelphia does anyone pay attention. Every pair of eyes seems to burn at him.

The suspicious guide steers the newcomer over to the city editor.

"Here's a man who says you've hired him," the guide reports, leaning heavily on the word "says," as if the city editor is obviously losing hold.

After an oblique glance, the city editor comes back biliously:

"Yeh. It's O.K. I hired him. . . . Siddown!"

What was to have been for the cub an exhilarating occasion, one for which he had waited, at least in these modern times, for years, seems powerfully flat. Self-torture sends live ants running about the cub's stomach. His equipment seems quite inadequate.

After all, he muses, a young doctor brings to his new office a set of shiny tools. The still-stiff brief case of the beginning lawyer is jammed with applications for writs, liens, show-cause orders, and other obstructions. But the cub brings only his still formless experience. Often he does not even have a pencil.

Let's call him Jerome K. Jones, just out of journalism school. Jones is compounded largely of myself and a distillate of many other reporters whom I know. Despite his seeming gawkiness, the compound of Jones is doing good work today, although it never seemed that way to me in the beginning or to the other men. Assigned to a desk, Jones finds in somewhat less than five minutes that he is not going to get the lead story. He sees that the mayor does not shoot the city's richest banker over a Hollywood cutie every day, nor DDT poisoning panic a filled cathedral and, if either happened, Jones would hear about it by reading it in the paper. No. Jones is told to rewrite several press releases.

The first few are easy: a charity drive in its twenty-eighth day reports current totals, an outsider is made an associate professor at the local university, but one is a bit knotty. In assigning the work, an assistant deskman mumbled something about a list of names in one item telling of officers elected at a late session of a convention not worth covering.

The nervous cub failed to catch the orders. He writes a windy piece made dull by his laboriously typing all the new officers, including those from Bountiful, Utah, and New Hope, Pennsylvania. After handing it up, the assistant gives the cub his first, albeit lenient, hell. The piece appears in the paper, completely rewritten with, as was requested, the names of the four local men elected.

These chores done, Jones lights a cigarette. The clinical eyes of the staff all seem to turn on him. Jones frames a fixed smile at them but when he does they turn away. All right, bucko, Jones thinks, I'll be your managing editor some day, your better, or at least your equal. It won't take long, either. Don't I, Jones goes on, have my friendly rejection slips, and haven't I hit several times with pieces of fiction?

When people talk I listen hard, he recalls. For some reason they all talk freely to me—gravediggers, upholsterers, tree surgeons and ferry-slip greasers. They've been doing it for years, including, alas, some of the most voluble, beat-up bores now operating. Now, I am going to put them on paper and into this newspaper. Maybe, someday, write stories that other reporters will clip and take home as, Jones knows well, he has done himself.

In the meantime, already hating the wheezing typewriter at his desk, Jones explores the desk drawers. Yellowed writing paper with the office letterhead is strewn about the top drawer. A copy of *Swann's Way,* its binding broken, and with a round stain that might very well be from a beer bottle, lies underneath. Broken pencils, the cap of a fountain pen, an ancient telephone-bill receipt, crusty expense blanks are in another drawer. Stuck on its side are a couple of two-cent stamps, unused but now useless. In the bottom drawer is a pair of overshoes, one with a hole in the right sole.

Fingering an unlighted cigarette, a pleasant man in his late forties ambles over from a group of staff men who stand in a friendly, but clannish, group near the city desk.

"Hello, there," he says easily, asking for a match which, Jones guesses, the man almost certainly has.

"I'm Henry Beneville," the man says, "and practically the only member of the staff without a police record. Just avoid what the city desk tells you and you won't go wrong around here."

After more hyperbole, Beneville tells Jones that the desk just assigned him once belonged to Lefty Coe. Lefty, Beneville says seriously, was a highly polished operator of pencil, telephone, and typewriter. Coe, he continues, covered the federal beat and had so many friends among judges, customs inspectors, revenue and F.B.I. agents that he was said rarely to have bought his own lunch. Fine, answers Jones, fine. Where is Lefty now?

"Dead," Beneville answers, as he is called away to take a story on the phone, ". . . heart trouble."

Jones is all set to brood over the unused stamps and the worn-out overshoes when, he, too, is ordered to take a phoned-in story. After adjusting a complicated headset, he hears a squeaky voice on the other end. Jones adopts a superior attitude to the correspondent, calling from Gatesville forty miles away. Discovering to his horror that he can barely understand the man, he instantly forgets his defensive superiority. The correspondent sounds as if his larynx were dripping rust.

In between the gibberish, Jones frantically gets the idea that the man is giving a good story. It's a report on a long-drawn-out investigation by a special state commission over elimination of three grade crossings where many persons had been killed and which had plagued Gatesville. The correspondent is a chronic repeater and expander.

That is, he repeats the same facts and, when not doing that, he expands on them, considerably changing their sense. The man on rewrite cannot be sure when to push his pencil. The phone torture over, Jones calls for a copy boy and asks to be shown the library because he knows that he will be using it frequently. Like every library staff in the country, the workers are friendly, indulgent, and helpful, although they are convinced that reporters' heads are made of Indiana limestone. Quickly, they ferret out the clips. None of them is short and the story is obviously important to the paper.

The correspondent reported that one of the crossings is approved for elimination by one of the three commissioners who sat at the day's hearing. That man's recommendation, however, must go to the state capital for review by the full commission before final action. Briefly, it is not the biggest story of the day, yet even Jones knows that it must be deadly accurate.

Given a half column to write the story, Jones digs his spurs into the typewriter, eases up on the reins, and is off to the races. Tantivy, tantivy, tantivy! His cascading words pour out: death, blood, weeping parents, the dastardly railroads, and the Great White Father of the special commission.

Not until approximately 8:00 P.M. three days later does the smoke clear and Jones admit in his secret heart that he was dead wrong. Meanwhile, of course, Jones had felt aware enough of his surroundings that, after handing up his story, he watched it being given to a prematurely fat rewrite man. The man snickered slightly at Jones's gem and, running his typewriter faster than most stenographers can, clicked out the story.

When Jones cooled off three days later, he knew that he possibly had committed gross libel, certainly had editorialized, but, worst of all, had incorrectly located one of the three grade crossings. Only that the city editor benevolently remembered that he, too, was once a cub prevented Jones from being fired. Perhaps, too, the city editor reckoned that the desk man was careless in giving the story to a new man.

Not that a new man is necessarily incapable of good work. Sometimes his very newness gives him a tenacity that an older reporter lacks, and wins him his first gentle applause. Benching Jones for a moment, I can still get a certain pleasure recalling the pat on the back I got soon after starting with *The New York Herald Tribune*. I was sent on a suicide committed by a young, deranged father who lived in an exclusive section of New York. The youth turned a .22 caliber rifle toward his heart at three in the morning and pulled the trigger. Details were meager because, as reporters soon discover, police quite fairly show little interest, professional or otherwise, in suicide. Once they are convinced, as they were in this case, that murder is not involved they close their notebooks and return to the station house. At such times, they have learned, families are in enough torment without having husky strangers, such as policemen, standing around too long.

But suicide is news and I had to hold on. The detectives gave me the name of one of their informants. That was Freddy, the night superintendent of the apartment house, a tubby, watery-eyed man who was pale from years of nightwork. He lived near the apartment house in a typically dark, New York walk-up apartment. A ring at the doorbell brought his wife. Yes, she said to my extra-civil approach, Freddy was in but he was asleep.

I expected this. Could I drop around later, after Freddy was up and had breakfast? Well, the wife hesitated, she guessed that I could try, but Freddy was up very late the night before and she wasn't sure whether Freddy wanted to see reporters. I put on my hat and left. Understandably enough, a telephone call to the family yielded little news but there were scraps of information to fit into a jigsaw. The dead man's age, twenty-five, his son's name and age, the fact that the father was being treated by a doctor. Like some two million other people I was to meet in the next few months, the relative on the phone maintained that the family were terribly intimate with officials of my paper and knew all sorts of high policy men who were, for the most part, mere names to me.

The detectives had said that the young father had been running around the public hall in his pajamas. There must have been a fine free-for-all in that apartment house, I guessed, before the man pulled the trigger. If I could get that from Freddy, it would give the reader the key, the Big Why of the tortured man's self-destruction. At first, I was hesitant about leaving the street where Freddy lived for fear that I would miss him; then I realized that I wouldn't know him if I fell over him. A foot in the door approach? No, I decided as I walked about the neighborhood, Freddy and I would have to be sitting down to get anything out of Freddy.

Two hours later, I was admitted to the small apartment. Freddy was still eating lunch. At last, he came into the living room. Cigarettes were lighted and Freddy started by saying that he could not talk, then proceeded to talk. He told how the dead man had begun by throwing things at his wife, then at his parents, and how he ran out of the apartment into the hall and was coaxed back. Finally, he ran out into the hall and this time refused to come back. The family called Freddy, for in the years that the family had lived in the house the young father had developed a liking for Freddy. Freddy came upstairs, he recounted, and pleaded with the man in his quiet voice to go back to bed.

"O.K., Freddy. I'll go to bed for you," the man said. As the superintendent said that, I knew that my time had not been wasted. I would have been content to have been told of the disturbance because it showed the suicide's mental state but the man's promise was even more pointed. A call to the family physician brought out that the suicide had been under treatment for an unspecified ailment and that the elderly doctor had to walk a dozen or more blocks to the house when he failed to get a taxi. The shot was fired before the doctor arrived but after Freddy had returned to the lobby, certain that all was quiet once again.

More than anything else, however, the man's promise to Freddy showed the suicide's hostility to his surroundings, justified or not. I put the line in the story as quickly as I found a place for it. Next day, the city editor himself came over and repeated it. Grinning like a cat, he asked me how I got it and, I said, it meant nothing more than a two-hour wait.

It was by no means an unusual story but, once all possible sources are run down, one to be treated with compassion. And such a story is a signal that the generic Mr. Jones is moving into deeper water, using his water wings less and less. He is getting his share of the brute work of journalism. That meant taking a copy of a speech to a dinner, luncheon, or convention as a second man for the paper's experienced men, following Senator Hardblow's prepared speech word for word to make sure he stuck to the text. The reporter writing the story near deadline simply cannot be in two places at once, a biological weakness of man which annoys city editors.

It meant, too, covering union headquarters or management offices, again as stooge for the veteran reporter, because a strike call or settlement was due, as always inappropriately seems to happen, near deadline. It meant, still for these cursed darlings, hanging around for hours in ether-drenched emergency wards after a disaster to get the best available list of dead, injured, and eyewitness survivor stories. Quite by whim, however, some of these top reporters gratuitously tell the city editor that he would not have been able to beat the *Morning Opposition* but for Jones's faithfully sticking on the job and keeping his eyes open.

Deviously, these good reports get back to Jones. He feels wonderful. Even he knows that there's a good deal more hoeing to be done, and already he has learned that a reporter should consciously pretend on every assignment that he is bucking for the Pulitzer prize. Unmistakable signs indicate that he is not so alien to the paper. The surly old receptionist, for example, who first brought him into the city room (which, curiously, does not seem noisy any more), now is a genial old party who says "Ga, morning," as Jones gets off the elevator. Other reporters let him in on their ceaselessly variable likes and dislikes toward the deskmen, always in proportion to the yield of their assignments. The Five Star Final, a saloon across the street from the paper, probably will not cash a check—yet—but it won't be long.

More chilly was the rough-and-ready disregard Jones got on his first bath as a police reporter. Here, he decided, was the last vestige of the true tribal spirit. Sunday feature writers get bunions climbing the inner fastnesses of Tibet and the backwoods of Tennessee, or plodding among the Indians of the Southwest looking for antisocial clans. They are running up unnecessary expense accounts. All they need do for their research is to live for several days among police reporters. Whether on East Side, West Side, or night headquarters, the police reporter stares at the newcomer and, before he has opened his mouth, turns thumbs down.

As Jones came to see, the men, for one thing, are generally expert in their line. For another, over the years they have developed sources, some of them good and some of them completely wet, and dislike letting the likes of a whippersnapper in on them. Too, police sometimes open up to friendly reporters too much for their own good and an avid newcomer might lovingly quote them verbatim and by name, making them a risk for a departmental trial. All this Jones learns later. During the red-hot present, about all Jones gets to phone to his office is what crumbs this *cordon sanitaire* sweeps his way.

In the end, Jones finds many of them tremendous workers. A few are mulishly dumb and have been generously carried for years by their alert fellows. Some are sick at heart with the crime they cover: the most sordid, bestial murders; the assaults committed by dirty little psychopathic punks; the weird sex offenses, and the toothless, numbskull wife-beaters. While the little offices of some police reporters may be in the shadow of their own newspaper's plant, some among them have the fear of the AP stringer in Outer Mongolia; that they'll be forgotten and cut off the pay roll in the first economy wave.

Another phase begins for Jones. Some of the deskmen call him "Jerry," in place of merely "Jones," or, perhaps, "Hey, you." Longer stories are given him and they are moving closer to page one. That is, solo jobs. Goodness knows, Jones has been out front innumerable times but as a dog robber for other reporters. He knows by heart that desk rigmarole on such assignments: "Jones, I want you to . . . and give it in to Glotzback, he's been handling this sort of thing."

Jones's slowness is disappearing in his writing and his passion for minutiae is gracefully dying of experience. Only recently Beneville, now his good friend, told him that he would wind up in the booby hatch or at least get occupational ulcers if he tried to get the name, shield number, and previous meritorious record of every one of two hundred policemen who made a mass gambling raid, as well as the arrest record and sentence served of those picked up. But, alas, Jones is still being rewritten.

At the typewriter Jones has the sensation of the hick from Seedville with his suit four sizes too small. Hurrying back to the office, he hits on his lead idea and has burnished off phrases that positively terrify their inventor. They also terrify the deskman reading copy. Over and back goes the pencil, cutting out the gems. For several days Jones will peer in the editor's face to see if, behind that placid façade, there lurks a secret madness. Obviously (reasons Jones) the holdup-man type, behind on his morphine payments.

This violent deduction wears off when, even though it was a long, agonizingly long time, Jones gets his first story out front. An auto manufacturer, anxious to preen over his firm's war record, writes the city's mayor, asking if the firm may exhibit two Sherman tanks in the city. The mayor is dee-lighted. Appropriately, one is moved to Sherman Square, the other to the Argonne Monument. To Jones it seems a mighty small story that will fit under a picture full of gaping kids. With the company's handout and a visit to the tank at the Argonne Monument, where he noted an innocuous sign about the tank's manufacture, Jones has plenty of information.

After a debate with himself over whether to waste another twenty minutes, Jones walks over to Sherman Square and right into a municipal hornet's-nest. A park regulation bans any advertising within park limits and the great tanks are given three hours to get out. The tank maker's press agents are there in full force and one gives Jones a quick look at the mayor's letter of invitation. Jones copies it word for word. He hurries back to the office, digs up the park director and obtains an apoplectic statement from him. The mayor, too, now sides with his park chief. Jones does the story, a simple straightforward job.

The story is handed in to the same editor who, Jones thought only the other day, was losing his grip.

"That's all good stuff, Jones," says the editor.

"Aaaaaah, it was nothing," Jones assures the boss. "I've worked harder on more difficult stories."

Jones looks hard at the editor, wondering if a certain Thing is going to Happen and whether the editor will mention anything about That.

"By the way, Jerry," the editor says chummily, "I would have put a by-line on that piece but we have it made up for a three-column cut with the story starting underneath for a couple inches and jumping inside. It's a style we never use a by-line on."

After Jones says that It's Perfectly All Right, the editor starts back to the chopping block that is the city desk. As he moves away, he says that a by-line will be forthcoming soon. Soon.

[3] POLICE REPORTER

by Walter Arm

THE New York police reporter is as far removed from the popular movie version as Manhattan is from Hollywood. The big-city newspaperman who covers crime news may be as dashing, as handsome and as sickeningly puckish, sometimes, as any screen replica. But he rarely, if ever: solves a major mystery; badgers gangsters into confessions; cleans up a town singlehanded; tells the police commissioner what to do; or tells his boss, profanely or otherwise, where to get off.

In the first instance, he hardly ever gains such a complete knowledge of a case that he could solve it. As for the second, he rarely meets a gangster (most criminals are stumble bums), and, if he does, he does not badger, because the gangster's chums might badger back—with a blackjack. As for cleaning up a town alone, or any other way, he soon learns that New York is awfully large and awfully dirty. He seldom tells the police commissioner anything because he considers himself lucky when he meets that elusive gentleman and luckier still when the P.C. talks to him. As for telling off the boss—well, jobs are getting scarce again; his wife and children would not like it.

No. The police reporter is not a grotesque nor superhuman character. He is, for the most part, a conscientious, hardworking newsgatherer, who tries to get the story, and the reasons behind it, as quickly and as accurately as possible. He is handicapped greatly in this endeavor by the size of his city. Unlike crime reporters in smaller localities he is not pampered by police, nor so chummy with them that he can invade their territory indiscriminately. There are so many reporters and so many policemen in the city that friendships are rare between them and, in New York, getting the inside of a story is based primarily in most instances on such friendship.

The police reporter is a man with a knowledge of the police and their methods; and has become, through experience, impervious to rebuffs from them and from other persons from whom crime news is dragged. The news he deals in is more colorful and exciting than most newspaper subjects but it is also dreary, sordid, and gruesome. Such news must be coaxed from heartbroken, suspicious, or otherwise reluctant people, including the police.

The only time a story comes easily is when a quick arrest is made or a major crime finally solved. Then the police officials, most of whom had nothing to do with the case, preen themselves, clear their throats and rattle off reams. But when the crime fighters are stumped, their mouths clamp shut, their eyes harden, and the police reporter is given short shrift.

It is here that the crime reporter proves his value. If he is capable, he tries to get his own facts from witnesses and principals in the current melodrama. This, tied up with the tiny bit he gets from the police, generally adds up to the story. If he is experienced, as well, he may be aided by one of those rare creatures—an intelligent officer who understands the value of publicity and appreciates a bit of help himself. If he is neither capable nor experienced, he depends on the scanty information the official police source may dole out, or cribs news from other reporters, and comes up with the routine, the ordinary, the colorless story.

A police reporter soon learns—or should—when the person he is questioning is lying, or evading, or embroidering a story for his own benefit. He learns to sift the fact from the fiction; the logical from the illogical, and to spurn the percentage men who try to use him. The things he sees and hears make him a skeptic, ofttimes a cynic, and give him a low estimate of the human species. But if he wishes to remain an asset to his newspaper and a human being as well, he retains some feeling and compassion as a balance.

Sometimes he finds reporting in the largest city in the world a bit repetitious and humdrum. But his working hours are spiced by the thought that at any time something might happen which would drive the cobwebs from his mind and the foreign news from page one.

His daily work consists mainly of wading through the unending series of incidents which occur in the metropolis at the rate of about one every five minutes.

A child is missing; an automobile accident occurs; there is a gang fight; a despondent man jumps to death; a fire bursts into fury; a man kills his wife and puts a bullet through his own brain; a storekeeper is robbed and slain.

Items like these, not items but heart-rending reality to those involved, flash constantly across his vision, like drug-maddened insects in a flea circus. They happen in all sections, throughout all layers of the social scale, and sometimes become grist for the news mill. Their news value is judged by the newsworthiness of the actors in them, the unusualness of the situations, or some rare angle which a reporter knows will appeal to the hearts, the tear ducts, or some other sense that newspaper readers possess. Mainly, he weighs these stories and finds them wanting in interest other than routine. And while he checks them and then either telephones them to his newspaper or writes the story himself, he is looking constantly for that outstanding story to come along. Each item may hold the germ of such a story, but only investigation and questioning can uncover it.

During the lulls in his work-life, he cultivates his contacts among the police, if he has any; makes new ones, if he can; and gets to know his city and its laws so that he can answer intelligently any questions asked by anyone—particularly his boss.

As has been said many times before, New York is a big city. Its thousands of streets are jammed with millions of family units, and bubble continuously with incidents and events which sometimes reach the public through the police and the press. For a newspaper to watch constantly all of this activity is impossible. Even to try to cover it by telephone and automobile is a superhuman task. And so New York, for the purpose of better police work and police reporting, is cut into segments, like a gigantic pie.

Most dailies divide the city by borough, assigning one man to each. They reserve for Manhattan, apparently the magnet for mass madness of one type or another, additional subdivisions and extra reporters. The borough of Manhattan is generally cut into three districts. The first of these covers the lower section of the city from the Battery to Fourteenth Street. The second and third split the island up Fifth Avenue and are known as the West and East Side districts.

Like the newspapers, the police department also divides the city—but for a different purpose. To protect 7,500,000 residents and their visitors, who average another million daily, it employs eighteen thousand policemen who patrol eighty-five precincts daily, in three eight-hour shifts. The largest number of men are concentrated in the busy and most important parts of town but all areas are linked together by telephone, teletype, and radio. A policeman no longer summons aid by striking his night stick on the curb. Modern science does the calling for him.

Heart of this vast signal and information system is the telegraph bureau on the top floor of police headquarters, 240 Centre Street. Every occurrence large or small which necessitates the calling of a policeman finds it way to the bureau. Here, almost every minute of the day and night, the police announcers call instructions and orders to the hundreds of radio patrol cars and patrolmen, and move miniature replicas of the cars on a huge map, like so many chessmen.

For the police reporter this is his initial source of news. This, and the police teletypewriter in the lobby of headquarters which taps out the events of the day in grim, unemotional phrases.

Compared to police reports, the reputed phlegmatic Englishman is a chatterbox. The most unusual and important stories and the ordinary variety comes through the teletype in almost identical language, and it is here that experience and instinct count and the police reporter is measured. He must be able to decide within a matter of minutes whether the bare facts outlined in a police slip, generally in about ten words, may be worth looking into or whether it should be ignored. If he were to decide to play safe and check each slip, he would soon find himself sliphappy. So he studies the language, spots the location as newsworthy or not—although this is not always the best basis for judgment—and makes up his mind whether to follow or forget.

Of course not every slip means such a mental coin-tossing operation. Some of them speak for themselves, and knife through dull language like a searchlight through a sewer. Even the police cannot hide, if that is their intention, the really outstanding stories. On July 28, 1945, for instance, a slip came through at 10:00 A.M., which read: "14th [West Thirtieth Street] Precinct. Smoke observed on upper floor of Empire State Building."

Only a few minutes before a B-25 Army bomber had crashed into the seventy-ninth floor, killed fourteen persons, and sent tons of debris crashing into the street. The slip made no mention of an airplane, or crash.

Yet even the lowliest beginner can tell you that a fire, any kind of a fire, in the world's tallest building, is worth covering. That is why reporters rushed to the scene before the teletype had ceased chattering and were there before police had time to establish their lines.

As in the case of the Empire State crash, important stories cannot be hidden behind dull police language. Good stories, not quite as important, can and are. The police reporter must rely on instinct to unearth them.

For example: This writer was watching the police teletype one dull night several years ago and could find nothing that seemed worth a story. He glanced idly at a slip which said: "Mrs. So-and-so, of 214 East Third Street, dead in bed. Contagious. Nothing suspicious."

Normally such a slip, especially when it bears the last two words, would be passed over. Too many people die in bed. But this writer kept returning to the item. The word contagious intrigued him. What kind of disease did she die of?

The house where the woman had died was not too far away. The writer hailed a cab and was there shortly. He found a police sergeant at the door of the room, who said, "Aw, there's nothing to it. There's nothing contagious. The cop on the beat made a mistake. He was told not to let anyone touch the body until the medical examiner arrived and thought this meant she had a contagious disease."

The reporter shrugged and thanked him and was about to leave when the sergeant remarked: "If it was contagious, her kids would have been sent to Willard Parker Hospital; as it is they've gone to the Children's Shelter."

"Kids?" the reporter asked. "What about kids?"

"Well, it's like this," the sergeant said. "This poor dame's been dead about three days and her kids have been in the house all the time. They thought their mother was asleep and they'd still be there if the neighbors hadn't complained about the smell. You don't think that's a story, do you?"

The reporter did and soon learned that the children, a three-year-old girl and a one-year-old boy had been living on scraps of food and waiting for mother to wake up. The story made page one.

The police seldom recognize a story or what makes a story. But a policeman is not paid to recognize stories. So far as he is concerned he is paid to do his job, which is to stop violence, capture evildoers and put in his eight hours a day without getting reprimanded. When his work is done he wants to go home, dip his tired feet in hot water, and forget everything connected with the job.

Most policemen believe a reporter spells trouble. They were told to have as little as possible to do with newspapermen, when they were taught the rudiments of police work, and they live up to that warning—that is most of them do.

A reporter means questions; questions mean answers; answers may be embarrassing, and embarrassment is something a policeman can do without. For years the stock answer of many police has been, "Aw stop asking so many questions."

This does not apply to all. Many policemen, and the majority of detectives, are part of a new generation; a generation with more education and a better understanding of the world than the old-time cop. Police are beginning to realize that a good case and good publicity can bring commendations and promotions. They are changing for the better, from a newspaperman's point of view—slowly but surely.

But the "brush off" is still one of the crosses a police reporter must bear. He is "brushed off" so often that he has come to expect it and if it doesn't happen he gets suspicious.

There are different kinds of "brush offs." Some are polite; some are sarcastic; and some are downright rough. The police, however, are learning to shy away from the latter and use it only in emergencies.

Luckily most police are poor psychologists and when they use the emergency "brush off," a reporter assumes, and rightly, that they are hiding a story. It is often an odds-on bet that the story concerns another policeman.

One such example comes to this writer's mind: police reporters find it helpful to visit the station houses in their district just to pass the time of day with police lieutenants and detectives and in the hope of picking up a story.

One New Year's Eve this writer dropped into a Harlem police station just before midnight. He greeted the desk lieutenant with a smile and the customary "Anything doing?"

He was not a bit disturbed when the officer answered his greeting with a jerk of his head and growled, "No."

He passed the lieutenant's desk and headed for the rear of the station house and the staircase which led to the detective squad room. He was barred by a patrolman before he could reach the stairs.

"Whaddya want?" asked the cop.

The reporter identified himself and told him.

The patrolman answered, "No one goes back there. I don't care who they are."

This reporter had been going "back there" for years. This was the first time he was ever barred. He knew something was up and tried to pass the policeman. He slipped under the cop's arms and just had time to see a matron stretched on the floor, her head blood-soaked, when he was treated to a sample of the emergency "brush off."

For the moment he was helpless. He could only glare at the officer, smooth his coat and ruffled feelings, and retreat.

Outside the station house he noticed an ambulance and questioned the driver. He was able to learn that the matron had been struck down by a prisoner who had escaped.

Armed with these facts he confronted the lieutenant and demanded more. When this was refused he called the inspector in charge of the district and that official soon appeared on the scene. He knew that the story was partly out and ordered, "Give him everything." The lieutenant outdid himself.

Like many secretaries who brush people away from their bosses in the mistaken belief that they are protecting him, so the policeman thought he was protecting the good name of the department by trying to cover up an incident which was no one's fault but the prisoner's. Incidentally, the prisoner was captured a day later.

Many times obtaining a story depends on luck. Reporters call them "breaks." It may be the break of getting to a story first or, it might even be the break of getting there last.

For instance: Two oil-filled tankers collided in New York Bay one February morning in 1945 and caused the deaths of 40 seamen and injuries to about 150 others. All survivors, many badly burned, were taken to hospitals in Staten Island. The early reporters on the scene rushed to them to get the survivors' story of the disaster.

This writer was hours late. So late that when he arrived the fire was completely extinguished and all survivors had been taken away. That is, all but one. He was a seaman who became lost in the hold of one of the burning ships and stumbled into a refrigerator for safety. He remained there until the fire was put out and was brought ashore just as the reporter arrived. The story of his experience led all the others.

Not all police stories are bloody. One day in the 1920's three elephants wandered away from a circus in Harlem and entered the West 123rd Street Station House. They tramped ponderously past the desk lieutenant, whose eyes widened in amazement, and on into the back room where a group of patrolmen were filling in reports. The policemen took one look and dived into the courtyard from near-by windows. The lieutenant called the emergency squad and when he told them why he wanted them, they laughed and refused to answer his appeal.

Finally, he convinced them and the emergency squad found it had quite a job on its hands. It took three tubs of lard and the combined efforts of ten patrolmen to coax and push the pachyderms out of the precinct.

The 1920's were a lush period for crime news. Almost daily some gangster or another was taken for a ride and the killings became so monotonous that they soon rated little more than a paragraph. The killing that stands out in this writer's memory is that of a gentleman named Petey Redshirt. Petey was slain as he crossed 116th Street between Third and Lexington Avenues, one cold, rainy night. His body fell in the center of the street, exactly in the middle of two adjoining police precincts—the East 104th Street Station and the East 126th Street Station.

Police and detectives from the former precinct arrived first and they found that Petey presented a problem. He was in neither precinct. The problem was finally solved by a shrewd sleuth who ordered the policemen to drag Petey over to the north side of the street. "We've got enough unsolved murders," he said. "Let's give this one to the other boys."

All the interesting people are not other newspapermen, but some of the funniest are. For instance there was a district man on the old City News Association who was called into the office one night to do rewrite.

He was asked, "Can you use a typewriter?"

"I certainly can," he replied, and started to walk out of the office with one of the machines. He was sent back to district reporting.

One reporter for an afternoon newspaper, a veteran of twenty-five years, was extremely conscious of his lack of formal education and always trying to overcome it. As a result he bent over backwards, used big words in the wrong places, and talked in heavy tones, with all the dignity he could muster.

One night a group of police reporters rushed to a hotel where, they had learned, a woman had killed herself. She had signed the register "Jane Doe" and there were no clews to identify her. Detectives finally consented to allow one reporter to take a look at her.

The evening newspaper reporter was chosen. He returned soon, his folded copy paper filled with descriptive notes. The other reporters gathered around him and he began:

"Gentlemen, the corp was dressed—"

"The corp?" one of the reporters interrupted. "You mean corpse, don't you, Johnny?"

John lifted one long finger and replied scornfully, "Singular, gentlemen, singular."

[4] GENERAL ASSIGNMENT

by Peter Kihss

THE Boy Scouts' motto "Be Prepared" could as well be the motto of every reporter.

I remember one assignment when the Duke of Kent arrived at La Guardia Field en route to visit President Roosevelt in the darker days of war.

One reporter outshrieked the hubbub as the duke's advisers sought to spirit him away from inquirers.

"Why can't I ask just one question?" she cried.

The duke heard her, and told her to ask it.

Feebly came the only thought of the moment: "How is your dear mother, whom we all admire so much?"

A reporter must be prepared to take advantage of opportunity, his story planned like a campaign, his strategy allowing for tactical changes in a fluid situation.

Any number of questions might have produced a worth-while story in the Kent case. Most obvious was: "Could he say a few words on the purpose of his trip to the United States?" Or: "Was he carrying a message to President Roosevelt?" Or: "Could he tell us his impressions resulting from the inspection of Canadian air-training facilities, which he had just concluded?"

A reporter must also—elementarily—be present.

After seventeen outstanding years as a Washington correspondent, Raymond Clapper turned columnist. In a magazine piece I did on the change, Clapper said there were three clews to getting scoops:

1. Luck.

2. Keeping in circulation.

3. Studying up the situation so as to know what to expect—and when to get your hunches.

Not only does a reporter have to know his sources. He must be on hand when the story is ready.

The alphabet of reporting contains two *p*'s—preparation and presence—as well as the five *w*'s of who, what, when, where, and why.

Stories attain print because they are either interesting or important, sometimes both. The interesting is important to a few; the important is interesting to a few. But a newspaper has a responsibility to print the important, and it blazes its own trail in deciding what is interesting.

In setting out to cover a story, there is first the problem of equipment. Pencils. Paper. Ridiculous as it would seem, there always seems to be some reporter on a story who is trying to borrow the ordinary tools of his trade.

Ordinarily, reporters use copy paper, folded twice the short way, for taking notes. But on assignments that may last several days, such as a court trial or a conference, many reporters have taken to employing hard-covered stenographer's notebooks, an item which was snubbed some years ago. A notebook can be especially handy on out-of-town assignments, where it assures against loss of old notes and acts as a substitute filing cabinet.

The general reporter finds himself assigned to stories which technically fall into three categories:

1. ACTION, such as a fire, a crime, a court trial, or even a meeting, consisting of speeches and debate.

2. SITUATION, such as the maneuvers involved in politics or strike threats, commodity shortages, holiday travel, and what newspapers sometimes label surveys and sometimes laud as crusades.

3. **Personality**, commonly an interview, sometimes the obituary of an outstanding individual.

In all stories, the more the reporter knows in advance and the more he knows what to expect, the better off he is. He should read his own paper thoroughly, his competition as fully as possible. Every bit of background will come in handy some day.

A general reporter should at least get acquainted with every outlet from which a story may emerge—police stations, courts, fire departments, city hall, state and federal offices, business and industry, transportation, health, food, aviation, the armed forces, hotels, sports. Someday he'll be shot out suddenly on any one of them.

He should know his town. A reporter hearing the fire alarm clang at the press room in police headquarters generally has a book which identifies the location of the call box.

John Riseling, night city editor of *The Washington Post,* started me out on a first alarm one midnight, a fire call from Twelfth Street and Pennsylvania Avenue, two blocks away, a hub of the District of Columbia. Almost anything at that location would be of interest to Washingtonians.

It turned out that the new Post Office Department building was afire, and our cameraman and I got there with the fire chief, before the engines. We got inside the building, and started tracking down the source of the smoke clouds rolling from the sixth floor. That fire lasted eight hours, with forty firemen overcome, water pouring spectacularly down walls, stairways, and elevator shafts. We covered it from inside the building, phoning from the office of the Federal Communications Commission chairman, one of the advantages in starting out fast.

Make a list, mentally or on your notes, of the places you're going, and what you've got to find, or what you hope to find. Where is the fire? When did it start? Who turned in the alarm? Who got hurt? Who performed outstanding feats? What burned? What was the cause? What was the damage? How was the fire fought? How long did it take to control?

A police commander on the scene is normally the first source of news. Next, get the fire commander. Then try for anyone who sounded like an interesting story from the first checks.

And keep looking.

When a Mitchell twin-engine bomber crashed into the Empire State Building, every newspaper in New York flooded the story with reporters. Everybody who could get inside went to the seventy-eighth and seventy-ninth floors, where the plane struck.

As a morning newspaper, *The New York Herald Tribune* had the benefit of ample time. Several of our staff, therefore, decided to scour all the floors above, and as many as possible of the floors below, to scoop up additional angles. On the eightieth floor, I went through a suite whose walls had been seared. Even a cactus plant had shriveled in the heat. In the innermost office, I saw an oval hole, broken two and a half feet high through a four-inch wall.

It had possibilities. The desk pad revealed the name of the tenant. A phone call to the city desk started a reporter out to his home. It turned into a dramatic yarn. A girl operator had been blasted out of her elevator. She fled into the office. Two men swung the door shut on the flames leaping behind her. One of the men seized a claw hammer. He smashed open an escape way through the back wall. He had the strength of desperation. I know; I tried hammering the wall myself, and with only academic stimulus, all I could do was dent it.

The reporter has first to size up his story, and frequently, in an afternoon newspaper or a press association particularly, to telephone a bulletin. He must be conservative. I remember one paper I worked on when a new reporter telephoned an excitable rewrite man. It was a fire and explosion in a three-story downtown building. "The building's a goner," the reporter cried. "Razed?" the rewrite man pressed. "Sure," rejoined the reporter.

That's what the first edition said. Another reporter was on the job by the second edition. Only the first floor had been wrecked. In the second edition, we put up the building again.

A few elementary points in telephoning will make any rewrite man's life happier. Know what you're going to tell him, and how. Summarize: "This is a fire story—fire and explosion, three-story building, first floor burned out, nobody inside." Sometimes it's better to telephone a story as if dictating the actual copy, lead first. Sometimes it's more comprehensible to give it chronologically, the way it happened.

Remember the fellow on the other end is taking notes, and it's all new to him. Especially on names, and on quotes, be sure you understand each other. There are lots of variations of almost any name. Lewis might come out Louis, if you don't check.

Too many reporters dismiss a story simply with the obvious. There is a "why," not only in national and international stories, but in what goes on in the next block. One day a mother and son committed suicide in Washington. At the scene, it developed that the apartment contained considerable literature from a pacifist organization. A telephone check showed the mother had frequently visited the organization in recent days, and was well remembered. The last time she'd gone there, she said she knew war was coming, and she couldn't stand the possibility that her son might have to fight. That extra item certainly offered strong circumstantial evidence of the thinking that ended in the tragedy.

Whatever else happens, the reporter on an action story has to realize that he has a communications problem. The best story in the world won't mean much to the paper, if it doesn't get printed. The reporter has to know his deadline situation. He has to hunt out several available telephones. Or he has to set up telegraph service on an out-of-town assignment, and allow for delay in transmission.

Some fantastic things can cause delay, and he must keep watching his service. Once I was working in Montevideo, Uruguay, covering a Pan-American conference. We wrote our copy and filed it early, about 5:00 P.M. New York time. Next day, we had a cable reminding us in strong terms that we were working for a daily newspaper, and that our entire file arrived two hours after edition time. Some genius in the cable office had heaped all the press copy in a stack, filing from the top down—so that the latest copy he received was dispatched first, and the earliest last.

The situation story is one that frequently allows for plenty of time. Often it is developed in the office, by sheer arduous telephoning. Often it takes the most effort; often it is the least rewarding in terms of reader interest.

Preparation for such a story is immeasurably aided simply by keeping comprehensive lists of sources checked on previous occasions. Situation stories have a habit of recurring. Every holiday, a city desk craves a story about the condition of transit lines, the attendance at beaches, the tallies on accidents. A list is not only convenient, but it is a check to assure that you have covered all the major possibilities.

For instance, in a roundup of food conditions, such a list would include federal, state, and city government officials in the field; trade associations representing producers, processors, wholesalers, and retailers, and any consumer organizations. Not all the sources on the list would have to be checked daily. But during the war, my list of news sources on meat problems alone ran up to some fifty names for the New York metropolitan area, and a day's necessary checks involved a dozen calls and more.

In situation stories, there is a lamentable tendency among reporters to begin quoting "officials" or "quarters" without using names. This is often mere laziness in failing to get an elementary fact—a man's full name or his title. In the first place, a name always lends authenticity to a story; in the second place, it establishes the validity of the source.

As a jest which elsewhere might have been founded on experience, the administrative officer of the American delegation to the United Nations Atomic Energy Commission once posted a cartoon on the wall at the office entrance. The cartoon showed a man passing a girl at a switchboard. On the switchboard was this notice: "The opinions of our receptionist are not necessarily those of the management."

How true. And how often the opinion of a subordinate fails to represent the responsible opinion of an organization whose views are to be depicted in a newspaper.

Sometimes, particularly in a diplomatic story, the source refuses to be quoted. If enough sources are checked, the item can be verified sufficiently to be printed as a fact without qualification. At least, there may be some other way of writing around it, such as that "thus and so was understood" or "the company public relations office reported."

A situation story is the kind that often determines whether a newspaper—meaning the reporters behind it—has responsibility and balance. A story can be handled in a variety of ways, but not all of these ways would represent the whole truth.

There was, to cite a case, the tale of the dramatic relief from childbirth pain, derived from the technique called continuous caudal analgesia. That relief was definite news. It was widely recounted and heralded. Equally as important was the necessity to point out that only a distinct minority of American mothers could benefit by it. As of May, 1944, for example, 60 per cent of American births took place at home, where there were not available the safeguards required for that technique. Of hospital births, 10 per cent of the cases arrived so late that the method was inadvisable. Of the 30 per cent left, the method was contraindicated for specific reasons in two-fifths. And of the 18 per cent then remaining, delivery could be comfortable naturally, or one of four other anesthetic methods might be preferred. All this should have been pointed out in full coverage, as well as the fact that the physicians trained in the method were relatively few and widely scattered.

Nowhere is a newspaper's power and its responsibility to the public demonstrated more speedily than in a situation story. In his classic autobiography, Lincoln Steffens tells how he and his fellow New York police reporters built up a crime wave.

First, Steffens scooped the town on a humorous burglary yarn, in which the two crooks persuaded the policeman on the beat that they were moving household goods—and got him to help them. Next day, Jacob Riis reported a burglary Steffens knew nothing about. Then the whole group of police reporters had to go out to get the best possible exclusive crime stories, as a defense against city-desk outcries.

In a trice, the police were being excoriated for inability to cope with the rising tide of lawlessness. The truth was that there were even fewer crimes than normally, and arrests were on the increase.

It was all in the matter of selecting what got into print.

Basic to any reporting is the interview, commonly a personality story, sometimes important for its color, sometimes for its substance, often only the elementary acquisition of fact in an action or a situation story.

In many cases, no reporter was on the scene when a story happened. He has to reconstruct it; he has to be sure of the reliability of the person to whom he is talking.

He has to learn elementary tact in talking to his sources. Courtesy is not apparently one of man's instinctive graces, and yet there is no God-given right of newspapermen to invade a man's privacy, or to ply him with multitudinous questions. A first rule would be to treat a subject as you'd like to be treated yourself, and to convince him of a good reason for taking the time to talk to you.

A reporter's contacts grow by his manners and by the way he has handled past stories. Such stories need not always have been favorable. Raymond Clapper wrote a book, *Racketeering in Washington,* which exposed nepotism and the other varied little grafts characteristic of the capital. He named names. Men respected Clapper, his fairness, and his facts. They kept talking to him.

Every source is a different problem. Some men will be glad to sit down and explain a problem from the beginning. Most men like to consider themselves authorities on a subject, with the inquirer a learner at their feet. Mayor La Guardia, of New York, on the other hand, was a genius, who found it difficult to be patient with the mediocre. It was a mistake for a regularly assigned city-hall reporter ever to ask temperamental La Guardia an elementary question which could be answered by looking up the city charter.

It is the interview, the personality story, which allows the freest hand to a reporter, the yarn which often makes reporters' reputations as craftsmen and writers. One of the best, Joseph Mitchell, of *The New York World-Telegram* and later *The New Yorker* magazine, said once that he just let his subjects talk. The more they talked, the better the story got. There are various tricks of priming the interview pump. Sometimes a man will get started on a significant line simply by a question about what he considers the most pleasant thing that ever happened to him.

It is not always mentioned out loud in nonjournalistic circles, or even in schools of journalism, but one of the facts of reporting life is the existence of pools, or reporters' combines. This is a system evolved in practice for one of two reasons—either because the particular reporters have to cover too many places to be physically in all of them when a story breaks, or because some of them are just plain lazy. It is frequently used to intimidate a non-co-operative or overenterprising reporter by holding out stories and beating him with the combine's joint effort until the city desk howls, and the nonconformist gives way.

It's a bad system, which sometimes can't be helped. In New York, the pool has probably gained its acme of development. The number of daily newspapers—nine major dailies as well as the local service of the Associated Press—means that a news source could be so inundated by individual questioners that he wouldn't talk to more than one or two reporters a day, if he wished to preserve his sanity.

Thus, one reporter will make one call for the combine, while another reporter checks a second source, and the product is pooled before edition time. Bellevue Hospital became so habituated in years past to the work of Robert Dwyer, of the old City News Association, that hospital officials of all grades virtually declined to talk to other newsmen, insisting on their getting clearance or information from Dwyer, the only regularly assigned reporter at the building.

Up against a pool system, a reporter can easily find himself in considerable trouble because of misrepresentation or misquotation. Not all reporters in a combine have an equal passion for accuracy, and I've seen cases where reporters at the same press conference heard different answers to the same question, or said they did.

In a libel action, it would be a fine coup for a complainant's attorney to tell a jury about the carelessness with which second-hand charges against his client's reputation were accepted and circulated by the defendant newspaper's reporter.

Up against the pool problem, the reporter ought to use any information from his colleagues only as a tip source—going out to check it whenever possible if he is going to use it. Wherever possible, he would be better advised to be the one to go out and get the story, passing it out to the mob if necessary, but at least relying on his own ability.

The more a reporter learns about the way stories are got, the better off he'll be. This is one of the great advantages of that occupational characteristic of newspapermen—talking shop. Learning how another reporter went after a particular story can afford a hint for another day, suggest a new source or a new tactic.

A fire flared one night in a top-notch Connecticut Avenue apartment house in Washington, just ahead of first-edition time. I was on rewrite, and I started making telephone calls to neighboring houses, police and fire officials in an effort to accelerate coverage of the story. (Such calls, incidentally, are made by use of the reverse telephone directory, which many large cities enjoy, and in which numbers are listed by addresses first, instead of names.)

A few calls established that the two-alarm fire had been rapidly controlled. The directory also showed that two Supreme Court justices, a senator, and a former ambassador lived in the house. The building had been largely evacuated during the fire, but for luck, I thought I'd call their numbers. I'd read somewhere about some one doing a stunt like that in Philadelphia.

It turned out that the celebrities had generally stayed in the building during the fire. Justice Willis Van Devanter hadn't even known there was a fire. Justice Benjamin N. Cardozo classified the fire as minor, and remained reading law books in his library. Mrs. W. S. Culbertson, wife of the former ambassador to Chile, even went up to the roof for me to get some detail on the damage, the kind of helpfulness a reporter dreams about.

There are occasions when a story is almost entirely made over by the fertility of a reporter's ideas, and it is then that a reputation is born. Chicago journalism has enshrined the memory of Frank W. Carson, a city editor of the flamboyant "Front Page" era. The hanging of Carl Wanderer, killer of his wife, was on hand. Carson thought it should be a memorable hanging. "What hobbies has he got?" Carson asked Charles MacArthur, then a reporter. "Nothing," said MacArthur. "He just kinda sits in his cell and hums."

Carson's brain fevered. He went to the murderer, and induced him to sing a song as he stood on the gallows. It was: "Old Pal, Why Don't You Answer Me?"

[5] GIRL REPORTER

by India McIntosh

DURING the sixteen years since I bludgeoned my way into the newspaper business with a timid smile and a few modest exaggerations about my ability, I have read, and listened to, at least two-score reasons why women should not be reporters—and I have gone on being one. So have hundreds of other women, neither brave nor foolhardy. So will hundreds more.

The explanation for this is simple enough: To the woman who wants to be a reporter, there is only one world—the newspaper world—and there are no forces within that world strong enough to keep her out of it.

Fortunately for the modern girl reporter, a handful of hard-working newspaper women before and after the turn of the century established a beachhead in this once masculine realm and so softened up the opposing forces that today the battle is a mock one. The girl reporter is still in a minority, but she isn't an enemy; fraternization is no longer frowned upon, and the garrison of the city room is a benevolent one.

Under the old law of the ill wind, World War II and the man-power shortage hastened this happy state of affairs. The woman reporter got the biggest chance she had ever had to prove that she could cover, at home and abroad, anything that came under the heading of news. Today, some skeptics will sit back and say: "So what? She didn't achieve complete equality with men reporters." My reaction to that is: So what? Give her time. After all, women haven't been asking for equality of any sort for very long, but have you noticed them lately?

The modern woman reporter holds as firm a place in the newspaper business today as her masculine colleagues. The public takes her pretty much for granted, and there is a decided decline in the number of quips she hears about sob sisters and the woman's angle, whatever that is. She is seldom reminded of her sex or her supposed limitations by the men with whom she covers fires and homicides, meets ships, shares taxies, and sits in on that diabolic institution known as the press conference which is geared to the lowest and slowest mentality present (not hers). Most of the men in her office seem to like her.

The big question then is: How are women treated by the city desk, that upper-case POWER which can annihilate with a word, a knitted brow, or a pantywaist assignment every minor triumph that the girl reporter has gathered unto herself?

In general, I would say that the city desk today tries harder than it ever has before to look upon its men and its women reporters with equal eyes; it succeeds on every score but one—assignments. The general-assignment girl is joshed, instructed, bawled out, or complimented in the same manner as a man; she is considered stable enough physically to endure any hardship, and stable enough mentally to decide whether or not a story exists in the set of facts which she has gathered. Glancing back over my own experience to the days when most girl reporters were considered a damned nuisance, I find myself wanting to slip off into a beautiful complacency about the whole thing: The girl's at home in the city room and folks there like her and nobody is trying to push her out and what more does she want?

But that is only momentary. The one thing which the girl reporter must yet achieve is the right to carry a man's full load of responsibility. On the whole, the stories which she covers are one-day stands; they are tidy little episodes which can be packaged in three-quarters of a column and then forgotten. With hungry eyes, she watches the men reporters draw most of the running stories—the big stories, with many facets, which splash page one for days or even weeks, surging to a climax or boiling over into half a dozen stories or fading to a one-line head as imperceptibly as the Cheshire cat faded to a grin. The city desk, with all its democratic leanings, is wary of the woman reporter's emotional equipment, and it seldom dares to put these traditionally unstable factors to a test which might smear up the front page.

Personally, I am willing to concede that the city desk has a point there. Despite the heroic records of a few Page One Girls over the years, and especially during the war, woman's stamina in the deadline squeeze is more or less an unknown quantity. Women suffer more openly on the deadline than men do. Being a woman, I know that tearing one's hair and groaning aloud do not interfere with a girl reporter's efficiency. But I am reasonable enough not to expect a man to know this. The city desk is masculine; therefore it harbors man's innate distrust of woman's emotions. Let us not quarrel too much with this attitude for the time being. It, too, will pass.

Meanwhile, the general-assignment girl gets around and for every dull day there is a bright day lurking just behind the city desk. Her by-line may not glitter too frequently on page one, but in virtually any given month she will see more of life than most women see in a lifetime. Hers is a glamorous profession and if she doesn't know this, then it isn't her profession.

Certain stories seem to the city desk to fall naturally into woman's province. Broadly speaking, these naturals involve women or babies or both. The girl reporter is by no means limited to such stories, but she gets a lot of them and if she is smart she makes the most of them. Women and babies wangle themselves into every type of news: murder, politics, disasters, barroom brawls, war stories, human interest yarns—the procession is endless. In their ignorance of city-desk policies, women and babies even get on the front page. No woman reporter should ever destroy the desk's belief that she has a special gift for writing about women and babies; as a matter of fact, she has.

With the exception of the stories which lead the paper (usually involving politics, labor, major disasters, or big-time crime) and the women-and-babies stories, it seems to me that the news around the city room is rather equally distributed among the men and women. Perhaps the general-assignment girl gets a little more than her share of the Worthy Causes (during the war that was certainly true); but she can console herself in her boredom that this is a tribute to her new-found accuracy, her painstaking attention to details, her modern reliableness. She can console herself thus because the woman reporter was once under black suspicion on all these counts; yet the Worthy Cause story frequently is what is known as "a front office must." That means that it must have more commas in the right places and more names spelled right than any other story.

During the war I poured my heart's blood into Worthy Causes. So did every other woman reporter. We pleaded in hundreds of thousands of words for the public to buy war bonds, support Red Cross campaigns, join the various nurses' corps, and give to the Army and Navy, their men, their women, their dogs, and their spyglasses. We griped a lot but deep down we knew that those stories were important and we were sort of proud of the job we did on them. They seldom bore a by-line, but a lot of them graced the front page.

The public today accepts the woman reporter, but it can't refrain from exclaiming every now and then, "But you don't look like a reporter!" That brings us to the question: what does the woman reporter look like? She looks like any average, wide-awake girl. She isn't as sleek and brittle as the secretary-to-the-first-vice-president type of career girl. She is seldom an intellectual and she doesn't look like one. The jittery, tough-talking, picture-snatching girl reporter of the mystery thriller is rarely seen in today's city room; the few of her number that exist are regarded around the office as "characters."

The general assignment girl is at home in police stations, courtrooms, public offices, hospital emergency wards, a lower East Side tenement, or a suite at the Waldorf. She covers the whole field of human relations, but she doesn't let the rough side of these things get under her skin any more than a man does. She interviews famous people and people who think they are famous. She stands with veteran shipping-news reporters on icy piers until her feet seem nonexistent, her mind numb, and her ambition dead. One day she goes down into the Tombs to talk to a seventeen-year-old who murdered his mother; the next, she sips cocktails at the Plaza as she listens to a thirty-nine-page lecture on The Art of Keeping a Speech Brief and To The Point.

These assignments are familiar to every man reporter. They are the newspaper business. The girl reporter is in it almost up to her dreams.

There are some definite advantages in being a *woman* reporter. Policemen, judges, important executives, and elevator men get a certain elation—the old knighthood spark, I suppose—out of giving "the little girl" a break. The modern newspaper girl, as a rule, is too enlightened, too proud of her near equality, to indulge in feminine sorcery for her ends; but she has common sense enough to know that being pleasingly feminine, in the better sense of the phrase, won't hurt her any, and it frequently helps her.

Every general-assignment girl can recall dozens of instances when she received extra little tidbits of news merely because she was a woman. They weren't scoops by any means but they made for more complete stories. To produce a superior story, a reporter knows that he not only must outwrite his rivals; he must dress up his yarn with details or scraps of information that everybody else overlooked. Since these scraps are usually in the possession of men, it's no trick at all for a girl to get them.

About two years ago, a B-29 Superfortress overshot a runway at La Guardia Field and crashed in flames in Flushing Bay taking its crew of five to their death. As soon as the bulletin flashed into our city room, I was dispatched to get the details and telephone them in to a rewrite man. Far across the maze of runways, I could glimpse the smoldering wreckage afloat on the water. There seemed to be only one way to get there in a hurry, so I took it—a beeline across those runways. Naturally I looked around to see if any planes had the same idea and they hadn't. I was halfway to my goal when I was spotted by Vic Barden, chief of the control tower, who took after me in a patrol car, siren screaming. He was a very angry gentleman when he took me into custody and told me what ought to be done with reporters who cluttered up runways.

Now, I am certain that if I had been a man, Mr. Barden would have severed all relations between us—at the least—after delivering his lecture and removing me from his airfield. I am certain because he said so. But because I was a woman, a pitiful looking creature, red-nosed and shivering in the frosty wind, and obviously repentant for my grave misdeed, the chief of the control tower hadn't the heart to toss me off the field as I deserved. Instead he drove me to the wreck and during the ride he gave me a complete account of the accident, including details which could only be known to the control tower. Mine was the only story which told where that plane was going. The other reporters had to be content with an Army handout but I got my facts straight from headquarters; the finished product showed it.

Certainly, I wouldn't advise women to go around breaking rules on the strength of this hovering gallantry. I never purposely broke a rule in my reportorial life, but when a reporter is chasing his story he sometimes steps over boundary lines before he is aware of it. When these infractions arouse the choler of a policeman, a pier guard, a fireman, or a court clerk, it is better to be a woman.

If a woman is well enough informed to prove that she scratched around for background before tackling her subject, financiers and bootblacks will explain the intricacies of their trades to her with infinite patience. They don't expect her to be bright enough to swallow their story in the fast gulps meted out to men. The girl who doesn't step into the library before she goes out on assignment does a tremendous amount of harm to all newspaper women; she is a menace and there are too many of her. I'll mention just one case in point, admittedly an extreme one. I could list a hundred lesser cases.

Several years ago, when I was working in San Antonio, Texas, I went around to interview Franklin P. Adams, who was there on a lecture tour. This veteran newspaper man was in one of the worst Adams rages of all time when I arrived. He was so mad that he wouldn't even tell me what he was mad about. Fortunately, there had been a witness to the episode which upset Mr. Adams and from this witness I obtained the facts which were later verified by Mr. Adams himself. A bright young thing from one of the other newspapers had preceded me by a half hour. She was a cub, but that could not excuse her error because her newspaper had a morgue with plenty of clippings and reference books. With notebook ready and pencil tip neatly moistened, she opened her interview with the brisk, businesslike question: "Now Mr. Adams what did you do before you went into the movies?"

The only way I could get my interview with Mr. Adams in the black wake of my little rival, was to promise not to ask him any questions at all. That is something of a handicap in an interview.

Newspaper women, like newspaper men, never seem to be able to remember anybody's experiences but their own when they spin a yarn. I am typical in this respect, so the rest of this story will be splashed with a lot of personal pronouns.

I started in the newspaper business sixteen years ago, but during the 1930's I took time out to marry and have children. When I resumed my career in 1940, I found that a lot of changes had taken place during my eight-year absence. The woman reporter was on friendlier terms with the city desk and she was accepted by the public. But remembering my lonely cub days, the change which impressed me most was the new attitude of men reporters toward the girl reporters with whom they covered assignments. During the war, this new attitude grew vigorously.

The woman reporter who acts as a working reporter should be accorded exactly the same treatment a man is accorded by nearly all the newspaper men she meets on assignments and in public press rooms. In return, she pays her way, she doesn't lean on the men either mentally or physically, and she shares or withholds news in strict accordance with that unwritten code of newspaperdom under which a reporter is entitled to keep certain facts to himself but must impart others to his fellows except in cases of exclusive stories or exclusive angles. This rule can no more be defined than that elusive quality "a nose for news." Every good reporter knows it but women used to violate it a lot. A few of them still do.

For the sake of the well-behaved general-assignment girls in New York, I want to clear up one matter which seems to be cloudy in the minds of certain newspaper men I know. Every big press conference and press tour brings forth a multitude of women who carry press cards but who are not reporters. I have never been able to discover just what they are, but I know that the men heartily resent them. They come from some of the more glamorous magazines, from trade journals, from radio, and some of them just seem to come from nowhere. They are sleek, broad-A girls. They wear Chanel No. 5 and Lily Daché hats. They usually act as if they are at a cocktail party.

A couple of years ago, I was on a tour of an Army air forces convalescent hospital with a few bona fide reporters and a horde of these glamor girls. There were at least a hundred press cards present so the party had to be divided into groups of twenty, each with a guide. One group, made up entirely of lovely ladies, was about to get under way when the guide called out: "Wouldn't the *Times* and the *Herald Tribune* like to fill out this group?" Meyer Berger, one of New York's better newspapermen whose treatment of women reporters is decidedly democratic, was the *Times* in this case. He edged over to me. "Let's not go with that outfit," he grumbled. "It's nothing but a bunch of women except for you and me." This was not my accolade alone. It belongs to the general-assignment girls, all of them. And bless their hearts, here's another bright and silky feather for their battered bonnets.

Not long ago, a bulletin flashed into the city rooms of newspapers in the metropolitan area. A ship, unloading ammunition, had exploded at the dock of the Naval depot in Earle, New Jersey, causing a mighty blast which took six lives and shook the countryside. Reporters and photographers converged on the installation and piled into Navy trucks assigned to take them to the site of the disaster, the tip of a mile-long pier.

In one truck, along with twenty-odd men, were two women reporters assigned along with several men from their offices to gather up the details of the story. As the vehicle rolled onto the approach to the pier, a shore patrolman flagged it to a stop.

"No women allowed on this pier," he said bluntly. "The girls will have to get out here."

Before either of the women—one of them was Ara Piastro, of *The New York Daily Mirror;* I was the other—could protest, a photographer whose face was familiar but whose name was unknown to us, spoke up impatiently.

"These aren't women," he explained. "They're reporters."

Nobody else spoke. The guard hesitated a moment, apparently trying to figure out whether there was any levity in the flat statement. There wasn't. He waved the truck forward.

[6] CITY-HALL REPORTER

by Robert J. Donovan

DAY in and day out throughout the year few reporters write so many stories for a newspaper as the city-hall reporter. His field includes all local legislation and taxation, the city budget, zoning, public transportation, civil service, local welfare and relief, all manner of public works and municipal activities and, to a limited extent, local politics.

The city-hall reporter is chronicler of the mayor's policies and peregrinations. While it is only a rare reporter at city hall who is a deep student of subjects like taxation and franchises, every seasoned city-hall reporter is an authority on the idiosyncrasies of the mayor. The number of intimate facts about the mayor which he is expected to know is incalculable. The mayor's weight and height, his haunts and hobbies, likes and dislikes, are only a few of the more obvious ones. In nearly five years at City Hall I believe I was asked at least a dozen times to include in certain stories the size of Mayor La Guardia's ten-gallon hat.

Covering city hall often entails writing about some of the baldest buffoonery in American public life.

Some United States senators and representatives and members of state legislatures act like clowns often enough, but it is on the floors of councilmanic and aldermanic chambers that the so-called democratic process is translated into the most ridiculous antics. The less important the business, the more extreme the shenanigans and billingsgate.

A few years ago reporters sauntered into the Council Chamber of City Hall in New York for what was to be a meeting on utterly routine affairs. It seemed impossible that any item on the calendar conceivably could make news, much less front-page news at a time when page one was filled with war stories. There were messages from the Mayor requesting the Council to ask the State Legislature for authority to reimpose certain taxes and to condemn the Second Avenue elevated, but these issues had been thrashed out long before and, in any case, the items were for reference to committee and not for immediate consideration. There was the general run of miscellaneous bills and resolutions, one asking the Mayor to post a $5,000 reward for apprehension of the murderer of a policeman and another declaring it to be the sentiment of the citizens of New York that arms and food should be sent to Eire.

Then there was the customary list of proposed changes in the names of streets and public places, none of which, in this instance, were of general interest.

When the Council got around to this part of the calendar, however, the place was suddenly in an uproar. The Council had been thrown into turmoil over the naming of a sliver of park land in Brooklyn. At the instigation of Italian societies three councilmen had introduced a bill to name the plot Amerigo Vespucci Park, while another councilman at the request of his Irish-American constituents and the American Legion, had put in a bill to call it Callahan-Kelly Park in honor of two local war heroes.

The result was one of those squabbles that no amount of shouting could settle. Someone, however, conceived a way of tossing the whole business into the lap of the Mayor without any embarrassment to the Council. The idea, which the Council readily approved by a vote of seventeen to one was to pass both bills and hand the Mayor, who must sign or veto local laws, the task of deciding whether to offend the Irish or the Italians. So in the form in which the legislation was passed and sent to the Mayor, it gave the tiny piece of land the ludicrously bloated and incongruous name of Callahan-Kelly Amerigo Vespucci Park.

In the morning papers next day the story was on page one.

City hall produces many stories of this type. Name-calling stories are another product of city hall. "You dog," "you Ku Kluxer," "low louse," "political stinker" are a few of the epithets that have dignified the government of the largest city in the United States in the last several years and given city-hall reporters something to write about.

Somehow or other the local political arena seems to provide a marvelous climate for the growth of personal animosities, creating news where otherwise there might be none. Several years ago a city-hall reporter, after watching a couple of city officials punch each other all around the multi-million-dollar monstrosity that passes as City Hall in Buffalo, New York, returned to the office and in the manner of a sports reporter at a world-championship prizefight, datelined his story RINGSIDE, CITY HALL, August 1. Whatever the fight was about probably would not have made a jot of news, but the fight itself was a front-page story.

Another aspect of covering city hall, and one least relished by most reporters, is the everlasting civic ceremony. The mayor is always being made an honorary chief of some Indian tribe, or buying the first Buddy Poppy, or breaking ground for a comfort station, or pinning a medal for heroism on a street cleaner, or receiving a Boy Scout group, or being the guest of honor at a luncheon, or doing something else to get a little publicity for himself, or—as is more often the case—for somebody else. A reporter wouldn't mind these affairs once in a while, but they come without end, often two or three a day, and it is not only an inconvenience to cover them in the midst of other work, but a nuisance to write about them at night after all other stories are out of the way.

And yet good stories sometimes come out of these ceremonies

if the mayor happens to be a man with a little imagination. He may, for example, use the occasion for a groundbreaking for one housing project to announce plans for two new projects, or the visit of Negro welfare workers to announce the appointment of the first Negro magistrate in the city, or the award of a police medal to roar at the underworld, or the signing of a bill to tear the hide off the opposition.

The mayor is potentially the best news source in town, and even on the quietest days a city-hall reporter can't take the afternoon off without an uneasy feeling that the mayor may explode some bundle of political dynamite in his absence.

A large proportion of the stories covered by the city-hall reporter are stories about public works. All newspaper readers are interested in new projects for their town, whether the project happens to be a new subway line, installation of parking meters, substitution of buses for trolleys, a new jail, acquisition of newfangled garbage trucks, a new cancer hospital, war memorial, or demolition of an old landmark to make way for a market.

The first announcement of such projects usually is made at city hall. But that is just the beginning of the story. Almost as much a part of many municipal projects as the brick and steel they are constructed with, is the shrill controversy that echoes about them at every stage, keeping the story alive for months and sometimes years.

One day, let us say, the mayor announces that the city is going to build an airport on a site that was to have been converted into a park. The city-hall reporters immediately have a front-page story on their hands. The next day taxpayers organizations flood the press room at city hall with statements depicting in the hack language of professional outrage the dire state of the city's finances and calling on all citizens to oppose this reckless new outlay before the city is bankrupt. Then the chamber of commerce jumps into the controversy with a statement praising the mayor's farsightedness and warning that if the city does not keep abreast of the air age with a new airport, it will lose its commerce to another city. The day after this statement has been issued, however, one hundred mothers in the neighborhood of the proposed airport picket city hall demanding that the land be used for park purposes, as originally planned, so their children will not have to continue playing in the streets.

Then a month or two later the public hearings begin. First one body, say the planning board, holds hearings. The chamber is jammed. A former Army colonel representing the Taxpayers League is ejected for shouting out of turn. The mayor is called a liar.

From the planning board the matter may go to the council. The council holds hearings. The chamber is packed. The public works commissioner throws a bombshell into the proceedings. He charges that the Citizens Committee To Defeat the Airport Plan is represented by an ex-convict, a man who forty years ago served a penitentiary term in New Orleans for gambling. The councilman whose constituents want a park instead of an airport brings in a wheelbarrow full of earth from the site, contending in a three-hour speech that the ground is unsafe for an airport.

From the council the matter goes, let us say, to the budget director, then back to the mayor and so on. Amendments are offered, opposed, finally adopted in compromise form. Many stories are written about them. When opponents have lost their last battle in city hall, they turn to the courts for an injunction.

They lose in the courts also, and the city at last can start building the airport. The mayor makes a speech, ground is broken and work begins. After probably a couple of years of hearings, squabbles, statements, speeches, and lawsuits the city-hall reporters rejoice at being quit of the matter when suddenly a jurisdictional labor dispute breaks out at the project. Shall the plumbers or laborers lay terra-cotta sewer pipes? With this the story comes back to city hall where it started, and the city-hall reporters, heartily sick of the whole subject, resume the tedious task of grinding out news about it. Nor even then is the end in sight, for when the airport is nearing completion a couple of years hence, one faction will wish to name it Eisenhower Field and another faction will want it named Patrick O'Toole Airport in memory of a late county Democratic boss, and city hall will be rent with the controversy.

It does not take many controversial projects to keep city-hall reporters occupied on and off for months or years. In New York a whole generation of city-hall reporters wrote about the city's plans and maneuvers to bring all subway and elevated lines under municipal operation, a goal finally achieved in 1940.

And it is not only large projects like tunnels, bridges, and airports which keep a city-hall reporter busy. Every year a city undertakes many projects that are small in themselves but affect residents of particular neighborhoods so keenly that they come to city hall and put up the most bitter opposition. Construction of a new parkway may force hundreds of persons to move. Maintenance of a garbage dump in an outlying section may give offense to thousands. The closing of a school may compel many children to walk an additional two miles each day to attend another school. The changing of a bus route may almost isolate a small community.

Persons thus affected have real grievances, and they often proclaim them with a conviction and eloquence that one does not always hear in discussions of supposedly loftier issues. Stories about these situations do not usually make page one and they are not very interesting to readers from other neighborhoods, but they are the stuff of a city-hall reporter's work and a true part of the current history of any city.

Most city-hall reporters, I believe, would agree that the most harassing day in the year is the day the annual city budget is made public. It is a day of toiling over figures and tables and charts, and of trying to reduce the mass of arithmetic to terms that will make sense to a reader. In larger cities, at least, the budget is a ledger of dictionarylike heft, crammed with nothing but page after page of figures. These would be typical entries:

Junior Civil Engineer..............	2 at $3,230	$6,460
Postage		13,000
Repairs for school organs, pianos.....		21,000
Pension Fund		700,000
Food, forage supplies for zoo		50,000

Here in this ledger is the whole catalogue of what the city will spend in ordinary expenses in a fiscal year. The total is usually enormous. Although the budget is a dull, incomprehensible-looking document, most of its lines have a vital meaning to somebody, and the total, because of its bearing on the real estate tax, is important to a great many people. If, for example, the line for Junior Civil Engineer read "2 at $3,000" instead of "2 at $3,230," the two engineers, possibly young men with families, might not be able next year to buy new furniture or new coats for their wives. If the appropriations for the board of education made no allowance, say, for new teachers to compensate for increased enrollment, your child would have to sit in a class of perhaps forty instead of thirty-five, receiving just that much individual attention. If the budget total rises sharply, you probably will have to pay higher taxes on your home, if you own it; or higher rent if you do not.

Of course, all the details do not come out in the first story. The city-hall reporter is swamped on the first day with the main facts: the grand total, the mayor's comment, which as likely as not shoulders the blame for a higher budget on the state legislature, new fiscal policies revealed in the budget, a summary of the major items and curiosities, and perhaps one or two of the first indignant outpourings of the taxpayers' groups.

The budget is not a one-day story, however. For two or three months it is the subject of feverish debate, and there is never such a universal clash of interests at city hall as on the days of the budget hearings. Then the dramas hidden in the pages of figures flare into the open—the plight of a street cleaner with ten children trying to get along on $1,800 a year, of a school teacher who has devoted years of study to her profession receiving $3,000 a year, of interns and nurses working long hours in crowded city hospital wards for paltry sums. Then the groups who want new schools, new health centers, new sewers, more police protection are pitted against the real estate interests which would suffer from a rise in real estate taxes and those who believe it folly for the city to spend more than it receives.

Every year this conflict yields many stories for city-hall reporters. Some of them, like the stories about the hearings, may be lively and interesting. But as the debate drags on, most of them, based on handouts from various factions, are insignificant and dull. For it is generally the case that despite all the subsequent hubbub and press releases, an administration will stand on a budget in substantially its original form.

A city-hall reporter's work would be simpler if he had nothing else to bother about than the budget, the mayor, the council planning board, and public hearings. These are his principal sources of news, but they are not the only ones. A city's business, in the main, is transacted by city departments, and each department is at least a potential source of news. Knowing the way around the maze of city departments, knowing which officials are in touch with particular subjects and which ones will give out information about them is the everlasting concern of every city-hall reporter.

If my own experience was any indication, a reporter probably will find that some obscure, quiet, white-haired gentleman hidden away in a corner of the department of finance, or the corporation counsel's office, or the department of public works knows more about what is going on in the city government than all the councilmen combined. A reporter who seeks out and cultivates such officials has a good chance of breaking certain stories before anyone else has ever heard about them. And what is more important, he stands a good chance of being saved from writing stories that are untrue. For one of a city-hall reporter's most valuable assets is the confidences of an official who may not volunteer information, but who will put him straight on information he has picked up himself.

Except that it takes time at first to find one's way around, to learn which officials know what they are talking about and which are phonies, and to develop a working knowledge of city affairs, covering city hall is much the same as any other local assignment.

On the credit side, a city-hall reporter does not have to write obituaries and can manage to stay somewhat out of reach of the city desk. On the debit side, he has to write a lot of stories that are woefully dull to a great many readers, and to write them over and over again each year.

On the whole, though, city hall is one of the best and most responsible assignments on the city staff. If it is any compensation, a city-hall reporter, I believe, comes to feel that in a sense he is in the public life of his town. He mingles with its officials, attends its ceremonies, follows its progress from day to day, is identified with stories his paper publishes about the city government. And if some of his stories are ignored by other newspaper readers, they are not overlooked by the men who run the city, and it may be that some city-hall reporters in an indirect way exert a modicum of influence in their towns.

[7] COVERING POLITICS

by Murray Snyder

POLITICS is a sport, a game run by and for professionals. The men who engage in it do so at first because of the fun of working on the "team" and sharing the limelight with the politically great. Later they forego amateur standing and look for spots on the public pay roll.

Most of those who are good at it could be more successful financially and enjoy greater security if they devoted their talents to private enterprise. But few businessmen get their names in the papers. Publicity is to the politician just about what it is to the professional ballplayer—perhaps more. Nobody pays $4.40 for box seats to see Joe Soapbox get out the vote and few would know Joe had any batting average at all if it were not for the newspapers and, to a lesser degree, the radio.

For the preceding reasons, the political writer should, as far as possible, regard opposing political parties as he does rival ball clubs. The contestants fight like blazes during the season for the glory of the club—and a share of the political equivalent of World Series revenue. But after the election is over, they're likely to be pals, drinking companions, or even law partners.

Of course, this is more generally true in the relations between the established parties, the Republicans and Democrats. The minor groups, reform outfits and such, have a more serious outlook and they tackle the problems of the day with a zeal which burns brightly, but usually not for very long. The history of these minor parties is that they usually split up instead of growing stronger, and the splintered units fight each other as much as they do the powerful intrenched organizations they set out to destroy.

Again it is emphasized that in politics as in sports, nothing should be taken too much to heart; it has all happened before and will again. Upsets, landslides, swings to right and left, revolts, scandals, reform administrations, and reversions to the old machine control. Much of the fighting within the parties and between them is phony, a disillusioning discovery the reporter makes very early. Many a contest is settled on a business basis, before the names go on the ballot, and many election rivals are excellent friends between campaigns. Many a Republican district leader will give his Democratic opposite number a helping hand to turn back an upstart Democrat on primary day, and next year the Democrat reciprocates in kind, if called on. The gentlemen are definitely professionals at the game and no simon pures need apply.

Appreciation of these basic principles is important to the correct understanding of the politician, whether he operates in clubhouse or White House. It is also important to remember that not only does politics make strange bedfellows, but only the lucky few hold onto their beds very long. Changes are frequent and abrupt and due far more often to public whim or political caprice than to any demonstrated failure on the job. Yet those are occupational hazards, like the base runner's spikes or the beanball.

To write politics well, a reporter has to like his sphere of activity as much as the sportswriter does his. He has to like people generally and to enjoy mixing with all kinds. The best way to get the hang of the political machinery is to start with the people who work at its lowest level—the so-called rank and file. The men and women who work in the districts are the troops who do the party's sweating and win the elections.

Too few of our citizens realize just how important this lowest echelon is. Operating from district clubhouses, the election district captains and their subordinate doorbell pushers keep tab on the several hundred enrolled members of the party living within their zone. They tackle them, year after year, for cause after cause. Signatures are required for the petitions which enter candidates in the annual primary election. Next the party members must be shepherded to the polls on primary election days. Naturally, the party is interested in getting them out only if the vote can be counted on to be "regular." If the voter shows signs of possibly supporting an insurgent against the party man, he is left free to forget all about the primary and his civic obligations, as 75 to 85 per cent of our qualified voters do every year. Last comes the actual election.

To a majority of the voters, the campaign begins only when the speechmaking and promises do, some time about four or five weeks before election. In many states, where one party or the other has a vastly superior enrollment, the primary of the predominant party is, in effect, the election. That is also true of hundreds of villages, counties, cities, and other subdivisions in all states. The handful of citizens who vote in primaries pick the administrative or legislative officers of these areas. So the political writer must know the complexion of the parts of his sphere of activity before he can do a good job of covering the whole.

The mechanics of lower-echelon politics is important, but so are the people, unimportant as they may appear individually in the large-scale campaign picture. The smart ones don't remain small fry very long. They climb the ladder either as operators of the party machinery or as office-holding "front men." Many top-ranking political writers and correspondents in state and national capitals find that politicos whom they knew back in the hinterland are top-notch news sources, due to a long established mutual respect and trust.

Other writers have gone out of town with local delegations to party conventions, or to cover their state legislature, and developed good news relationships with the traveling politicians. The night-

and-day business and social contact does the trick. When they all get back home, the web of information lines is well laid.

The camaraderie about legislative halls, which transcends party lines and even extends to the press room, serves to give the reporter invaluable news contacts in remote sections of his state. When he makes his pre-election scouting tours, to test political winds, his weather vanes are spotted through every county. And to double-check on the politicians, he has fellow correspondents to confer with in the major cities.

This brings us to Axiom Number One of the business: A political reporter is only as good as his news sources. He knows little more than what he has been told, so far as the nonpublic happenings in his field are concerned.

This is as good a place as any to attempt to set down a few points that might make up a sort of code of behavior for political reporters. Here it is:

1. Maintain strict impartiality.

2. Establish a reputation for trustworthiness by protecting sources of information and respecting off-the-record confidences.

3. Don't be a free loader; pick up your share of the check; your paper can afford it.

It is obvious that until the widest and most representative circle of friends and news sources has been established by a political reporter, he cannot cover the field satisfactorily by telephone. Smart politicians just don't unbosom themselves to strangers over the telephone, even if the inquisitive character has the unlisted phone number. It's a "legman" job.

Besides, the best political stories don't always come as the specific answers to specific questions. The fellow who keeps pushing for answers often misses the by-products of a general political "bull session"—the background knowledge and opinion of veteran politicians—which sometimes lead to much better stories at a later date.

This article opened with the observation that politicians like publicity the way they like their pay checks. A good policy for a reporter responsible for the news from a city hall or a legislative body is to lay down the law at an early date to his own local representatives in the governmental agency. If he doesn't do it, one of his editors should. The proposition should be stated like this:

"You, the politicians, depend on us, the local newspapers, to get your pet stories before your public; these reports help elect you and perpetuate your organizations. Just so long as the news is legitimate, we print it without bias or distortion.

"You also have access to a great deal of valuable political news, other than the mimeograph product that everybody gets. That sort of exclusive information, printed in advance of competing newspapers, would make us (the newspaper which helps make you, remember?) a more respected and influential publication. We think you owe us a break on any of this stuff you can give us without violating confidence or jeopardizing some important public undertaking."

No editor or reporter should feel reluctant to suggest that sort of reciprocal arrangement to the local delegations to Congress, state legislature, city council, or to state and national political conventions. Besides all other considerations, it is a civic duty on the part of these officials to boost the local newspaper, or papers as the case may be. The smart politician operates along these lines without coaching. But many of the old-school boys still think in terms of the plush days when some newsmen were parties to their graft, and served principally as press agents.

On this same theme, it should be made clear that the political reporter is establishing news relationships with officeholders on a long-haul basis. He is going to be on hand a long time, unlike the special writer who does jobs from day to day in different fields, but is not held responsible for a continuing situation.

Just as sports writers have their pet pitchers or quarterbacks, so political writers have their favorite politicians. Press-room welcome mats are dusted off for the men with a willingness to divulge important news, for men of honesty, ability to clarify muddled issues, or natural capacity for making copy. Jim Farley as national chairman of the Democratic party, was for many years the idol of literally thousands of newsmen from coast to coast. Perhaps it was because he spoke so freely, trusting everyone, at off-the-record press conferences; perhaps it was merely that he seldom failed to remember a reporter's name, or anyone else's for that matter, once introduced. The reporters worked with him and he helped reporters in their constant effort to print political news before it reached the handout stage.

By contrast, there have been important political figures, some in high elective office, whose chaotic relations with the press were notorious. Frequently when a politician dislikes or mistrusts newsmen, it is because of his basic dishonesty and his sensitivity to public reaction, which necessarily must be critical at times. Unfortunately, some of these inaccessible or uncommunicative politicians either make or possess news of great value.

But there are more ways of attaining an objective than by frontal attack. There is at least one "leak" in every office. Sometimes the head man knows about it and encourages dissemination of tidbits of information through selective channels, usually to newspapers politically friendly to him. Hints are dropped of probable future appointments to administrative or judicial posts. Advance information is supplied concerning possible firings, action on legislation, or on contemplated public improvements, which are always politically important.

Here we come to the institution known as the "trial balloon." It is a device used by politicians, sometimes directly and sometimes through their favorite "leaks," to test public reaction to official actions such as those listed above before the die is cast. Until the official pronouncement is made, confirming the "dope" story, the responsibility for its accuracy is all the reporter's. And if the public reacts adversely, the idea can be dropped—and often is.

Hence the rule for handling the "it was learned" sort of story, unless the reporter has been shown convincing proofs, is extreme caution. The more important the news, the more the reporter should attempt to check its accuracy with other sources before printing it. Even then, "escape clauses" should be employed if there is any doubt. For instance, while today the leaders of a political group may be virtually agreed on John Doe for Mayor, minds may change overnight and so may candidates. Until definitive action has been taken, the newspaper account of the situation should state that it is subject to last-minute change, that William Woe is still an active contender and has support from certain enumerated sources.

In other words, the rule is: Don't go overboard, unless you are sure. The political writer with a low batting average on forecasts gets himself into the class of some Broadway columnists, who print their sweepings with equal positiveness, whether they involve prospective births in Hollywood or cabinet appointments.

The news of the moment is the thing on which headlines are built. But the veteran political writer rarely writes of today's developments without applying to them the measuring stick of the past. The issues, candidates, enrollments, prospects and—finally—the vote—of one election are always compared with preceding years.

This is where the morgue, the newspaper's "memory," fits into the picture. Few who have not worked on a well-run paper realize the immense value of the vast facilities of this department. Its mountains of clipping files, bound volumes of other years, innumerable reference volumes, Who's Who annuals, and the skilled librarians who work around the clock keeping things up to date, are used constantly by the news staff. They make up for a great many gaps in the background of the stranger to the local scene.

Even the veteran political writer seldom trusts to his memory. It is always safer to look at the record.

What are some of the things to look for to bolster a political story already in hand? Check the clips on the key individuals involved. Today's white hope sometimes turns out to be yesterday's black sheep. Or his prewar views on our foreign policy might be worth checking against his current opinions. It is not uncommon to find the same politician screaming for tax reductions in one speech and for increased public improvements in a succeeding one.

Where a district, county, or state is involved in an election-campaign story, the recent history of that voting area helps give the picture of the trend, if there is one. The vote in a comparable election a few years back might be broken down to indicate the problems of the current candidates in certain sectors, due to racial strains, influx of new population, or personal popularity of certain candidates.

In these days of cramped news columns and a growing aversion on the part of editors toward gabby writing, getting the story is not enough; the reporter's second job is to get it into the paper, displayed as well as possible. He has to sell it to his city editor.

Editors often pass up political stories which are too technical or possess an appeal as reading matter to only a relatively few professional politicians. Perhaps they reject too few of them. Where the subject matter is technical, the reporter can do a civic job by translating it into layman's language. There is much that should be more widely understood in the esoteric realm of the election laws. Some of it can be written far more interestingly than it is today. Much of the bitter scrapping by election lawyers is actually amusing.

From the standpoint of the editor and publisher, it is their public responsibility to increase the general knowledge of things political and to encourage greater participation in the selection and election of candidates. It is just as important to keep the spotlight on the organizations and the people who run local government as it is to campaign for reform of police, health, and education departments after they have been run down.

The political writer shares this responsibility with his chiefs. The theory is that if enough people are sufficiently informed, they will go to the polls and do the right thing. At least they will be unable to complain that they did not know the facts of life around them.

[8] THE WASHINGTON BUREAU

by Bert Andrews

HEAD OF THE WASHINGTON BUREAU OF

THE NEW YORK HERALD TRIBUNE

WASHINGTON is a reporter's paradise, but it puts a competitive strain on a reporter perhaps greater than that imposed in any other city. Its temptations have ruined many great reporters and many, many more who could have been great. Yet it dangles rewards that are solid enough to make the steady men, the reliable men, the brilliant men take strain and temptation in stride.

There is no mystery about what makes a reporter deserve that best-of-all praise—the casual but meaningful accolade of a colleague —"So-and-so is a *good* reporter," concurred in by the men who hear it. The reporters who earn the right to that adjective *good* usually begin earning it in journalism classes or in their cub days on newspapers, whether small or large.

On the specific topic of Washington, I write as one who has been chief Washington correspondent of *The New York Herald Tribune* since June 2, 1941—an assignment that came after seventeen years of experience in the United States and abroad, in Sacramento, San Francisco, San Diego, Chicago, Detroit, Paris, and New York.

Here a reporter has ready access to the great and near great. Most of the officials in Washington are politicians of one stripe or another, but they are big-time politicians. State legislators or town councilmen are usually harder to approach than top-flight men in government agencies. The latter realize what some of their small-town brethren never learn—that they must be affable, polite, and helpful, even to correspondents of papers vehemently opposed to them.

A good reporter in Washington gets opportunities for magazine writing, for radio appearances. There may not be much money in it at first, but each new venture adds prestige. If a reporter remains in the capital, his income should show a continuing increase over the years. If he doesn't want to stay, chances are he can step into a job in press, radio, magazine, or publicity, for Washington is conceded to be one of the best training grounds for allied activities.

The pitfalls are there, however. One is the old curse of some weaklings in the profession—the bottle. More social drinking, with more intelligent and charming people of both sexes, can be done in Washington than in any other city in the world. But a reporter can't keep up with all the social drinking available and with his work, too. A sensible balance, obviously, varies with the individual.

A second danger is laziness. A reporter can walk miles on Capitol Hill, for example, just to get to see two senators and two congressmen. True, he frequently can get to people on the telephone, saving his time and theirs. It causes some reporters to relax in their offices, pump the telephone, suck their thumbs, and come up with ponderous "think pieces." But there is no substitute for a good pair of legs. Good sources talk most frankly to men they know in the flesh, who aren't just voices on the phone.

A third evil, swelled-headedness, afflicts the very young Washington writer who thinks he has been mysteriously transformed from a "reporter" to a "correspondent," merely by having been assigned to the capital. The old-timers have been around long enough to know that it doesn't pay, in politics or newspaper work, to relax too much too often. There are plenty of good men coming along all the time. A by-line in a metropolitan paper out of Washington is no God-given right. It can be taken away, and it will be taken away if the individual isn't careful about what appears under it.

This is as good a place as any to mention the liaison that must be maintained with the city desk in the New York office. Washington is the nation's official capital; New York its economic and business heart. So much of what goes on in Washington ties in closely with the news originating in New York that it's often a tossup whether a story is "Washington" or "local."

Sometimes the city editor does the quarterbacking; sometimes it's the bureau chief. It might almost be said that the bureau is part of the city staff, or the city staff is part of the bureau. A Washington story today may be a New York story tomorrow. Or the same story may be breaking along different lines in both places. The two organizations must work together.

The White House is the news crossroads of the nation and even of the world. Almost any news story, even one involving a relatively obscure development in some out-of-the-way corner, may be exploded into front-page headlines if the President does or says something about it.

No other beat, perhaps, demands so forcefully that the reporter who would do a good job covering it keep himself well informed. The newsman who must ask, "What is this all about?" when the President or one of his press secretaries announces that the White House has acted on something, starts out with his competition far out in front of him.

It means reading the newspapers, and something besides the fiction in the magazines. A reporter with a lot of friends on newspapers in other cities is a valuable man to have around. Ofttimes they come up with advance tips on stories of local or sectional interest that may suddenly acquire national importance as a result of White House attention.

The need for speed in White House reporting is obvious. For the wire service or radio man, White House stories always break on the deadline of some paper or station. The stories frequently take precedence on the wires over all other news. The reporter who must take five or ten minutes pondering over a lead—or rewriting it a couple of times—won't last long at the White House.

The White House reporter frequently must turn out copy under difficult conditions—particularly when the President travels. He must be prepared to bat out his story with a portable typewriter bouncing on his knees in a crowded automobile in a parade, or in a pitching ship's wardroom. Covering a Presidential speech, he must turn out his story, complete with color and audience reaction, while the speech is being delivered—and have it all in the hands of a telegrapher a minute or two after the President finishes.

The attributes of all good reporters—persistence, willingness to do leg work, and, above all, imagination—also take on extra significance in covering the White House.

Stories which break at the White House usually have repercussions in Washington and through the nation or the world. The White House's reporter's job is only half done when he records what the President has said or done. He then must go to work to find out what prompted the President's decision, who advised him to make it, what the effects may be, whether it will solve a problem or create new ones. The man who turns up some of these answers produces stories which please his editors and colleagues and keep his readers informed.

The most valued—and dangerous—task of the White House reporter is the forecasting of events and Presidential decisions. To accomplish it, he must have highly placed friends who have the President's ear. But he must also look beyond the happenings of today to see what they portend for tomorrow.

The routine of covering the White House is simple. At 10:30 A. M. every day the President's press secretary has a conference with the beat men, discussing who is going to see the President that day, at what time, and for what. Once a week the President himself holds a press conference (Roosevelt used to have two a week), at which no holds are barred save that the President may not be quoted directly without express authorization.

Presidential callers enter and leave through the executive office foyer, off which is the press room. They are "braced" on the way in and out by reporters. If they are important enough, they also face a barrage of camera flashbulbs on the White House steps. The usual rule is for White House callers not to reveal what the President said to them, although they may reveal, if they like, what they said to the President. However, many a story comes from a man just about to see the President, or who has just done so.

Covering the callers is just one example of the vital necessity for background and thorough reading of the papers. The very fact that Congressman Zilch has an appointment to see the President is enough for a story for the reporter who has kept on top of developments.

Contacts with the various special assistants to the President—some of whom have their offices elsewhere than in the White House—pay off handsomely in beats. One of these may tip a newspaper friend that the Secretary of State, for example, was hastily summoned to the White House late in the afternoon, and bustled in and out a side door without being spotted by newsmen. That's a story in days of recurrent international crises.

The State Department, once considered the haunt of bespatted, tea-drinking "journalists," rather than working newspapermen, is a top news source now. More than ever before the news desks now realize that diplomacy is the nation's first line of defense. When it fails, either appeasement or war must result.

The routine of covering the State Department begins at the White House press conference. Most State Department newspapermen go across the street to the White House executive offices for this conference, because major diplomatic decisions are so closely allied to the President's activities.

At noon daily the special assistant to the Secretary of State in charge of press relations holds a press conference. He answers questions, or refuses to comment if the matter is too delicate, about the many facets of international affairs constantly developing throughout the world. He issues the routine statements, or handouts.

Twice weekly the Secretary of State, or, in his absence, the acting Secretary, has a press conference. Questions may be submitted in writing in advance, or thrown at the Secretary without warning. The Secretary of State, however, may not be quoted directly except with his express permission—an honest error in quotation might subtly alter the shade of meaning and cause international complications.

When the Secretary of State wants to be quoted directly, he makes a speech on foreign policy, or issues a formal statement, or makes public the text of a note sent to some foreign power.

But the real stories broken out of the State Department are not from the press conferences or handouts, important though these are. Good newspapermen covering the State Department daily talk with such key officials as chiefs of divisions, men on the various "desks"—French, British, Russian—who frequently cannot tell all they know, but who give a keen reporter guidance on handling information he may already have picked up from other sources.

Most men covering the State Department for large newspapers and press services find themselves invited to teas, cocktail parties, and other social affairs at the various embassies and legations. Smart reporters accept the invitations, nibble at the really delicious food, drink very sparingly of the excellent liquor, and keep their eyes and ears open. Many a tip, and many a beat, has been obtained at a diplomatic cocktail party.

On the diplomatic run the reporter not only has the competition of American newspapers and press services, but that of Reuter's, the British agency; Tass, Russian; France Presse, French, and a dozen special correspondents of individual newspapers. Foreign or domestic, the competition is rarely mediocre.

In order to cover the activities of Congress, the reporter must have credentials from the Standing Committee of Correspondents, which administers the press galleries on behalf of the House and Senate.

This five-member committee has functioned since 1884. It is elected for each Congress by the membership of the press galleries of the two houses, numbering more than five hundred. To obtain admission to the Congressional press galleries, each applicant must submit an application blank and a letter from the responsible editor of his newspaper. The press galleries are distinctly a daily-press institution. Separate galleries are provided for radio commentators.

The decisions of the Committee regarding admission to the press galleries may be appealed to the speaker of the House and to the Rules Committee of the Senate. In few, if any instances, have the rulings of the Standing Committee been overturned.

Incidentally, the two major political parties have for many years turned over to the Standing Committee of Correspondents complete control over press stands at the national Presidential conventions, including the distribution of credentials to the newspapers of the country and the arrangement of press facilities. The White House and State Department also rely on the Standing Committee to handle credentials for international gatherings, and even to pass on qualifications of those who attend White House or other press conferences.

Capitol correspondents work from the House and Senate press galleries, located above the House and Senate chamber floors. Each consists of a tier of seats where correspondents sit when listening to debate, and an interior office lounge with facilities for working and loafing. The galleries are staffed with employees who answer telephones, take messages, provide copy paper and stationery, get copies of bills, documents, speeches, and releases, and keep a running account of the day's doings on the floor.

Correspondents covering debate on the floor may order a transcript at any point merely by asking a press gallery attaché to notify the official reporters' room. The correspondent's newspaper is billed for this service. The press gallery employees' service extends to committee hearings as well. At hearings, the employees reserve press space, provide releases, paper, and other essentials.

The galleries are the clearing house for all news of Congress. Speeches are sent there for distribution to newspapers, and all notices of press conferences and committee meetings are posted. In the House, correspondents have access to the Republican and Democratic cloakrooms just off the chamber. Here they obtain much of their news or background by interviewing members. In the Senate, reporters send their names in to senators, who come out to the President's room to be interviewed.

These three, the White House, the State Department, the Congress, are the most important beats in Washington. Covering them, or any other beat, requires specialized knowledge, as has been made apparent. But no reporter can afford to envelop himself in his specialty to the exclusion of general news. He never knows when the ramifications of a story on his beat may take him into outside channels, where a good all-around man can knock the ears off a specialty expert.

When news is popping all over the place, or in short-handed times, he may find himself covering an outside story—a sudden controversy of political importance in an otherwise obscure bureau, or even a local crime of national interest. A reporter who has confined himself so strictly to a specialty that he's forgotten the techniques of his police-beat or civic-club days is apt to be almost helpless against rivals who still can turn a hand at anything that comes along.

Whoever he be, beginner or old-timer, a reporter must know

how to get information quickly when a story breaks in the shadow of a deadline, and what comes naturally to a seasoned man must be learned by the beginner. Only the veteran is likely to know offhand the right people around town to call in a pinch. But a new shooter can sometimes make up for his lack of contacts by his familiarity with standard sources of information.

A youngster who has diligently studied the *Congressional Directory,* who knows how to find an agency in the telephone book, who can snatch a fact from the *World Almanac* without spending the night poring through it, may turn up the material for a story in a crucial situation.

The beauty of it is, that the fact snatched from the almanac may turn up on the front pages of every paper in the country a few hours later. The most satisfactory thing about Washington is that everybody is watching. It is a challenge and, for the good worker, it makes the job worth while.

[9] FOREIGN REPORTING

by Joseph Barnes

FOREIGN EDITOR OF

THE NEW YORK HERALD TRIBUNE

WITH the end of the war, the corps of American correspondents abroad collapsed even more quickly than the armies they had been sent to report. There were many reasons for this, beyond the truism that war makes new headlines every day while peace makes a banner line only once. The end of wartime surtaxes on corporation income led accountants to look somewhat more carefully at the expense accounts of foreign reporters. The vast press relations apparatus of the fighting services quietly stopped, and jeeps, air priorities, and press hostels stopped too. Editors all over the country decided almost overnight that readers wanted to forget the war.

Even this sudden change was less profound than other changes which had been taking place since 1939 in the business of foreign reporting. For even after many of the war correspondents had gone home, the professionals were left. They are a group of men already sufficiently typed in the public mind to offer stock characters to Broadway, to Hollywood, and to the novelists. The reality behind the type, however, had changed since 1939, more perhaps than for several generations.

Reporters who earn their living abroad are still, for the most part, hard-working men. They are seldom well enough educated for the job they do, and they may include, as fiction and scenario writers appear to believe, more than their share of prima donnas and exhibitionists. They operate too much as a fraternity, and their reporting suffers from insufficient competition as much as from the short memories of their readers. They still work long hours and honestly at helping the United States understand the world from which it can no longer escape, and they are probably closer kin to their readers, both in ideas and in language, than the foreign reporters of any other country.

Some of the changes in this fraternity are clear and simple. It includes more native-born Americans than ever before. Many of the foreigners with scholarly knowledge of their subject but little of the American idiom, who had all but taken over the foreign service of some newspapers before World War II, were among its casualties, either physically or professionally. Their successors are, on the whole, markedly younger. The fraternity still drinks too much, perhaps, but it has lost a good many of the sodden attributes of—say—a Robert Benchley portrayal of a foreign correspondent. American reporters abroad still baffle many of their foreign colleagues by their refusal to accept money and their reluctance to accept discipline. In both these prejudices, they are continuing old American traditions of idealism abroad. But this idealism is, probably, far less romantic than it used to be. During the war, forty-odd American newspapermen lost their lives, and those who survived have more memories of the sound of a V-1 or the feel of a jeep on a mined road than of roistering in the cafés of Paris.

They found their assignments changed. After World War I, an enterprising American reporter abroad might have dreamed of an expedition through the North African desert to find Abd-el-Krim, or of telling the true story of Queen Marie of Romania. A generation later, the ambitious correspondent wanted an interview with Vyacheslav M. Molotov, Soviet Foreign Minister, who was no farther away than a Paris hotel, or a comparison of occupation policies in Germany, which was often enough directly under his nose. The great story which would splash itself across the front page was certainly no easier to get, but it was a different kind of story.

The technical problems of reporting have also changed. Radio communication has given American newspaper readers spot news from areas earlier reported only by camel caravan. Costs have not fallen correspondingly, but newspapers are more willing to pay for the qualifying adverb, and really tight cablese is becoming as lost a journalistic skill as shorthand. Airplane transport has given modern reporters a mobility beyond the wildest dreams of Richard Harding Davis. It has also immensely widened the peephole through which editors at home look at the problem of reporting the world. Comparative reporting of news in different countries, by men who can now have the dust of Athens still on their shoes in Warsaw, may in the long run change the business of reporting the foreign world more deeply than anything since the invention of the telegraph.

Not all the technical changes have been for the better. The American hunger for speed in news transmission has played into the hands of censors all over the world, giving them bottlenecks easier to cork than ever before. Fast transport has weakened the nineteenth-century tradition according to which a correspondent settled in one foreign country, to learn its language and its people. As a result, some of the more esoteric countries of the world have grown still more esoteric in the American mind, and the reputation of being "Oriental," "quaint," or "enigmatic" can be used by shrewd politicians to close a country as tight as a corrupt city hall. Finally, the war has left a world of ruins and red tape in which a foreign reporter may often spend nine-tenths of his waking hours acquiring food, shelter, transport, and legality, with only the fag end of the day for his essential business of reporting.

In a few large foreign cities, reporters for the press associations and the bigger papers still work in bureaus organized very much like any Washington bureau. Some of them are specialists, covering diplomatic news, or economic developments, or local politics. In other cities, one-man bureaus are the rule and in these cases a reporter's office is often inside his hat. In either case, a foreign reporter is expected to use more ingenuity in developing news leads, and more responsibility in writing stories, than his colleagues in a city room. But if he overfiles, the business office at home is usually not slow in helping him trim his prose. And all his copy, whether long or short, must run the gauntlet of the copy desk and the night desk. The notion that a foreign correspondent writes exactly as he pleases is a conceit that sometimes rallies his self-esteem, but which no good reporter at the far end of a cable ever really believes.

In London, Paris, Mexico City, and Buenos Aires, the work of a foreign correspondent differs from that of a reporter in the United States chiefly in the fact that he, or his bureau chief, must guess what will interest his readers most on any given day, how long the story should be, and what its lead should emphasize. Otherwise, the daily routine of his job is pretty much that of a reporter anywhere. If he is an exceptional reporter, the business of learning or perfecting the local language will keep him out of the bars for part of his free time. If he is even normally curious, the daily life around him will keep his eyes and ears open longer and wider than at home, and send him to bed more tired. If he is one of the real professionals, the line between work and recreation will tend to disappear, and he has a chance of finding the kind of all-absorbing immersion in a new experience which some men would pay money for, instead of asking for a salary, and which is the ultimate reason why some men still want to be foreign correspondents.

The reporter abroad who works outside an established bureau in a big city must have a little masochism in him. To arrive in Warsaw, or Belgrade, or Jerusalem, or Harbin, and to prepare to describe the life of peoples and to explain the destiny of nations is a little like going to work on your own head with a heavy mallet.

There are men who like it, and there are men who do it extremely well. For the most part, they are veterans who have learned by experience to look for a bed, for a cable or wireless office, for some way of getting out of town again, for food and drink and local currency, and for some native citizens who are not too dishonest, in about the order named. There is little rhyme or reason to the job; knowledge is acquired by a kind of osmosis which would make any good sociologist, economist, or public-opinion analyst shudder. Sometimes the results can also make an intelligent reader shudder. When the job is done well, it is distinguished foreign news. Getting news in this way has never lengthened the life of any reporter who did it long.

Counting allowances and expense accounts, foreign correspondents are on the whole better paid than local newspapermen. None of them grow rich until or unless they go over the great divide into public lecturing, radio work, or writing for the slick-paper magazines, but they are considered quasi-diplomatic representatives of their papers and are given a standard of living somewhat higher, at least in relation to the cities where they are stationed, than reporters at home. They work longer hours; there is no five-day week and no overtime pay for a reporter abroad. And even if his cocktails are more expensively mixed and drunk in more expensive society, a reporter living abroad gives up many of the amenities of life in America. In many cases, especially since the war, he takes his chances with bad diet, no heat in winter, no new clothes, and the corrosive psychological effect of knowing that, wherever he is stationed and whatever his pay, he is a bloated aristocrat compared to the people he has been assigned to report.

There is an element of insecurity in the life of a postwar foreign correspondent which helps him at least to avoid the evils of complacency. One of the most striking paradoxes of the United States at present is that the world's greatest power, with more than six million men recently returned from some kind of foreign experience, with leadership in both political parties committed to increasing involvement with the world's affairs, has fewer newspapers maintaining an independent foreign news service than at any time in recent history. The correspondents themselves argue this curious phenomenon, and they have so far turned up no explanation on which all agree. There is little doubt that many publishers have been trying so zealously to spot a trend towards isolationism that they stand in grave danger of creating one. There is also little doubt that the recent competition of what has been called "processed and packaged foreign news," prepared by rewrite men in the United States from press association copy, propaganda handouts and front-office rumors, has temporarily, at least, decreased the market value of an authentic dateline and a first-hand report. The press associations have recently rediscovered the foreign market for their news reports with an enthusiasm of salesmanship which has not reinforced the independence or the confidence of their newsgatherers. These are problems serious enough to make conversation in press camps and hotels all around the world, but if they have deterred any considerable number of reporters from wanting to be foreign correspondents, this is not observable on the foreign desk of any big newspaper still engaged in its own world reporting.

It is these reporters who write foreign news. It is the mixed and often obscure motives at work inside them which define in the long run the kind of foreign news Americans get and, therefore, that part of our future involvement with the world which will be conditioned by what we think. It is in this speculative area that the most interesting recent changes have taken place in the style or fashion of foreign correspondence, changes which promise to reflect and to help produce a new relationship between the American mind and the world at large.

In the period between the two wars, the best American foreign correspondents were men engaged, like America itself, in a search for knowledge of themselves. It was no accident that the most influential book written by one of them was called *Personal History*. Their divorce rate was high; bullfighting and drinking and modern painting were staples in their conversation; Marxism, Union Now, the Spanish Republic, intervention in the war, and some of the drawing-room versions of fascism all won adherents and crusaders among American reporters in Europe between the two wars.

This was itself a sharp change from the search for adventure which had drawn reporters of Richard Harding Davis' generation to work abroad, and from the search for an older civilization with more stable values which took William James Stillman, for example, in a still earlier generation, from *The New York Post* to a foreign correspondent's job on *The Times* of London. It was not so long ago, as newspaper generations are counted, that something like Stillman's career, or Davis', was the pattern of a young foreign correspondent's secret dreams.

Each of these patterns was the reflection of an American generation's concern with the foreign world. The last of them, which dissolved in September, 1939, had drawn many hundreds of bright young men and women to foreign countries in a personal search for something more than the news they were paid to get. The epidemic of personal books which they later produced made it clear that they were looking for what they thought were rules of human justice, or a formula for world peace, or a blueprint for prosperity. It may really have been a knowledge of themselves, and the kind of adult self-confidence which is expected of reporters from a major world power.

It would be tempting, and wrong, to report that the newest, post-1939 generation of American correspondents abroad has at last found this self-confidence, and is now looking for objective truth. All that is clear is that the job of foreign correspondent, and the motives which lead men into the trade, have changed with the country for which they write. American reporters abroad now seem, for all their youth, more mature, more cynical, less vulnerable to "causes," probably more dangerous people. They know themselves better. Filing a dispatch to New York or Chicago from Helsinki or Nanking is less like dropping a pebble into the Grand Canyon. They can hear it land, and sometimes, if they are good and lucky, they can even hear an echo. They listen for it, anyway, and this is something new.

So, for one thing, crusading has tended to go out of fashion. Consider the candor of one of the best of them, Homer Bigart of *The New York Herald Tribune*. This Pulitzer-prize winner has written an excellent description of the central problems of foreign reporting. The fact that he included it in a routine news dispatch to his paper, admitting frankly that he felt no omniscience, no objectivity, and no compelling urge to shout: "WAKE UP, AMERICA," is a minor landmark in the cultural history of our time:

"A reporter cannot stay two weeks in the poisoned atmosphere of Warsaw without developing a bias which, perhaps unconsciously, is bound to color his reports, and there is no correspondent in Poland today who hasn't in his heart aligned himself with either the Communist-dominated government or the now open opposition of Vice-Premier Stanislaw Mikolajczyk's Peasant party.

"It is important that the reader remember this, for although the reporter is obliged to 'give both sides'—few newspapers would keep him very long if he didn't—the bias creeps in. Sometimes it's in the clever stressing of one side's arguments over the arguments of the other. Or perhaps in the sly omission of a damaging fact. . . .

"Most correspondents who go to Warsaw are, like the present writer, somewhere left of center. They are willing to concede that Poland lies well within the security sphere of Russia and that Moscow has every right to demand of Warsaw a government it can trust. If Poland wants Communism, that is no business of ours.

"You would think, therefore, that we would be embraced by government propagandists with glad cries of 'Comrade, you're our meat!' Instead, we encounter distrust and suspicion at every turn.

The slightest deviation from the government line draws a stream of abuse in which 'liar' is the mildest epithet. And any correspondent who hopes to wangle a room in government-managed hotels had better shun Mikolajczyk. . . .

"For the first week or two a correspondent somehow manages to write nothing bad about anybody except the Ukrainian bandits, which is quite safe, since none of the Poles likes them anyhow. You can also do a piece about the United Nations Relief and Rehabilitation Administration and the Polish famine—provided you shut your eyes to the government's inequitable system of food distribution. But from there on you run into trouble because everything else is political.

"You cannot lift a story from the Warsaw newspapers, because not one of them can be trusted. You cannot completely trust your sources, because no matter how well informed they may be you can be sure they are telling you what they think the Western world should hear.

"It takes days to confirm anything and, meanwhile, there is the dreadful temptation to send it off and the hell with it. Apparently anything can happen in Poland, and even the most lurid tales have a plausible ring. Moreover, if the story is antigovernment, it will be blandly denied by the government, no matter how true it is.

"You find yourself running back and forth between government and opposition, accumulating all the while a great stack of accusations and denials. There is no middle ground, no impartial witness. Battle lines are drawn and everyone has chosen his side. It is a war over the definition of democracy—East versus West—and because you have been conditioned to Western concepts you find yourself drawn irrevocably toward Mikolajczyk.

"You do it with misgivings, fully aware. . . ."

There it is, complete from prejudice through leg work to misgivings. It is a thankless job, with only a phony lecture-platform glamor to look forward to; no foreign correspondent has ever yet made a fortune or been elected to public office. But it has its rewards. It offers, to all but its timeservers, engrossment and excitement on a twenty-four-hour basis, something like reading a *War and Peace* which never ends, and this is a restless hunger in those who want it. It is still possible that in no other business can a man be so much a part of his own time.

[10] THE REFERENCE LIBRARY

by Robert E. Grayson

I AM burgeoning like a flower. A book about the newspaper business, with a chapter about the library? And the librarian himself to write it? It's the millennium, and I plan to file it, accordingly, under "M."

Only a newspaperman really knows how much a library means to a newspaper, and he seems reluctant to tell about it. When he becomes an ex-newspaperman and begins to write short stories, he usually includes one touching bit about something he calls a "morgue," where a superannuated editor dodders about, clutching tattered clippings. That may have been the picture once, but few active newspapermen today go back far enough to remember it.

Just to show how far the picture is from the fact, let me throw a few fast figures at you. The biographical file of *The New York Herald Tribune* is housed in 1,000 steel drawers. In it, carefully indexed by name, are clippings dealing with 1,000,000 persons. Near by are 750 more steel drawers, in which stories are filed by subject instead of by name. There are 4,000 entries in these drawers, with 7,500 subdivisions, and a 20,000-card cross index. If you want to look up volcanoes you simply have to look up "Volcanoes—General," or "Volcanoes—America," or whatever other phase of volcanoes happens to catch your fancy at the moment. To keep these files current, a staff of twenty-four men and women works almost around the clock.

Off to one side is a carefully selected library of four thousand books; an even larger library of pamphlets, government and otherwise, and several drawers of maps. Altogether, that is a quick bird's-eye view of the library, although as I continue you'll find me referring to some of our other possessions.

The whole organization is devoted to one purpose—to answer questions, answer them fast, and answer them correctly. The newspaper depends on the reference library for its accuracy, the scope of its information, and the background authenticity of its articles. Men and women daily must write stories remote in time or in place from their own experience. The library makes it possible for them to do it.

The questions come in steadily throughout the working day, easy and hard, clear and confused. One may come from a feature writer who has two weeks in which to prepare his copy, and the next one from a night rewrite man who is right on deadline and has two or three editors reminding him of that fact. As a rule, the feature writer who can wait asks the easy questions, and the rewrite man races in to ask the tough ones—or am I just getting bitter?

The librarian never can outguess his questioners, and never knows what the next question will be. First, reporter Jones comes in: "What was Claude Pepper's plurality when he was first elected to the Senate?" Easy. We look that one up in the Congressional Directory, under Pepper. The senators always put those little things in their biographies, about the elections they win. When they lose, they omit it.

If only all the questions were like that. But the next visitor may be reporter Smith: "Bob, you remember that man out in Queens who broke his ankle last month when he stumbled over a trash can? I think it was Queens. Maybe Brooklyn. Yeah, last month or the month before. You remember the story, don't you, Bob? Get me the clips on it, will you?" So we get them. It doesn't surprise the reporter. But it surprises me sometimes.

One thing is certain—the story is in the files. Every news story that appears in the *Herald Tribune* is in the files at least once. It is filed under the name of each of the principal characters in the story, whether they number one or one hundred. It is filed also in the subject files, if it concerns any one of the four thousand subject classifications.

Even if it wasn't in the *Herald Tribune,* there is a good chance that it is in the files. For one thing, eleven other newspapers are read and clipped daily by the staff, and any worth-while story that fails to appear in the *Herald Tribune* is snatched from one of those papers. Twelve national magazines are clipped, principally for biographical material or factual stories. The magazine material duplicates to some extent material we clip from the dailies—and for a good reason. The man who wrote it probably used somebody's newspaper library for his research work. But he ties the whole story up in a neat bundle, which is sometimes of considerable value to our own men who want a quick survey of a man or a matter.

Filing the story would be a barren occupation, if it ended there. A library becomes valuable only when it is used—when the reporters and editorial writers are encouraged to use it, and the staff of the library proves itself willing to help. One of my deepest prides lies in the fact that no reporter on the *Herald Tribune,* so far as I know, hesitates for a moment about using the library. He is welcomed into its chaste precincts, whether he is working on a story or, during the lazy hours, feels like dropping in and running through the back issues for his own entertainment.

This fellow feeling between the library and the staff shows up in stories. The procedure used on the *Herald Tribune* is a good one, and has become almost automatic with the years.

When a reporter gets an assignment, his first port of call is the library. Most assignments involve a name or two, and the biographical folders are immediately turned over to him. These are complete—there is no confusing cross-reference system to complicate matters, since if a story must be filed twice, it is clipped twice.

Let's suppose (to pick an idea out of nowhere) that a reporter is being sent out to interview Doris Duke. In the library he gets her clips, and leafs through them rapidly, getting an over-all view of the subject. Some he reads, for they seem to have considerable pertinence. He notes the many court battles between Doris Duke and her ex-husband James Cromwell; the fact that Miss Duke's money comes from the American Tobacco Company; the statement that she is the richest woman in the world.

Having made a few notes, he calls for the librarian again, and discusses the clips with him. The librarian scurries around, and comes back with more clippings—the envelope on James Cromwell, so that the reporter can make himself current on that gentleman's activities; clippings on the American Tobacco Company, so that he can see how business is in Lucky Strikes these days. Books, too—perhaps a brief history of the American Tobacco Company, and a volume on great American fortunes.

When the reporter leaves for his interview, he is primed. He knows a good deal more about Doris Duke than the lady suspects. He knows what questions to ask, and how to frame them. He needn't waste precious time with questions that have already been answered in the clips, and every minute granted him at the interview becomes a valuable minute.

That is one way in which the library serves the reporter, and the most useful way. But the clippings serve another great purpose, and although they may not serve it quite so often, it is likely to be a big thing when they do.

Every day thousands of names pop up in the news—names that mean nothing to the editor who sees them. But as a matter of routine, every such name is sent to the library for investigation if the story has any potential value at all. We check the files, hundreds of times daily, and send back the inquiry stamped "No record in reference library."

But then, one fine afternoon, the files yield a gold mine. There, under the name of the unknown gentleman, is a treasure of yellowing clippings. He was an important witness in a famous murder case years ago, perhaps, or a great musician who has since fallen on evil days. The envelope of clippings, by itself, has turned an obscure item into a page-one story. It happens, time and again. Many an editor, many a reporter has made a reputation because an old envelope turned a routine story into a sensation.

Reporters are not the only clientele of the library. The copyreaders, too, learn to lean on it, for it is the responsibility of the copyreader to let no misspelled name, no error of fact, no false title or date get in the paper. A good copyreader has a valuable talent for smelling out errors, and he comes at once to the library for confirmation.

Then there are our outside customers. Some of them are newspapermen who have moved on to broader fields. If they don't abuse the privilege, we give them occasional access to our files. A little more erratic are the inquiring members of the public at large. Most of them, of course, are readers of the paper who are stumped by a question, and who suddenly bethink themselves of their favorite paper, with its air of daily omniscience. They call us, and we always do our best to answer. One particular segment of this outside public is familiar to every newspaper library—the men and women who call, late at night, and usually from a bar, with some such conversation as this:

VOICE: *Herald Tribune*?

LIBRARIAN: Yes.

VOICE: Who were the original Four Horsemen of Notre Dame?

LIBRARIAN: I'll look it up. (Long Pause.) Miller, Stuhldreher, Crowley and Layden.

VOICE: You sure it wasn't Frank Carideo?

LIBRARIAN: Miller, Stuhldreher, Crowley and Layden.

VOICE: Thanks.

This is one line the conversation can take. It means that the questioner has just lost a bet. The other line comes when the voice says, after he has received the information, "Tell my friend that, will you?" That means the questioner has just won a bet.

We treasure the unusual questions, and the foolish questions, and we get our share of them. There was, for example, the excited young woman who telephoned in September, 1945, when we were beginning to print demobilization details. When was the Umpty-umpth Division due back, she asked. We checked, and told her that the division—and presumably her boy friend—would sail past the Statue of Liberty some time in the spring of 1946. "Oh, I know that," she said impatiently. "But what day?"

One of my favorites was the man who called up with a violent hang-over and wanted to know where he lived. It isn't as complicated as it sounds. The gentleman had arrived in the city and turned to the classified advertisements in the *Herald Tribune* to find a rooming house. He found it, moved in, and celebrated by getting roaring drunk. Some hours later he decided to go home, and discovered he had forgotten where the room was. We were able to tell him.

The radio has recently loosed a plague upon librarians, and if it continues newspapers will be forced to discontinue their question-and-answer service for the public, which has always been willingly and courteously given. But more and more programs are coming on the air in which the announcer propounds a question, to which listeners are invited to send the proper answer and "a letter of not more than twenty-five words. . . ." Then, of course, the listeners hasten to their telephones to call the newspaper libraries and the public libraries for the information.

As soon as we find out what the radio question is, we refuse to answer it. This isn't bad temper—it is only that we must discourage such calls. A library is busy enough with its own work, and any public service is an overload, although it's an overload we are glad to labor under. Answering questions for lazy listeners is another thing entirely.

But this is drifting pretty far from the newspaper business. Let's get back to the reporter. How can he get the most from his library?

By using it constantly, for one thing, but we have gone into that sufficiently. By using it imaginatively, for another thing. If one clipping suggests an idea, he should get the clippings on the idea. Maybe it will be a waste of two minutes, maybe it will make a story. Is two minutes so precious?

Let the librarians perform as much of the work as possible. This may sound like treason to my own profession, but there is a good reason. A good librarian is trained to ferret out facts. Once he finds out what kind of information is needed, he can get it faster and better than the most talented amateur.

More important, however, he will keep his library in order while he is doing it. The quickest way to destroy a library is to put things back in the wrong place. Misfile an envelope and it might just as well have been thrown away. The librarian knows where things go, and how to put them in there. He can handle fragile clippings without destroying them. His books are classified according to a system, and only he knows the system well enough to handle it.

So I want my files kept sacred to my staff. The *Herald Tribune* is a big paper, and has the luxury of a big library staff, so we forbid reporters to use the files on their own initiative. On other papers it may be necessary once in a while, but it should be avoided as much as possible.

And please! those of you who at one time or another take clippings out of a library, bring them back. Lost clippings are gone forever. Just remember you have them, remember where you put them, and when you are through with them, BRING THEM BACK. It doesn't seem like much to ask.

Anyway, that's how a library works. As you can see, it is a major factor in a newspaper's success. Most papers realize that now, although they didn't always feel that way. The war of 1914-1918 first made it apparent, and brought some great librarians into the field. Such men as David G. Rogers of the *Herald Tribune,* Joseph Kwapil of *The Philadelphia Inquirer,* William Alcott of *The Boston Globe* and Ford Pettit of *The Detroit News* blazed a trail that is being followed more and more conscientiously by papers throughout the country.

One of the great prides of the *Herald Tribune* is a contribution made to library work by Mr. Rogers. In 1932, he consulted Recordak, a subsidiary of the Eastman Kodak Company, on the possibility of adapting microfilm to newspaper files. After several years, the Eastman technical staff developed a machine that films newspaper pages rapidly, and a projector that shows them clearly in full size.

In 1935, filming of the *Herald Tribune* started, and we now have every paper, from *The New-York Tribune* of April 10, 1841 up to last month, on microfilm. Copies are in public and college libraries throughout the country. Eastman keeps the original film in special storage, and should our positives be lost or damaged, they can be replaced immediately.

Reporters need no longer fumble with the delicate pages of dusty bound volumes. A reel of film can be slipped into the projector and viewed, page by page, with no more effort than is involved in turning a hand wheel. Our entire film file rests in metal cabinets that take up only a fraction of the space that bound volumes would require. The method is being widely copied, but so far as we know, the *Herald Tribune* was the first to put it into effect.

[11] SCIENCE REPORTER

by Stephen White

THE newspaper-buying public likes to have its newspapers written in a language it understands, and to fulfill this desire the publisher must employ translators. Not translators from the Polish or the Lithuanian, although at times such paragons would be worth their weight in gold. The need is greater than that. The publisher must find himself a corps of men who can translate the mystic—and at times abominable—dialects spoken by the world's scientists, aviators, and physicians, to name only a few of those who preen themselves on the possession of languages of their own.

Make no mistake—their languages are distinct ones. The ordinary American would have far more difficulty understanding an American protein chemist, for example, than that same chemist would have understanding a Russian colleague. As a working reporter, I have covered (in the days before the whim of a city editor made me an expert on science) many an assignment which took place entirely in a foreign language of which I had no knowledge. It was difficult, but it could be done. Heaven defend the man, though, who without a knowledge of nuclear physics is called upon to attend a meeting of the American Physical Society. I'd choose an intimate interview with an Iranian general. At least the general gestures.

Science has to be covered, and so do all other specialized fields. They are becoming more important day by day, and the public is becoming equally more demanding in its desires. If the intricacies of modern science turn out to be far beyond a science reporter's ability to simplify them, and beyond the readers' patience to struggle through them, it does not alter the fact that those readers want a good solid whack at it, and the newspapers should be happy to provide it.

Perhaps you think I exaggerate the difficulty of the problem. Let's see. I reach into my desk and take out a recent copy of the *Physical Review*. This is a magazine published once a month for physicists. Sooner or later, every major discovery in physics appears between its covers. I read it regularly, and find a story in it frequently.

Take this tidbit, on page 74—"Schwarzschild Interior Solution in an Isotropic Co-ordinate System." Or perhaps you like the thrilling essay on page 89, "Activation of Ag (225 d.) by Resonance Neutrons." On page 98 the title is more terse, "Helium Cryostat."

Unless I underestimate the public seriously, none of these stories will be snapped up on the way into the subway. The problems of making an honest dollar, getting fed and housed, and finding a place to go in the summer don't leave enough time for the ordinary citizen to allow him to be posted on isotropic co-ordinate systems.

That's a statement of fact, and I don't expect anybody to take issue with it. But it's no less true that the same public that lacks the time to understand the *Physical Review* demands that the *Physical Review* be explained to it, clearly and accurately, and without delay. That's why *The New York Herald Tribune* hires me, and most other major papers hire somebody like me.

I don't know about the masterminds on the other papers (although I have my suspicions). But let me make a confession. I don't know what those titles mean myself. I may have a dim suspicion of what they mean, but I don't know. Yet, I have to understand them in a hurry, and if any one of them is that vague thing known as "a good story" I have to get it down on paper—fast. What's more, I usually do. So do my colleagues. That's how you know what happens in the world of science, and—admit it now—you DO have a pretty good idea, don't you?

Why don't I know what they mean? you may ask. After all, I'm hired for the job. Yes, but look. . . .

It takes a good man his whole lifetime to understand fully any one segment of the subject known as physics. It takes a whole college faculty to know the whole field of physics. It takes another faculty to know chemistry, and then we still have biology, geology, astronomy, bacteriology, psychology. It is apparent that under no conceivable conditions could I ever learn all those fields, or even a tiny proportion of them. If I could, I wouldn't be in the newspaper business—I'd be in the circus.

Even if I knew as much as the most recent Nobel-prize winner, the necessity for spreading my knowledge over the enormous field of science would mean that I still knew virtually nothing in each specialty. And anyway, I don't know that much. Furthermore, I don't think any of my fellow science reporters know a great deal more than I do. Yet, on the whole we do a pretty good job.

Let's see how it's done. To begin with, I am going to talk about science, because that happens to be my beat. The problem is the same for a reporter covering aviation, or medicine, or any one of a dozen possible beats. The problem is the same, and the procedure is the same. Where I write "science" you can fill in any of the others.

Before going into how we do it, it might be well to summarize what it is we are supposed to do. I am expected by my paper to know, in advance, what is going to happen in the world of science in the near future, so that both I and my paper will be ready for it when it happens. I am expected to find out all about it when it happens. I am expected to write that information down quickly and clearly, so that he who runs may read. Finally, I am expected to be ready at all times to cover any scientific story that comes up suddenly, without the warning my newspaper expects from me.

I can't do all this by knowing science. Instead, I do it by knowing scientists. And in that pair of sentences you have the story of the specialized beat.

In every field of science, it is my business to know the great men of the past, who have made their contributions and are now the men who teach and inspire others. I must also know the men who are doing great work today, and the men who will do great work in the future.

These men cover science for me. The older men, by the nature of their position, know everything that is going on in their fields. They have a bird's-eye view of science, and in most cases they have the time and the desire to talk about it. The men who are at their productive peak are a little harder to reach, and not so likely to sit around chatting. In their specialities, though, they are willing always to let me know just what the story is and what it means. As for the younger men—I eat with them, drink with them, and go to ball games with them, when we both have time. They tip me off on the future, because they are the future.

That makes the whole thing sound easy, and it isn't that easy. Such a system of gathering news has its responsibilities as well as its delights.

To begin with, none of these scientists is going to talk to me if I am utterly ignorant. They don't expect me to know the technique of metallic shadow casting in electron microscopy, but they do expect me to know what shadow casting is, and what an electron microscope is. In other words, in all the fields of science that I cover, I must have a rudimentary knowledge of the terminology and the problems. Rudimentary is the word for it, but that little is vital, or I am in the position of a reporter interviewing a bridge expert without ever having seen a deck of cards.

More important, I must have the absolute confidence of the men with whom I deal. A reporter finds confidence essential on any beat where his news sources remain the same men from year to year, so there isn't anything special about it. But in the fields of which I write, the confidence is more difficult to win.

A scientist must live with his fellow scientists, and when you come right down to it, they are not the easiest people to live with. They tend to be a little jealous, and to examine every scientific claim with a most embarrassingly scrutinizing eye. The man who pretends to an important discovery, without rigorous proof that his discovery is actually and fairly established, is an outlaw. The scientist who seeks publicity is scorned as a charlatan, and he is doubly a charlatan if he seeks publicity by way of sensationalism.

As a result, the honest scientist—and he is the one with whom I want to deal—worries whenever he speaks to a reporter. The slightest misunderstanding, or the slightest misquotation, will cost him the respect of his fellows. He will not trust me, a reporter, until he is sure that I will neither misunderstand nor misquote him. And on my part, if I am to continue in business, I must be careful never to misquote him or to misunderstand him.

I must also trust his confidences. He will tell me of work in progress only if he knows I will maintain silence until the work is finished. If I do anything else, he is placed in the position of announcing a result before he himself is sure of it. In the world of science there are few greater sins.

Let us assume that I have learned the terminology of science, that I have established working relations with good scientists, and that for a spell I have shown myself worthy of their confidences. In the normal course of things, I will automatically learn what new advances are to be expected in different fields. In the various scientific publications (and how many there are!) my eyes will be open for technical papers bearing on those fields. I know very well I won't understand one when I find it, but I am fairly confident that I will recognize its importance, even though I can't follow it line by line.

Now, and only now, I am ready to go into business. Let us

suppose the business comes—that I find in the *Physical Review* a technical paper entitled "Production of Proton-pairs in the 2,000,000,000-volt Electron Accelerator." (I'm on safe ground with this supposition, since there is no 2,000,000,000-volt electron accelerator, and there isn't likely to be for some time.)

Well, first I filter this through my vague knowledge of terminology. Protons are matter—as a matter of fact, hydrogen gas is nothing but a lot of proton and a little electron. So if they are producing protons, it looks as if they are producing matter, which should be a good story. The rest of the title tells me that they aren't producing them from orange marmalade, either, but they are actually turning energy into matter. This is a good story (parenthetically, it will be a hell of a good story—when it happens).

Then I read the technical paper, which isn't going to help me much. More than likely, I will be completely out of my depth by the time I get to the second paragraph. But I am not at all desperate. It is the next steps that are the crucial ones, and I hope I am ready for them.

I don't intend to mention any names, but I know someone at the University of Something who is an authority in the field of electron accelerators. I've had a few drinks with him, at a meeting of the American Physical Society, and I've dealt with him often. He knows me, and he knows I can be trusted. So what I do is telephone him. "Dr. Someone," I say, "look what's in the *Physical Review*."

And Dr. Someone tells me all about it. He tells me what it means, and what it may indicate, and why it is good work or bad work. I ask him questions, and he answers them as thoroughly as he can. By the time he gets through, I have a good basic knowledge of what that paper means. He usually concludes, "Don't use my name, will you? After all, I haven't read the paper, and I haven't checked up on the work." So I don't use his name. If I did, he wouldn't be in the next time I called.

Naturally, I don't let it go at that. I call Dr. Whosis, and Dr. Whatsis. The three men may disagree, but from them I get a sound story. I'm on my way into print.

One more thing, though. I call, if possible, the man who wrote the paper. By this time, I am primed for him. I know the angles and the objections. If he lets me, I cross-examine him on his paper. Usually he helps me out, but here again, I get the same last word—"Don't quote me on anything but what is in the *Physical Review*." I don't.

All this being done, I can write my story. Now, perhaps, you begin to realize why my newspaper carries so much pontification under my by-line. On Monday I am likely to be an expert on chemistry; on Wednesday I write learnedly upon bacteriology; and on Friday I give brief lessons in astronomy. The reason, of course, lies in those omnipresent last words "Don't quote me."

Since I am not allowed to say that Dr. Whosis told me all these nuggets of wisdom, I have to write them as if they came out of my own handicapped brain. At times it annoys me a great deal more than it annoys the least tolerant reader to find myself in the position where my by-line must act as authority for a column of erudite prose. It must be done that way, if it is done at all. It doesn't help at all to write "An authority said," since "authorities" must give their names and addresses if they are to be at all convincing.

There is a danger in this sort of thing—a danger I hope I have avoided so far, and that I am alert to avoid permanently. Pontification is an insidious habit. After a while, one begins to be convinced of his own infallibility. Too many experts in the newspaper business begin by seeking information and end by giving it. Me, I don't know anything about all these things I write about, and don't let me kid you. Most of all, don't let me start kidding myself.

Anyway, that's how I cover my beat. When news came that the atom bomb had been dropped, that is the way science reporters all over the country covered that story—which was, by the way, one case in which they hadn't the vaguest idea what was happening.

If you talk to the men who cover medicine and aviation and all the rest of the specialized beats, you will find it's the way they cover their beats. It's a lot of fun, too. We couldn't ask for better jobs.

[12] SPORTS

by Red Smith

EVERY hour on the hour, and at shorter intervals around the time of high-school and college commencements, beamish boys address the sports editor thus:

"I have always wanted to be a sports writer. I have always been interested in all sports, particularly curling. I played on the high-school lacrosse team and was sports editor of the campus weekly. I know by rote the batting averages of all players down to the Three-Eye League since 1930."

Depending on whether or not the sports editor's budget allows for a secretary, he (a) flings such appeals into the wastebasket or (b) dictates a polite note regretting that there are no openings at this time. If he had the leisure and inclination to play seeing-eye dog for these blinded youths, he would reply:

"Look, son, if you really want to be a sports writer, go hound the city editor for a job chasing fire engines. Catch on somehow as a cub reporter or copy boy. Learn to wheedle a photograph from a divorcee, and to interview a diplomat intelligently, and to find the real reason why the bloomer knitters are on strike, and to talk to a man in the death block. Develop some understanding of why these people make news, and some proficiency and taste in writing their stories.

"If when you've done that you do not consider it beneath you to report the scores of games, you'll experience no difficulty transferring to the sports department where they'll let you spread your wings."

It is unhappily true that a great many sports departments bear about the same intimate relationship to the rest of the newspaper as the iron mine bears to the open hearth. The inmates of the department are like aldermen or members of an exclusive club, withdrawn from and insulated against the turbulent city around them. And the trouble with most bad sports writers is that they have only the foggiest notion of what newspaper work is all about. That goes for many who have put in all their adult years drawing wages from the same cashier who pays off the police reporter.

The green sprout comes to the sports editor with two pieces of equipment: a desire to get into the ball game free and a pious resolution to expunge all traces of English from the stuff he writes. Faithful reading of sports pages—psychiatrists cannot explain why he chooses the models he does—has taught him that a base hit never may be called a hit but only a bingle, a safety, or a clout; that an inning must always be a stanza, canto, or chapter; a basketball player always is a cager; a soccer player, a booter; and a football player, a gridder; that the only printable designations for a baseball team in Brooklyn are Dem Bums and the Durochermen.

If, beginning thus, he never gets out of the sports department, the chances are he will go to his grave believing that with the possible exception of the story of creation, the most stirring news conceivable is that "All roads lead to Yankee Stadium today."

So the first rules are these:

1. Be a newspaperman first and a sports writer next. If there are a half-dozen top sports writers in America who did not serve an apprenticeship in the city room, their names do not come to mind.

2. The English language, if handled with respect, scarcely ever poisons the user.

Watching games and reporting who won is about as pleasant a way of earning a living as man has devised. If one doesn't get rich at it, one has at least the opportunity to lean back on a sunny summer afternoon and wonder what the poor are doing. One of the most gifted practitioners of this agreeable craft has a favorite saying: "Show me a better racket and I'll give it a try." Up to now, no one has.

It is a good racket. The sports writer has a working press pass (tax exempt) for the events that others pay to see. The best seat in the house is reserved for him except at a World Series, where his accommodations are less roomy than a strait-jacket, or at a big heavyweight fight, where he sits behind a movie star, a ward heeler, and a night-club operator. In some baseball parks a collation is served during the game and there is a press lounge nearby providing more stimulating refreshment. Most football foundries furnish a chilly frankfurter and cold coffee between halves, and make no especial effort to spill the mustard on the reporter's notes.

Except for these creature comforts, the only difference between the fan's lot and that of the sports writer is this: one is there to enjoy himself, the other to work.

When the fan leaps to his feet and cheers, the reporter ducks his head and scribbles a note. When the rooter rends his haberdashery in a transport of joy, the newspaperman frowns in concentration, mentally phrasing his opening paragraph. When the Old Blue in Section 8 goes snake-dancing across the field to tear down the goal posts, the sports writer rolls two sheets of paper into his portable typewriter and sets to work.

The job he has to do then has been compared to chipping off a small piece of his brain with a chisel, one piece per assignment. It isn't quite as bad as that. But the man who covers 154 baseball games in a summer doesn't always find it easy to make the story of today's game fresh, and readable, and noticeably different from yesterday's. Hardly anybody, finding him ankle-deep in crumpled paper which he has ripped out of the typewriter in despair, would envy him.

Once in a long while the sports writer rebels. There was one who accompanied a Philadelphia football team to a game in Orangeburg, South Carolina, which happened to be played on a Friday. The two best teams in the South were to meet next day in another city to determine which should go to the Rose Bowl.

Departing from Philadelphia, the reporter accidentally struck himself on the brow with a pinch bottle and lapsed into a semi-conscious state which endured until the party arrived in Orangeburg. There he disappeared entirely. Somebody else wrote his story for him and then a search was organized. The body was exhumed in the town's chief hotel.

"C'mon, Joe, wake up," the leader of the posse urged. "We're catching a train for Philadelphia."

"Whensa game start?" Joe asked, duty always uppermost in his mind.

"The game's over," he was told, "and your piece is in the paper. By the way, your boss asked over the wire whether you planned to cover the big game tomorrow and we told him no, you couldn't make train connections."

By this time Joe was propped up in bed on one elbow. He was a distinguished-looking man, silver-haired and erect. Now he drew himself up stiffly.

"That's right," he approved. "Only one game at a time!"

Ghostwriting for colleagues who have been taken unexpectedly feeble is not confined to the sports field but it probably is more common there than among, say, Washington correspondents. It is the basis of a fund of folklore. There is, for example, the story about a veteran who became incapacitated at the Saratoga races. For several days a friendly Western Union chief selected paragraphs from other writers's dispatches and patched together stories which he filed under the veteran's by-line.

At length the sufferer arose from his bed of pain and, weaving slightly, made his way to the Western Union office. In those days there were two telegraph companies.

"Listen," he roared, waggling a finger under the chief's nose, "if my stuff doesn't improve immediately, I'm filing Postal!"

Sports writers on rival papers willingly help one another out because, not only is there a camaraderie typical of the press box, but there is comparatively little competition for news beats. Most sports news is scheduled—the game is played or rained out; a team wins or loses, the score is posted, and there's no secret about it.

Consequently, the competition is in the writing rather than the gathering of news. That's why there are police reporters and war correspondents and so on, but only sports *writers*—the emphasis being on composition. A paper that hopes to attract readers through its sports pages must not only provide complete and accurate coverage, but the sports news must be presented in livelier, more readable style than in rival sheets.

The reader who turns to the sports page is looking for entertainment, exactly like the customer at the box office.

Appreciating this fact, the sports writer frequently falls victim to the occupational ailment of overwriting. He strains for the unusual "angle," gropes for the sprightly phrase, and, overreaching, pitches overboard into a purple waste of mixed metaphors. Some of the best writing that appears in newspapers shows up on the sports page alongside some of the most execrable.

There are no known rules to guide an apprentice along the path of rectitude. There is no established pattern to define, for example, the proper way to write a baseball story. Only a few basic principles can be stated.

Every ball game is different from every other ball game, if the reporter has the knowledge and the wit to discern the difference. If he can report the difference intelligently, every story will have a freshness without labored groping for an "angle." He ought to get the score right, describe the play simply, and make it clear why one team beat the other team. He should remind himself frequently that it's only a game, and that the natural habitat of the tongue is the left cheek. And he must shun the frumious cliché.

The job requires less muscle than digging ditches. The baseball writer's day needn't begin until shortly before game time when he visits the dugouts to check on the condition of the boil on the shortstop's stern. For the next two hours he records the plays in his score book, dictating to a telegraph operator if he must send play-by-play accounts to an afternoon paper. Then the morning-paper man writes his piece and is through; the afternoon man turns out a brief post-game lead and retires to compose his "overnight," which will appear in tomorrow's early editions.

This routine varies slightly with the sport but not much. Football is a more complicated game to report, and the writer notes its progress on a chart instead of in a score book. Most big football colleges furnish line-ups, statistics, and similar details.

Virtually all baseball clubs, some professional football teams, and an occasional college invite the press to travel to out-of-town games with expenses paid. Some papers prefer to pay their representatives' way. The Cleveland papers, *The Chicago Tribune, The St. Louis Post-Dispatch* all pay their own and so do *The New York Herald Tribune, The New York Times, The New York Daily News* and *PM*. It makes little difference to the individual writer. Although it is true that many baseball writers, being fans, tend to become more and more a part of baseball and less and less working newspaper men, it also is true that no writer pulls his punches because he is traveling at the club's expense.

For afternoon or early morning editions, the reporter who sends a play-by-play account of a football game misses most of the niceties of the line play, because he must follow the ball. He sees more, however, than the neophyte covering a track and field meet, whose time is consumed chiefly in scouring through the program seeking records and the first names of the contestants. A more satisfactory alternative is to sit next to Jesse Abramson, of the *Herald Tribune,* an incredible character who has known all track performers since the cradle and can quote every record clocked since *Pithecanthropus* first stood *erectus.*

An ideal sports staff would be composed of writers with the expert knowledge of an Abramson in track, a Stanley Woodward in football, a Garry Schumacher in baseball, and a Joe Palmer in horse racing.

However, the rookie sports writer will, as a rule, start on his first job knowing little more about his craft than the rookie bank messenger knows about compound interest. Both should learn as they go along. The chronically uninformed can always write the sports column.

[13] BUSINESS NEWS

by Harvey E. Runner

OF all news, that of business is perhaps closest to the consumer's pocketbook—and, therefore, of wide public interest. Yet, business news, as covered by newspapers, is a comparatively new development. It took a serious depression and a second world war to drive home its real importance.

For years, newspapers have covered the news of mankind, faithfully reporting births and deaths, describing man's joys and pleasures, and detailing his trials and tribulations. No interest—from society and sports to politics and crime—was neglected save one, that of business.

True, newspapers carried financial-news stories, side by side with daily quotations of stocks and bonds. Wall Street activities were well covered, as was news of interest to investors. Little attention, however, was devoted to business, industrial, and trade news and what did appear in print was written, in most instances, for a select few engaged in finance or industry. This news was of virtually no interest to the general public, except those persons who were holders of securities.

The possibility that the everyday developments in business could be of vital interest to the public—as much as sports, politics, or crime—was not considered by either businessmen or newspaper publishers.

Today, that is all changed. Business developments are viewed in a new light. The long depression of the 1930's, and the strikes and shortages which followed World War II focussed attention on the causes for such things.

As a result, it is now realized that what happens in the nation's industrial plants and mills and in offices and stores can spell a surplus or shortage or a change in price of many important living essentials at some future date.

Businessmen carefully watch their daily newspaper for information which will have an effect on their own business. They are interested in production figures, inventories, use of credit, prices, sales, profits, and company decisions of various kinds. They also are interested in government action, especially in an age which has given birth to so many federal controls.

Today's well-written business story is also of deep interest to the public, for more often than not, it will be on the business-news pages that the public will see its first announcement of new refrigerators, washing machines, or deep-freeze units. The business-news page also is likely to be first to tell of new developments in television or radio and to show photographs of the new models.

Moreover, if nylon hosiery, white shirts, men's suits, or Scotch whisky are to be in larger or smaller supply, it is ten to one the first news the public will have of it will come from a business-news story.

Before 1930, few stories concerning business appeared in the front section of the average newspaper and rarely did such a story reach page one. Now, scarcely a day goes by without one or more stories dealing with some phase of business appearing on page one and with anywhere from forty to sixty additional stories, big and little, being used on the back pages.

The importance of business news began to be realized on a broadening front after the disastrous stock market break of 1929. When the National Recovery Administration was formed, business news became page-one news. Therefore, it might well be said that business news did not arrive by way of the back pages, as most classifications did, but via the first page.

During the 1930's, attempts to raise the country out of the depression made important news, most of which dealt with steps to boost the level of business and create greater employment. It was during these years that the Washington bureaus of daily newspapers began to pay more attention to business news and even to assign one or two members of their staffs to watch developments in this field.

Some newspapers, including *The New York Herald Tribune,* have created a separate business-news department, which specializes in reporting daily the most significant developments in business, industry, and trade. This department is headed by a business-news editor, who like the city editor, sports editor, and other department heads, is directly responsible to the managing editor. Personnel of business-news departments runs as high as twelve persons on some newspapers.

The importance of business news was emphasized anew in 1945 when the Associated Press announced that its financial-news department would be known as the business-news department and its editor as general business editor. Previously, the department head had been known as the financial editor. The Associated Press, in explaining its action, said that it was better to call it "business" than "financial" as the field of business included not only financial, but industrial and commercial activities as well.

In New York City, three newspapers, the *Herald Tribune, The New York Times* and *The Sun,* have separate business-news and financial-news departments, each with an individual editor. The two departments, while working closely together, are entirely independent of each other. The fields of coverage are clearly divided. Each department is allotted its own space daily and determines which stories are to be used and the relative play each is to receive.

On other newspapers throughout the country the activities of the two departments are combined and under one head. Up until the war, the department head was known as the financial editor but in recent years some newspapers have changed the title to business-news editor.

Where there are two departments—business news and financial news—each has its own fields to cover. On the *Herald Tribune* this work is divided as follows:

Business news: Broadly speaking, business news, among other phases of business management, covers production, planning, sales, advertising, promotion, purchasing, pricing, merchandising, and wholesale-retail distribution. Specific industries covered include: automobiles, rubber, tires, food, liquor, textiles, men's and women's clothing, shoes, leather, hosiery, radio, television, broadcasting, advertising, electrical appliances, heating equipment, pharmaceuticals, plastics, furniture, floor coverings, motorcycles, motorboats, office equipment, household goods, cosmetics, jewelry, toys, luggage, tobacco, and candy.

These are only the major industries for which business news is responsible. There are dozens of smaller ones which also are covered.

Financial news: Just as business news covers the management functions of industry, so financial news takes over the financial functions. These include the annual financial statements, bond and stock issues, dividends, and similar actions. In addition, financial news embraces the stock and bond markets and various exchanges throughout the country. It also includes the commodity markets, banking and insurance, and several industries, including railroads, aviation, petroleum, coal, public utilities, foreign trade, steel, iron, and chemicals.

This division of coverage in regard to industries varies slightly on different newspapers. For instance, on the *Times,* foreign trade is covered by the business-news department whereas on the *Herald Tribune* it is handled by the financial-news department.

Both the business- and financial-news departments have writers who specialize in one or more fields. Sometimes a writer will cover only one or two fields, but in most instances fields include six to ten industries.

For example, on the *Herald Tribune,* one reporter covers the men's and women's clothing fields. A second covers automobiles, rubber, tires, motorcycles, and motorboats; and a third, radio, television, broadcasting, sales promotion, and advertising news.

Business news concerns itself mostly with the consumer-goods industries—those industries which produce and sell the tens of thousands of items which the public purchases every day out of necessity or for pleasure. No other kind of news is so close to the daily life of the average person, and for that reason business news is not dull but alive and interesting.

Stories on food, clothing, and automobiles, for example, touch the daily life of nearly every individual. When these stories tell of price changes or report whether the supply is large or small, millions of people are interested.

Not all business-news stories are written by business-news reporters; some are handled by city-staff reporters and others by men in the various out-of-town bureaus of newspapers, notably the Washington bureau. Some of these men may be trained business-news writers, but most of them are not.

The city desk on the alert newspaper is acutely conscious of daily developments in business which affect large segments of the population. Scarcely a day goes by without several members of the staff receiving assignments touching on some phase of business. Usually, these men, where they work on newspapers having business-news departments, consult with the business-news editor before going to work on their assignments, asking for background information and the names of the most likely sources.

There is close co-operation between the city desk and the business-news desk on these stories. Sometimes, the city editor will ask the business-news desk to handle an assignment. When this is done the finished story is turned over to the city desk. At other times, a member of the business-news staff will develop or cover a story which obviously is worth page one and it will be offered to the city desk or the managing editor.

The ideal way of covering a business-news story is for the man most familiar with the field to handle the assignment. The average city-staff reporter, even though given the sources, is working under two distinct disadvantages. First, he does not have full background information on the subject. Second, his sources do not know him personally and he does not know them.

This works against a general-news reporter, for men in business and in finance usually are reluctant to talk with reporters who are unfamiliar with their subjects and whom they do not know personally. They have found, through experience, that the information they give in response to questions sometimes is misinterpreted or presented incorrectly, since the man on the assignment does not understand the situation as fully as would a specialized writer regularly covering the field.

Therefore, these sources frequently do not talk as freely to city-staff reporters as they do to the business- or financial-news writers whom they know. Perhaps the toughest assignment a city-staff reporter can get is to be put on a business or financial story which on other newspapers may be covered by the experts in that field.

The automobile field is perhaps the one outstanding industry in business news coverage where the reporter responsible for such news handles it for the whole paper. In the days ahead the tendency will be toward increased specialization in covering news and this will make the business-news writer a more important factor in the production of the more readable newspapers of the future.

All too few newspapers have business-news departments or specialists in that field on their staff. Those newspapers that have such men are doing a fine piece of work in keeping the public posted on scores of developments touching on the economic life of the nation, which a dozen or so years ago were not considered worthy of publication.

A fact not generally realized is that a majority of the writers on business news on New York City newspapers are men who broke into editorial work through the city staff. They are good reporters and competent writers, comparing favorably with city-staff men.

For example, two business-news writers on one newspaper have become foreign correspondents and a former business-news writer on another newspaper has become a news correspondent abroad for one of the radio networks.

There is a growing tendency today for the business-news departments to select men with city-desk experience when filling vacancies or adding to their staffs. This is a step in the right direction and reveals an interesting change in the reporter's attitude toward this type of news in recent years.

Ten years ago a man working on the city staff of the average newspaper rarely wanted to change over to business-news writing. Therefore, vacancies were filled either from the trade press or by men just beginning newspaper work. Today when a vacancy occurs, the majority of the applicants for the business-news vacancy are reporters and rewrite men from the city staffs of newspapers.

There are several reasons for this trend, the most important being the general realization among newspaper men that business news is becoming more important than ever and that a reporter with knowledge in that field becomes a better reporter, should he ever transfer back to the city staff.

Newspaper men also realize that business news, being a comparatively new field, offers many opportunities in the future. The average business-news story is not a one-day story, as so many assignments are, but a continuing, developing story in which facts learned and written about become background for the next story. Covering business news might be compared to getting an education in economics or a graduate course in some field of business—and at the same time being paid for it.

The business-news reporter, unlike the general-news reporter, is not wholly dependent upon his editor for assignments. While some assignments are given by the business-news editor, the reporter is mostly on his own and it is his responsibility to cover all news in the fields assigned to him. He should be the first to see a potential story in any industry he covers.

Through his daily contacts, he knows what is developing in his fields and usually plans his own day's work. A business-news reporter, therefore, must have plenty of individual initiative, make and develop friends and sources who will help to keep him informed, and be able to recognize any change or development in an industry which may warrant a story.

A business-news reporter gets an extra thrill in uncovering a good story which his competition may not have, because frequently the story is one which he personally has developed and not an assignment. Every business-news reporter is expected to turn in several exclusive stories weekly, in addition to doing a special feature for the Sunday issue.

The business-news field in New York City is highly competitive. Most of the dailies cover business news whether or not they have a separate business-news department. The business press also offers keen competition, with five dailies in the field. They are the *Journal of Commerce, Wall Street Journal* (now devoted largely to business news), *Women's Wear Daily, Daily News Record,* and *Radio Daily.*

The fact that newspapers in New York City have the competition of five dailies in the field of business alone is in itself strong evidence that newspapers were late in recognizing the importance of business news. Even though the business press has been doing a good job and is continuing to improve itself, newspapers are making themselves felt as an important medium in the business-news field.

Most newspaper readers, however, have yet to learn the importance of business news. This is because: (1) in many newspapers, it is still neglected; (2) in others, it is placed in the back part of the newspaper where it is not seen by many readers; (3) it needs to be presented more interestingly; and (4) it requires some promotion by publishers advising the public what they are missing when they do not turn to a newspaper's back pages.

Once the general public catches on to the fact that business-news stories are written for them as well as for businessmen and businesswomen, the readership of such stories will increase. A newspaper's back pages will then become must reading for the public just as they are today for business executives.

The prediction is made here that at some future date business news will rank with sports in interest to the reader. When it does, business news will have a staff as large as that of sports and its allotment of news space will equal that of sports. The potential audience is there. All that is needed is to keep business-news stories interesting and informative and to educate readers to turn to the back pages of their daily newspapers.

[14] THE CRITICS

by Howard Barnes

THE field of newspaper criticism is largely uncharted. While its practitioners usually enjoy reputations and rewards unshared by their anonymous colleagues, the function of their jobs is speculative. Even when reporting is, as it should be, the basis of approach to artistic endeavors, there is extreme latitude between popular appeal on the one hand and so-called objective standards on the other.

In some instances, notably the theater, critics wield an almost dictatorial authority. Their appraisals usually define the ultimate commercial success, if not the artistic recognition of stage productions. Literature and music are conditioned less directly by newspaper notice, although it is a hardy impresario or executant who can ignore the reviews. For years the screen has belittled the importance of journalistic evaluation, while examining it avidly and advertising voluminously in conjunction with it. The dance, art, and even the radio are conscious of the sometimes dubious distinction of spot coverage.

However singular many manifestations of newspaper artistic opinion may be, this branch of editorializing is firmly established in the pattern of reporting. Metropolitan papers devote space daily to reviews and features of the arts as standard procedure, while on Sunday one and frequently several special sections are dedicated to news and comment.

Reader interest is inevitably specialized, but it is intense and given to personal expression. A controversial critic, as George Bernard Shaw or more latterly Virgil Thomson will attest, is insured a large volume of indignant and approving letters from craftsmen and art-lovers generally.

Aside from knowledge of any art, a paramount quality of reviewing is enthusiasm. In this day of mass production, good, bad, and indifferent artistic expressions are scrambled together. Inevitably a critic's patience is taxed. His function as commentator and guide, however, becomes all the more vital. In this country, at least, the aloof pedant has little place in the newspaper scheme.

The late Percy Hammond, whose brilliant style and perception made him a leading dramatic critic of his generation, took a season off to go around the world in the early 1930's, leaving this writer to cover openings. He was jubilant about his leave of absence. "In a couple of months," he said, "you will be dragging yourself to one dismal flop after another. Me, I'll be standing in the moonlight, drinking in the beauty of the Taj Mahal. And do you know what I'll be saying to myself? 'Lord, I wish I were back on Broadway for that first night at the Bijou or the Morosco.' "

No matter how cynical he may become, a reviewer must beware of becoming tagged as jaded by the reading public. While it is imperative that he maintain a rigid integrity and refrain from being swayed by petty personal prejudices, he must keep his approach buoyant and even optimistic. He is observing a small show in the larger show of a newspaper's coverage.

The question with which a reviewer is most frequently confronted is the manner in which he assays a work. When it is an established composition, as is generally the case in music or fine arts, there is a fund of registered approval or disapproval on which to draw. With new works, particularly on the stage and in literature, the reviewer is very much on his own. Whatever objective and enduring yardsticks he may fancy employing, his personal reaction is of vital importance. To hold any large body of readers this must, of course, conform in measure to audience reaction, but over a period of time it may influence the popular point of view. As one who should know, this writer can flatly state that movie criticism had a minuscule impression on the industry or the public twenty years ago, but has now become a considerable force. In this instance reviewers thought and wrote with unique independence.

There are those who will object that a personal reaction is small guarantee of genuine artistic appraisal. On the contrary, it is the only factor which makes a reviewer something more than a factual recorder of a work and the audience reaction to it. Given experience and background and some sense of public taste, the critic is on safest ground when he is heeding his own enjoyment or displeasure. That this is usually based on an emotional response makes it somewhat unpredictable, but it also increases the chances of its being a common denominator to universal appreciation.

A critic of the theater has admitted that his judgment was partially swayed by his wife. "When she laughs," he said, "the chances are good that the show is funny. When she cries, it is moving, although perhaps corny. When she goes to sleep, there is more than a suspicion that the offering is dull."

Carried too far, this is a dubious distinction of artistic worth. First-night audiences are special, and often overeager in their approval. Since a newspaper write-up is designed for prospective spectators, readers, or listeners, it is a wise commentator who pays scant attention to the first round of applause.

Of all newspaper critical tasks, the reviewing of books is perhaps the most arduous. The sheer volume of published works these days is prodigious enough to appall a chronicler. It is true that this is one branch in which reviews are "farmed out," as it were, specialists from the staff or outside it being called upon to pass judgment on books in their specific fields. At the same time, a chief reviewer must read one or two new volumes a day to keep abreast of his field. Barring complete collapse, his chances of mental and emotional indigestion are high indeed.

Such a daily critic as Lewis Gannett must employ a superb sense of selection as well as a tremendous background in his job. The field in which he operates is in no way limited to literary works of art. Books have become distillations of all the material that newspapers bring to the attention of readers. The book critic must be close to the thought and feeling which vitalize his age.

The special sections, as already noted, permit far more collaboration than in any other artistic field. The Sunday book reviews may represent the opinions of many experts with diverse views and particular prejudices. It is the problem of an editor such as Irita Van Doren to make that collaboration a true reflection of the best thought in the most important fields that have inspired literary expression. Certainly the service to the average reader is infinitely valuable. Without newspaper reviews, he would be snowed under.

In the dramatic field, a commentator is called upon for considerable authority in all the arts. A theater critic who fails to understand and appreciate the enormous influence of motion pictures on people, particularly those who are denied access to the living theater, is making a mistake. With the so-called musical shows he is called upon to evaluate the dramatic potentials of melody and harmony. The increasing importance of the ballet in such offerings makes a background in the dance an important adjunct to his appraisals.

Efrem Zimbalist once summed up the difficulties of music reviewing by telling of a meeting with Deems Taylor. The eminent critic was all agog about taking a course in the violin. "It will help me to better understand chamber and symphonic music," he enthused.

"It will help him," said Zimbalist somewhat wryly. "But I've spent a lifetime learning the fiddle and I'm still learning."

A critic is peculiarly vulnerable in his relations with the craftsman in his medium. Only recently Irwin Shaw, in the preface to a play which had met indifferent Broadway success, complained bitterly that reviewers did not know anything about playwriting, acting, direction, etc. Aside from the fact that such commentators as George Bernard Shaw, St. John Ervine, and George S. Kaufman have set rather striking examples as straight stage artists to refute his charge, it is unfair. No one has to write a play or paint a picture to derive tremendous pleasure from it, or know whether or not he likes it.

I am certain that the less closely associated a critic is with technicians, the more objective and sound his opinions are. While he must always be a clearing ground for controversy about works or schools of art, his championship of anything but sheer quality must always be suspect. More than one commentator has wandered into the byways of political prejudice or esthetic battlegrounds to his inevitable detriment. His job may be highly complicated, but its ultimate objective is clear as crystal.

There are innumerable exceptions to any blanket warning against fraternalization between artists and their appraisers. Motion-picture criticism would be at a low ebb, indeed, were it not that conscientious reviewers have gone to directors and scenarists to discover the touchstone of film quality. Modern music, particularly that involving atonal or polytonal harmony, would have had far slower development were it not for the patient expositions of alert writers in the medium. The literary greats and the most audacious practitioners of the fine arts might still be waiting for popular acceptance had they not had their journalistic interpreters.

It seems idle at this date to stress the importance of newspaper reviewing as a continuous record of artistic achievement. Even when they have forsaken their journalistic podiums, it has been the spot reporters of music, literature, drama, or even radio who have established a consecutive pattern of works and wielded a profound, if incalculable influence over upswings in sincerity and quality. The journalistic judge may be fallible, but if he is worth his salt, he has an enormous and continuous responsibility to both his medium and his public.

A sense of humor is a valuable asset in his vocation. Like the prophet, he is likely to be wanting in honor in his own bailiwick. It is not often that he is compelled to violent defense of his stand, as happened to a New Orleans music critic in the last century who had to fight three duels after criticizing a beauteous soprano adversely. At the same time he must be able to take with something of a shrug such attacks as that of Maxwell Anderson, who called dramatic critics "the Jukes family of journalism," or the oft-repeated assertion, attributed variously to any number of famous showmen, that "the only good critic is a dead critic."

Before he is dead, however, the reviewer has to be very alive indeed. While it is of no real concern to the reader, on-the-spot criticism calls for tremendous speed and nervous tension. A drama critic for a morning newspaper has so short a time in which to write a review that the mere physical matter of putting it on paper becomes a job. Given no more than an hour in which to write on *The New York Herald Tribune* and little more than that on its counterparts, he must pass judgment, analyze, report, and collate in an incredibly brief time. St. John Ervine, when visiting critic of the old morning *World,* insisted on a full day for reviewing, but after a year the paper reverted to the standard deadline.

A question which is frequently uppermost in the minds of followers of newspaper criticism, especially journalistic aspirants, is how in the world anyone ever becomes a reviewer. It is extremely difficult to answer. Having been confronted with it innumerable times during twenty years, the writer can still only stress what may seem like intangibles to eager beavers. Enthusiasm and sincerity are certainly prerequisites to the calling of an artistic commentator. A background in the arts is essential, although too much academic musing may lead to pedantic expression in a field which requires clarity of expression and easy communication with readers.

One of the best bulwarks for a reviewer is a training in straight reporting, which is the basis of his job. There are occasional experts who come to journalistic criticism without any preliminary training in newspaper work, but many of the most celebrated have put in their apprenticeship on three-alarm fires or police courts.

[15] FASHION EDITOR

by Katherine Vincent

THE problems and duties of fashion editors on newspapers vary considerably.

Before I was appointed to *The New York Herald Tribune* staff ten years ago it was pretty clearly set in my mind what was expected of the fashion editor and of the department, in the way of daily and Sunday coverage, special features, and supervision of art work and layouts.

Every editor should be a reporter too. Even though I had experience in the fashion field both in this country and in England and France before my new appointment it seemed clear to me that reporting experience would make a more effective editor and in turn would make for a better, brighter, and more accurate output of work from all the members of the department.

Once you establish an audience which includes both consumers and the trade, it has a way of knowing from your story whether you were enthusiastic about a collection or whether it was "just one little dress after another."

Free of advertising pressure, thanks to the *Herald Tribune* policy, I have been able to develop in fashion writing what I think might be called a point of view. This does not by any means indicate that it even resembles the style of the music, art, or drama critics. What it attempts to be instead is a straightforward kind of reporting, peppered here and there with comments which may be either amusing, enthusiastic, or a little lukewarm. I admit that observations on several occasions in the past have reached a boiling point, because it was the only way to handle the problem with any degree of honesty.

This freedom in journalism should be guarded. Correspondingly unnecessary and unfair remarks for the sake of being funny or just to amuse yourself are unforgivable, and you as the guardian of this trust are not worthy of being a reporter.

As well as reporting, a good fashion editor in a certain sense must lead, not the way a professional crystal-gazer operates but rather with an open mind, a good solid consciousness of the basic aesthetic in styles as well as the utilitarian values for the present and the future. In your selection of merchandise which is to be reported in your pages you must not base that selection too much on just what appeals to you. If that mistake is made an integral part of the meaning of fashion will be sadly lacking and readership appeal is likely in time to be reduced.

I think that when young people go looking for jobs they should have some idea about the problems of the people they are approaching. For example the girl who tells me she is writing two Greek plays, an admirable project I admit, though slightly ambitious, is not the person that I want in the fashion department to write captions, take dictation, file, or do any one of a number of things that come up daily under the heading of "Musts for Today." It seems to me that writing one Greek play would be quite enough. However I do not want an exhausting young intellectual around the office. It baffles me no end that young people who sincerely want to work in one capacity or another on a newspaper cannot think in terms of our problems rather than theirs.

Every new job is bound to present not only its initial difficulties but a constant stream of problems as it goes along. I remember distinctly that during my first week on the *Herald Tribune* the editor of our picture department called me to ask if I would like a "double truck." I was sure that he was asking me to go dancing in Harlem, and needless to say was a little baffled. That however was not the case. A double truck, or a double spread as it is sometimes called, means two pages of photographs facing each other as bravely as possible.

Before appearing officially on the staff I was asked to call on Grafton Wilcox, then managing editor of the paper. He spoke about the American fashion industry. He seemed satisfied that my fashion experience met the necessary requirements and said it was a subject he did not know too much about anyway so there would be no more queries. Then he asked me what I knew about *Herald Tribune* style, print, and the composing room. My answer to that question was rather simple and to the point, "Not much, but I'm sure I could learn." His answer was simple too, "You'll do."

The places for women on a newspaper are by no means limited to fashions, food, beauty, and decorating.

Depend on your own interests, your eagerness to learn, and your ability to adjust yourself to people and situations that change constantly and the field is wide open. No newspaper man or woman can give you a pat formula as to how your personal talents or your capacity to work can be used to the best advantage for the organization or for you. Why should that be discouraging? In a sense it amounts to a challenge. Let us suppose for the sake of the argument that you want to be a combination fashion artist and writer in a small way. Let us say that you have attended a school of journalism and taken a course in fashion drawing. Have you ever considered taking your drawing pad and sketching the costumes of people in your home town or city and doing memory sketches of clothes that you see in the shops?

Naturally you cannot rush feverishly about, attempting to sketch the store's exclusive designs, even though your purpose might be at once innocent and harmless. Harum-scarum ambition of this kind winds up frequently with well-meaning young women telling it to the judge.

The field of fashion holds out enormous promise for young

women in the field of journalism but fashion jobs are not by any means restricted to newspaper work. There is plenty of work to do in fashion illustration and fashion writing, for advertising, publicity and promotional agencies. The radio and the newsreels have spots for fashion experts and when television gets going it surely must devote a lot of its time to fashions.

One of the most interesting things about fashion is that it is in constant motion, sometimes rippling slowly and with great tranquility to a minor change, and other times darting in swift leaps to a radical new idea. Fashion as a form of art is never static. In this respect it may well be applied to other arts that have changed through the years. Does the Empire State Building look like the old Flatiron Building? That is an example of the gradual and radical change in architecture. Can you mistake Renoir for Picasso or Dali? That is the slow progression—the moving expression of ideas in art. Do you find any difference between the great music of Mozart and the brilliant compositions of Stravinsky?

Now why should fashion as another form of art be criticized for its frequent if not constant changes? Music and art live through the ages, buildings seem to be quite sturdy, but beautiful or functional clothes have a very limited life span. A high percentage of the accusations that fashions change too quickly stem from the male of the species. I suspect sometimes that they are secretly pleased (in spite of the bills) because our interest in fashion is a subtle compliment to them.

Paris before the war was responsible for a rapid flow of fresh imaginative ideas, another part of motion. Now that the war is over, it will be again, but this time on a slightly different basis. American designers, manufacturers, and retailers have learned a lesson the hard way under wartime restrictions and, as we review the picture step by step or over-all, they did a splendid job. There is no trace of condescension in my tribute to their ingenuity, their talents, and their slavish adherence to regulations that were necessary to the war effort but sometimes confusing to follow.

We know from questionnaires, word-of-mouth reports, and our own personal experiences that fashion advertising in the *Herald Tribune* is read more widely by women than any other single feature. Retail stores and fabric manufacturers present their merchandise in our pages daily and Sundays marked with the distinction of fine art work and bright comprehensive copy that tells their story and gets to the point quickly.

The bulk of daily fashion coverage is spasmodic because showings come only in advance of each season. On the whole, executives of New York stores have done a good job of spacing their showings as much as possible to avoid overlapping. The fashion press does not consider that reporting one collection in the morning and another in the afternoon is an overwhelming project. It means good solid concentration and quite a little sprinting around, but the system is certainly far superior to the old one which blithely offered from three to four important showings in one day, each one newsworthy in its own right.

Paris quite recently was still guilty of this crime on more than one occasion. Its explanation was that American buyers could not stay too long in Paris with the result that the fight for "first come first served" was not so simple for the American press to cover adequately and justly. We did, however, at the expense of life and limb, frequently watching a parade of six hundred to seven hundred dresses and filing stories at one o'clock in the morning (if one worked for a morning newspaper).

The French dearly love *publicité* but they know very little about it. For example, fashion photography in France, with the exception of the work done by a few outstanding people, is deplorable. They are far behind the Americans, who know that a good fashion picture plus a clear, concise caption will best tell a reader the story of a dress. This does not mean that a large and important collection can be covered satisfactorily by printing just a layout of pictures. In this case the well-constructed informative story with a point of view is essential.

If you hope to embark on the perilous career of fashion reporting, the value of being able to take shorthand is not to be underestimated. The only other alternative is to develop speed in longhand and be sure that you can understand your own handwriting—a practical problem when the time comes to do the story.

When you write the story, remember not to indulge in guessing. Your job is to report what you saw. If some silly woman on your left or your right says "Obviously, my dear, geranium pink will be important this season," you can smile politely and say, "Yes, of course." But it is not your job to say what is to come, you are supposed to tell what happened and where. Fashion is news and should be treated as such.

The business of fashion reporting is definitely a woman's job: the average man does not know the difference between a peplum and a tunic. Competition with the male of the species is not to be considered, a point which is certainly in our favor. It is quite true that there are some men in the newspaper business who have a definite interest in fashion, and some of them have a fairly keen understanding of the subject; they are few and far between. In your relationships with the men on a newspaper or in the trade, think like a man and act like a woman. This may be a confusing statement, but you should approach your job objectively, you should be able to report accurately and you should be able to avoid emotional nonsense and scenes in the office. You should always be able legitimately to defend your own point of view, calmly, clearly, thoughtfully and with poise. If you fancy yourself as a Dresden shepherdess, stay out of the newspaper business, there is no room for you. You will not make the grade and in short you will be a plain old-fashioned nuisance.

A fashion job is fun and filled with interest for the woman who is equipped to do it. In many respects you must face tangling with men on various problems, but in the end, and sometimes after a hard struggle, if you manage to win their respect, you have beaten the major part of the problem and although your job still presents its difficulties, the worst of the battle is over.

[16] NEWS WRITING

by John G. Rogers

THE newspaper reporter is the most prolific and widely read writer who ever lived. From Walla Walla to New York and around the world he flails his typewriter incessantly as the first step in the mass production of news. He is male and female, and young and old, and he works twenty-four days a day, including Sunday, cranking out his short-lived wares—hot stuff today, shelf paper tomorrow. At best, his product is very good, dispensing information tersely, clearly, and accurately. At worst, it is confusion, cliché, misspelling, and falsehood. To a large extent people will read him whether he writes well or poorly. This consumer indifference is always depressing to reporters who work hard at the typewriter to give the story quality, but it remains a fact that the readers of newspapers are after information and not inspiration or beauty.

There is, however, a very special kind of beauty in good newspaper writing. Its ingredients are crispness, clarity, punch, and economy. In essence, good newspaper writing is an expert job of simplification. The reporter knows something—a piece of news. His job is to tell it to the reader and, of course, it helps a lot if, in the first place, the reporter actually understands what it is that he knows. But, assuming that he does, then he has to know how to tell it clearly. Doing this right is a sort of knack that some reporters come by naturally, that some have to learn, that some never learn.

Usually, the bigger and more important the story, the easier it is to simplify. Or, rather, the less it requires simplification. When the President dies, there is no need to struggle at the typewriter.

There is no way in the world to start except to say that the President died and from there on, the importance of the event makes every available detail a part of the story.

But, take a reporter who wrote a fine story on the President's death, and send him to cover a meeting of the Committee on the Development and Co-ordination of Intergovernmental Budgetary Finance. Let the committee sit for seven hours, discuss fifteen aspects of its heavy subject without coming to a conclusion, and then let the city editor ask for a column on the story. The reporter is likely to have a tough time. He has to select whatever is meaningful from a great mass of dull detail, and he has to simplify it, and organize it, and write it in such a way that a reader need not flee in frustration after crawling through a first paragraph. Writing this story is strictly a chore, but it is a much tougher test of the reporter's skill than was the one on the President's death.

Through long abuse, the worn typewriters of city rooms are lazy and pedestrian things. Their automatic reflex, when their keys are tapped, is to give forth the cliché, to take the easiest way out. "John Jones, 34, a shoe clerk of 738 Main Street, suffered lacerations and contusions last night when the automobile he was driving skidded and. . . ." or "Declaring that the end of the world within ten years is a virtual certainty, Prof. Felix Smith asserted last night in an address before the West Side Men's Club that. . . ." And so on. Such dreary stuff is all that any reporter ever will get out of his typewriter unless he sets to work with imagination to seduce something better out of the old apparatus.

Several aspects of newspaper writing are based on shortages. Usually, the story is supposed to be written as briefly as possible because there is a shortage of space in the paper. Then, the most important facts are supposed to be told first, next most important facts second, etc. This is because the reader has a shortage of time and must be told the essentials in a hurry in case he has to drop the paper in the middle of a story and run somewhere. Clarity, aside from the fact that it is a great ideal, is necessary because some readers have a shortage of ability to understand what they are reading. No slur on the readers here. This third shortage applies to reporters and editors, too, only more so because they are supposed to know something about everything whereas most readers have a limited number of specialties.

There is a good deal of showmanship in newspaper writing. The lead of the story—the first paragraph—is a sort of come-on. Like a woman's eyes or a barker's line, the lead must invite and interest or the suitors and customers may turn away. The best lead is usually the shortest one that reads well and sparkles a bit and is still truthful. Some papers, chiefly the tabloids, are famous for short punchy leads but in their frenzied quest for formulas that will entertain or shock, they too often use distorted or exaggerated leads. No matter how appealingly you wrap up the lead, it is no good if it gives a wrong impression or tells a lie.

The best lead has not only the fewest possible words, but also the shortest appropriate words and phrases. For every long and clumsy word or phrase that seems forever to come first into a reporter's mind, there are short and terse substitutes that are better and are waiting impatiently in the dictionary and thesaurus, aching to be used. The best lead gets along without a comma, which means that it has not more than one short clause to get in the way of the direct statement.

It is said that a good public speaker sometimes picks out one person in his audience and pretends that he is speaking to that person alone. This device might be borrowed by reporters. When a newspaperman sit down and stares at that old enemy, the blank sheet of paper in his typewriter, he might pretend that he is about to tell his story orally to a friend. If he were doing this, he certainly wouldn't use such atrocious words and phrases as "implementation," "thorough investigation of the situation," "virtual certainty," or "indications pointed unmistakably to." Now if he wouldn't use such aberrations in conversation, why must he use them in the paper? Newspaper writing, of course, can't be as completely informal as conversation but a pull in that direction should be a good thing.

Examples might be chosen at will from any paper that is printed, has been printed, or can expect to be printed. Rather than choose a whipping boy, a synthetic lead might be concocted, patterned after our daily sins:

The opinion of observers at the General Assembly of the United Nations, most of whom have devoted considerable time to an analysis of the problems facing the delegates and are in close touch with representatives of the various countries, is that, while the Russian proposals are likely to win some measure of support from the Baltic states and other Soviet satellites, the most probable outcome of the voting on the thirteen items to come before them one by one as they take up the specific settlement of the trusteeship appeals are these:

Ninety-two words and four commas, and the sentence is not over yet, although the paragraph is. And don't think that such a mouthful of mush isn't to be found daily in the New York newspapers. Aside from all considerations of the general beauty of short crisp sentences, consider this: In New York probably half the papers are read on jiggling subways or commuter trains, while the reader and his paper bounce up and down. Fewer commas and more periods should become a battle cry.

A few of the useful rules that make clear writing are almost too obvious to be pointed out, yet they are violated every day. One is to keep the verb as close as possible to the subject. Certainly the two friends should not be separated by long, awkward clauses. Another is to keep the lead free of too much cluttering. A pair of proper names each requiring a long identification is too much freight for most leads to carry. Make it easy on the customers by dropping one or both of them lower in the story.

The overuse of quotation marks is not a violation of clarity but it doesn't contribute to quality. Sheriff Jones began to "crack down" yesterday. . . . The sheriff can crack down just as hard without the quotation marks. The participle lead—asserting that, declaring that, etc.—is the weakest and easiest way to start a story and should be exiled to a limbo of sloppy craftsmen.

Much stiff writing in newspapers today can be traced to journalism schools. The prospective reporter is told, "Remember, the questions of Who, Why, When, Where, and What must be answered in your lead." Often, even after graduation, the student journalist concentrates so hard on this professional injunction that he gets into a mental straitjacket and loses all freshness or individuality of approach.

Another source of writing fault in newspapers is the competitive system. Doakes of the *Chronicle* and Brown of the *Blade* cover the same story and get the same information. Doakes is ambitious and wants to beat Brown. So, at the typewriter he begins to soup up the story, to stick the needle into it quite a bit farther than the facts will justify.

Doakes may write:

"In one of the most significant pronouncements of the year, Mayor Hoffenfeffer declared dramatically yesterday. . . ." And so on through "major implications unfolded against a backdrop of political warfare" and the spirit of it all is: Hold on to your hats, readers! You'll never get this in the *Blade*.

It is a plain fact that to some papers, the simple truth of the story is never enough. They dress it up and pump it up and they don't merely present it to the reader, they all but cram it down his throat.

[17] REWRITE

*by Robert B. Peck**

REWRITE on a morning newspaper is essentially a simple job. It is just a matter of fitting words to facts. The snugger the fit, the better the story. The rewrite man doesn't even have to get the facts. Somebody else digs them up and sends them in. All the rewrite man has to do is to marshal them, dress them up, and let them march. It is a pleasant job for anybody who likes to write.

It is not a job for the dyed-in-the-wool newspaperman, however. The passionate zeal with which the true reporter digs out a story is no asset to a rewrite man. It is, in fact, somewhat of a handicap. The rewrite man's value lies in his ability to turn out a lucid story to fit a given space in as short a time as possible. If he starts following out loose ends in the hope of getting a better story, he is likely to impede the progress of the paper from typewriter to press. Sometimes he may have to seek further information but, in the main, his task is to assemble a story with the materials at hand.

His job was born of the speed with which a metropolitan newspaper is put together. Speed remains one of the most important elements in it. It is a luxury seldom enjoyed by a rewrite man to get a good story to write early in an evening which is free enough of the pressure of other news to permit him to give his story the attention he thinks it merits. Generally he must content himself with the thought that the story he turns out is, at best, a makeshift—a thought which is a wonderful consolation to a man who probably

* Among newspapermen, Robert B. Peck has been known for a generation as one of the best of the rewrite men. There is no counting the young reporters who found in a Bob Peck rewrite of their stories a model of the way a story should be told.

could have done no better if he had spent thrice the time upon his opus.

The volume of news coming into a newspaper office makes speed in handling it essential. Otherwise it piles up. The night city desk of a metropolitan paper handles news written by members of the staff, news sent in by the Associated Press and other news agencies, news which is sent by telephone or telegraph by correspondents, and a great mass of material sent out by publicity agencies.

All this has to be winnowed and sifted. When the chaff has been discarded, the residue must be processed for printing. Stories written by members of the staff generally can be sent along to the copy desk for editing. There are members of the staff, however, who seldom and sometimes never write a story themselves. These are the men who cover the police districts of the city. They telephone their news. The stories sent by telephone are taken by a rewrite man.

Many stories which come over the teletype machines of the local news agencies are well enough written, but lack individuality. No paper wants to see its local stories duplicated word for word on a rival's pages. So most of the news-agency stories not dealing with matters to which staff men have been assigned go to the rewrite. Stories sent by correspondents, either by telephone or telegraph, go to the rewrite. Whatever publicity matter has been selected for use goes to the rewrite too.

Occasionally a story written by a member of the staff has to be rewritten. A conscientious reporter often finds it extremely difficult to keep his story within the bounds set by the editor. There are certain facts which he worked hard to get, certain facts which he wants to put in, not for their immediate significance, but because he thinks they may become of importance later or because he thinks, by putting them into his story, he will gain favor with the man who gave them to him and thus may get more important information later.

So the reporter puts all his facts in and, perhaps, exceeds his space allotment by 50 per cent. He turns in his story prayerfully and the night city editor, also calling on the Deity, hands it over to a rewrite man.

Clarifying a muddled story sometimes is a tedious job. It is a good deal like untangling a length of snarled and knotted cord. The first thing to do, after reading the story with some care, is to select an important point or loose end. With that point firmly in mind, the rewrite man can start his job of unraveling the rest and the task becomes progressively easier as he goes on. Sometimes, by the time he has got about half the story rewritten, he finds that the rest falls into place naturally and can be picked up intact.

Reconstructing a poorly written story generally is easier than clarifying an obscure one, providing, of course, that the essential facts are present. A poorly written newspaper story generally is merely a disarranged set of facts. Once the facts are set in their proper order, the story tells itself.

The rewrite man has a great advantage over the reporter when it comes to handling facts in that a great many unessential facts have been discarded before the story ever reaches the rewrite desk. Ordinarily the man who has covered a story returns to the office with at least twice as much information as he possibly can hope to get into his story.

When a rewrite man gets one of these discursive stories to rewrite, the unnecessary information in it, thanks to his training in trimming and planning stories to size, sticks out like warts and the story offers few difficulties. Laborious sentences, which were concocted with the idea of including a lot of collateral information, are simplified to little more than subject, verb, and object and the story gains grace and speed.

Writing to measure becomes more or less second nature to the rewrite man. Most of the stories he has to rewrite have been labeled for size—ten lines, twenty lines, a "short spread" (a half column or so), or, sometimes, three-quarters of a column. He may not always agree with the editorial judgment expressed in such marking, but generally he figures there is a reason for it. The amount of local space in a newspaper is limited and the man who marks the stories knows more about what he can afford to give them than the rewrite man does.

Only in extraordinary cases will a rewrite man question the space mark on a story. He does his best to get it into the space allotted to it and, in the course of time, a certain space sense develops which enables him to get the more important features of a story in, no matter how small the space allotted to it. Occasionally the very brevity of a story commands attention. A rewrite man who consistently exceeds his allotted space on stories isn't functioning properly. Nor is the rewrite man who consistently underwrites his stories. Either aberration upsets the calculations of the night city editor, who is trying to divide the space at his disposal fairly among all the stories which come to his desk.

Of course there are certain stories, mostly those sent in by telephone, which the rewrite man gets before the night city editor knows much about them. Unless such stories obviously are "shorts," he has to consult the night city editor before writing them and give him as good an idea as he can of their importance. There probably are few night city editors who care to have an unexpected "top" flung at them in full bloom.

The ability to gauge a story as it is told to him is fully as important to a rewrite man as to any other newspaper man. A good many of the stories that are sent in are pretty obvious, of course. Nobody could go wrong on them. There always is the chance, however, that the correspondent has misjudged the scope of his subject. If his story has been written or sent by telegraph, any such error shows up plainly.

If he is telephoning the story, however, the clew to its importance may be lurking in some phrase which he tosses in casually. It pays to be alert when taking a story by telephone, and it is an advantage also to know your correspondent. Some are more liable to error or more prone to meiosis than others.

All kinds of stories come in by telephone, of course, dinners and political meetings, action stories and features. Dinners and meetings generally fall into a groove. There isn't much that can be done with them except to write them in the routine way. Generally speaking, they are a tremendous bore to all concerned. Any rewrite man will tell you that one of the major afflictions of the world is that there is too much talking going on—all too often by persons who don't know what they are talking about.

Action stories and feature stories are different. It is in writing such stories that the rewrite man gets his occasional chance to cut loose. Frequently there is almost as much technique involved in taking such stories by telephone from district man or correspondent as there is in writing them.

If the sender is an experienced newspaperman, it generally is just a matter of listening to him, but if he lacks experience, he must be handled with some care—not befuddled by interrupting questions and not encouraged too much either. Interjection of questions may strike him dumb with stage fright or annoyance, and too much encouragement may lead him to try to embroider his story. The experienced hand sending in a story knows enough to leave the embroidery to the rewrite man. The attempt on the part of an inexperienced man to usurp that function is likely to disgust the rewrite man with the whole thing.

The rewrite man and the man at the other end of the telephone have to be in complete harmony to put a good story across. The best thing a rewrite man can do is to listen carefully, take down the salient facts, and meantime picture to himself as vividly as possible just what the situation was as the voice at the other end of the wire describes it.

This visualization is a tremendous help when it comes to getting the story straight in all its details. Questions can be saved until the end, and then the narrator can be led back to whatever spot appears a little hazy to the rewrite man, and an attempt made to clarify things. Generally such spots can be cleared up, but sometimes clarification depends upon facts which the correspondent has been unable to obtain. If the missing facts are not to be found in the office files or by telephone, it means that in writing the story the rewrite man must gloss over or artfully circumnavigate the treacherous ground. It generally can be done gracefully and unobtrusively.

Of course there always are details lacking in any story, and the ones which are important only for the color they lend often can be supplied by the rewrite man, if the correspondent hasn't got them. Once the rewrite man knows the general description of a house in which some interesting incident occurred he can put enough detail into his story to make that house appear real, whether he gets it from his informant or not.

The rewrite man knows how human beings react to certain situations and he can put in a few human touches that will be substantially true whether the district man was able to report them or not, and they will add some vividness to the story. If he gets around his town at all, he knows the general character of a good many of its neighborhoods and doesn't require a detailed description of the block in which the story is laid. If he does need any more information about it, his partial familiarity with it will enable the district man to fill any blanks with ease.

When a good district man sends in a story, it generally is so clear in the rewrite man's head when he gets off the telephone that, except for addresses and the spelling of names, he hardly has to refer to his notes at all, although he may have a couple of pages of them. Such stories are a pleasure to write and often they turn out to be easy to read too. As a general thing the rewrite man gets too much credit for them and the district man gets too little. They are, in fact, the result of teamwork and of experience at both ends of the telephone. Even the district man often is amazed at the way his story turned out in print, and he too is inclined to credit the magic of the rewrite man who, as a matter of fact, merely wrote the facts as they were related to him and filled in the chinks as he went along. The story was there all the time, but the district man couldn't realize its possibilities until he saw it in print.

The bane of the rewrite man's existence, the horror that recurs to him in dreams, is the story which obviously has great possibilities but in which vital facts are lacking. In such cases he just has to bull ahead and cover up the best way he can. He isn't writing with complete confidence and the weakness generally becomes apparent. Surmise won't do when it comes to essential facts and too much mystery weakens a story.

A rewrite man soon realizes his dependence on facts. Few things are more irksome to him than to have a lighthearted night city editor toss on his desk a few paragraphs of AP with the remark: "Here's a funny story. Got a parrot and a monkey in it. Write all you need about it."

It already was a tradition forty years ago that a story blessed with the presence of either a parrot or a monkey was a funny story. A story which has both these creatures in it, of course, is irresistible. As a matter of fact, it all depends on what the monkey or the parrot does whether the story is funny or not. Frequently the things they do would be much funnier if a horse did them.

Anyhow, it is poor psychology to tell a rewrite man in advance that a story is funny. The mere statement arouses skepticism and brings the bile to his fingertips. The mention of the monkey and the parrot is the last straw, and it generally is in a ferocious state of mind that he sets out to mangle that particular story.

Or maybe the psychology isn't so bad at that. Ferocity is sometimes an excellent state of mind in which to approach a story, especially a story labeled in advance as funny. It makes for lean and caustic writing, and sometimes the suffering rewrite man will turn out a funny story on the subject in spite of himself. Funny to other people, that is; in his own opinion, gall oozes from every sentence.

The big story that begins to trickle into the office an hour or less before the deadline is another cause of unreasonable bitterness to the rewrite man. He is inconsolable about the catastrophe, not out of human tenderness, but because it didn't happen a couple of hours earlier. Then, he says to himself, he could have done real justice to it. The probability is that he is entirely wrong. If he had got a stack of copy a foot high two or three hours earlier and found more coming in all the time, he probably would be in an even more confusing mess than he is and probably would write no better story, for there is no more powerful incentive than pressure of time.

As it is, he sits glowering at meager and contradictory bulletins until he sees signs of impatience on the part of the night city editor. Then he says to himself that he can't write what he hasn't got, and proceeds to do that very thing. The magic of it is that, invariably, when he begins to write, the bulletins begin to come in like homing swallows and perch insistently on his desk.

Gradually a suggestion of the story begins to take form. There are eleven dead or there are fifteen dead. That makes a lead anyhow, and a good one, too, because it always is possible to change the number at the last minute in case corrections come in.

By the time the first paragraph is finished the copy may be coming in faster than he can read it. It doesn't make any difference. He's going to have enough for the first edition. The early bulletins have given him the main idea—he hopes—and he just reads what is on top of the pile at his side and juggles it somehow into the mental frame he has contrived for the story. The copy on top of the pile is freshest and is likely to be the most reliable.

Somehow or other the story gets written and gets into the paper and actually runs for a column or more. It seems to stack up all right with what the other papers have and the rewrite man has time to catch his breath. Of course, as more information comes in, the lead has to be rewritten and inserts put in, all of which pain the rewrite man intensely, as he has come to take no little pride in that prodigy which leaped from his typewriter in his first burst of energy. He can see that it's going to be an exceedingly sour and disjointed piece of work by the time the last insert is in, but the stuff has to go in somehow. So in it goes and, miraculously enough, at the end it isn't nearly as bad as he thought it was going to be.

The big story that breaks late is one of the reasons for the existence of the rewrite job on a newspaper. Nobody knows when there may be such a story, but anyone can be fairly confident that there will be several of them in the course of a year. The rewrite staff constitutes the newspaper's insurance against such incidents. There may be nobody in the office to send out on the assignment, but police district men can be mobilized—generally a thoroughly competent set of fact-gatherers—and the rewrite staff will get the story written.

It often looks as though the rewrite man wasn't earning his pay. As a matter of fact, he frequently isn't. From a third to half of the time, he may be loafing. The main thing is, however, that he is there, just as the members of a fire company are there, whether they are responding to an alarm or not. Members of the reporters' staff, working furiously at their typewriters for an hour or two before edition time and recollecting previous hours devoted to covering their stories, might well put a rewrite man to the blush, if rewrite men blushed easily. They are not a sensitive lot, however. When they work, they work hard. When there's nothing to do, they loaf, a pursuit at which they are adept.

[18] SUBURBAN CORRESPONDENT

by John E. Frogge

THE suburban correspondent, the space man who covers some areas far from the city of his publication, or a county, or a suburban community, is the most picked on of human beings.

He wouldn't be a correspondent, working a forty-hour day with but little reward, unless he liked the work. He wouldn't be a correspondent unless he wanted to be one, for most of them can get—and hold—jobs on the best of dailies. Most of them have held those jobs, that's the reason they are correspondents.

The correspondent has no hours off—no days off. He likes to work for a newspaper, or else he would be jerking sodas, or fitting shoes, or heading a bank. With his varied experience, he could do any of those.

The suburban correspondent works for the day desk—and the night desk. He's up all night covering a murder story, which he never sees in print because late editions aren't delivered to his locality. He drops into bed exhausted after phoning that last bulletin that probably never made the paper anyway.

Then, promptly at nine o'clock in the morning, an alert, breakfasted, and shaven youngster on the day desk calls him to ask if he knows about that murder in his territory and will he please get a follow story.

Or, having worked all day trying to dig up a yarn for that same squirt on the day desk, some great idea that the day-side man had, he calls it in to the night desk, only to have an entirely new set of masterminds tell him, "Never mind that, there isn't much room in the paper anyway, but here's an obit. Better pick up a paragraph and call back." Odd, correspondents don't go crazy, though.

But a reporter, a staff man. That's something different. The staff man swaggers into the picture just when the going is hottest. When the story is at its peak. Sent out from the office to take over. He is cordial—just a trifle distant when he shakes hands with the correspondent. He is stern, impatient to be away.

The correspondent sits down with him to bring him up to date on the story. The staff man orders a beer and one for the correspondent, who usually drinks Scotch. They sit for a time, and the staff man assures the correspondent, "Of course, old man, I'll see that you get credit for all this." He needn't worry, the correspondent will see to it himself that he gets credit.

If the staffer is too overbearing, there's always a way. Call the office direct when a new angle breaks, tell the desk that you can't seem to find the staff man at the moment, but here's so and so. It's easy to be where important things break when you know the district attorney, the police chief, the cop on post, and the sheriff. Easier still, drop off the staff man at the corner spot, assuring him that nothing will happen. Then go to work.

The newspaper correspondent never sees his name in print. Never a by-line comes his way. Once in a great while, probably through some error in the composing room, the credit line, "By a Staff Correspondent," appears over one of his stories. For a full hour the correspondent gloats to himself—anyone else would think he was crazy. Then comes a call from the office with another obit to get. Obits take the starch out of anybody.

There may be correspondents who can make a living out of working for one newspaper. I've never heard of one. They work for anybody and everybody who has an odd dollar. But that complicates matters, and no correspondent can work for more than three newspapers.

By the time he has telephoned his story to three papers it begins to pall. He begins to drop details and to be sorry the thing ever happened in the first place. And by the time he has dealt with three rewrite men, he's ready to quit his job anyway.

If he writes and files his stuff, then writing three yarns and making them sound different and still contain all the same facts, make him dead tired. Three newspapers are enough.

Dealing with rewrite men is sufficient headache for anyone. A rewrite man may know his city, but he doesn't know all the territory surrounding his city, that part covered by correspondents. All the local geography has to be explained to him.

Names with which the rewrite man is familiar in the city mean nothing in the country. There are names to spell out. The rewrite man knows the district attorney in the city. The fellow in the country is a stranger to him, which sometimes results in misspelled names and general hard feelings.

And rewrite men ask questions at the most peculiar moments. They break in to ask them, when they could just as well wait until the end of the story. Correspondents talk over long distance telephone lines, where it's hard enough to hear anyway.

No correspondent is worth his salt to any newspaper unless he knows his territory. Nor is he worth his salt unless he is a newspaperman. Therefore, it is to be presumed that he covered that territory for some newspaper, perhaps a local one, before taking on the correspondence for the big-town sheet.

Which boils down to this—it's impossible to walk into a new territory and make enough to keep body and soul together as a correspondent.

The correspondent must know what goes on in the open, and, if he doesn't actually know what goes on behind the scenes, he must at least know where it goes on. He must have all sorts of friends in every part of his territory. His territory is usually far greater than that covered by the staff men in the first place. He may have a county suburban to New York City. Any of the suburban counties are greater in area than the city itself. Yet the desk doesn't hesitate to ask him to "Jump over to so-and-so and pick up this-and-that." That jump may be a little trip of forty miles, there and back. And the desk wants a call back in ten minutes.

Then, there is the exclusive story. Is that a headache! More than once, every correspondent of any account in this country has had two or three newspapers call him within five minutes, telling him that they have an exclusive tip that such and such had happened. What does the poor correspondent do? Well, the simplest thing is to tell the second and third newspapers that he has already had a call from another paper on just that. Then call back the first one and tell them that other papers are hot on the same story.

His calls are always received with a great deal of suspicion, because it always seems somewhat of a surprise to the city editor that his correspondent is working for someone else. That city editor doesn't stop to think of his budget and what the correspondent's income is. How could the fellow work for just that much?

City editors have the idea that the correspondent should answer the telephone at any time, day or night, whenever it's the pleasure of the city editor to call up. The city editor, or his assistant, never seems to remember that the correspondent's territory is sometimes three or four hundred square miles and that territory can't be covered sitting by a telephone.

Tickets! The bane of the correspondent's existence. Traffic tickets. Everyone in the newspaper office sometimes drives through the correspondent's territory. And, remembering that good old Johnnie covers that particular bit of the earth, the city slicker bears down on the accelerator. There comes the motorcycle cop and trouble. The man from the city mentions dear old Johnnie's name, but gets the summons just the same. The man from the city feels just a little loss of confidence in Johnnie, because the motor cop didn't recognize the correspondent's name and give him the freedom of the road, but not enough hurt to neglect mailing the summons to Johnnie—forgetting to enclose his driver's license—and ask him to fix it up. (I've had such offhand requests when the ticket was marked for eighty miles an hour and in the middle of a local safety campaign.) But always, it seems that Johnnie's pal in the city, whom he has probably never seen, never has to appear in court. Though they have been known to grouse about having their offense being noted on the back of the license, even when it is accompanied with the words, "suspended sentence."

Now, take some cases. Here is Nassau County, 252 square miles of lovely land, populated by about half a million people. It is bounded on the south by the Atlantic Ocean and on the north by Long Island Sound. On the west by New York City and on the east by Suffolk County. Nassau County is roughly square. Seems fairly easy to cover.

But, there are the county government, three town governments, sixty-seven village governments, and two cities. Not to mention several score special districts. All within Nassau County. The desk expects the correspondent to know everything about every one of those governments.

There is a county police department which has a detective division that covers all the county—every inch of it. But the uniformed force of the department does not dare encroach on the territory of incorporated villages that have their own police departments. And there are fifteen of them.

There is no county-wide fire department, but several score small, volunteer fire departments that may or may not accord in their boundaries with village lines. They have no central reporting station. Each is independent and jealous of all the rest.

There are planning commissions in the county, the towns, and many of the villages. Some apparently do not plan at all. There are fire districts, sewer districts, sidewalk districts, sanitary districts, garbage districts, school districts, and lighting districts. The commissioners of each meet every now and then; and probably, at least once a year, there is a story that the metropolitan readers would like to read, in each one. It never gets in the paper, for the correspondent isn't twins. That wouldn't be enough. He'd have to be a member of the greatest multiple birth in the history, to have one part of himself present at even half of these meetings.

And the sanitary district lines never accord with those of the sidewalk district and there may be five fire districts within one school district. The correspondent just keeps quiet about the stories that do break in those board meetings, when he does hear about them days later, and hopes that his desk never finds out.

Most correspondents cover for a newspaper or two and also for one of the wire services. It never pays to work for two wire services—they keep too close watch on each other.

That results, invariably, when a story is breaking, in the correspondent's having to make a decision. It's almost press time on one of his newspapers, and yet, his wire-service customer wants the news so fast as it can get it. It may seem a trivial matter, making that decision, but is it? The necessity for it invariably arises. Who wins? The office with the fastest rewrite men. Get the story to that office first and let the office that has the slowest staff, the rewrite men who never seem to know what is going on, wait until the last.

Competition between correspondents is much more real than that between the reporters working in the city for rival papers. The reason probably is that the correspondents know each other and are not suffering from the politeness due to strangeness when they meet.

Then, beats are easier to get when you are a correspondent. Beats, in the city, are seldom the result of the individual reporter's efforts. In these days of mass interviews and handouts, every paper fares about alike. What beats do occur usually come from office tips, anonymous telephone calls, and the like. The correspondent gets none of those. He gets his stuff by being on the job, by having a special friend somewhere or other, or by a tip from someone he has met.

But those tips are personal affairs, not the kind that are telephoned by some constant reader to the city desk. The correspondent makes the most of his tips. The correspondent's story has a special lure for the man on the desk, for it comes from a far-off place, whereas, that desk man has just turned down an equally bloody murder around the corner.

Then, Nassau County, for instance, is the abode of great wealth. The man on the desk seldom knows anything about the community which the correspondent mentions, whereas he does know that a murder at Tenth Avenue and Fortieth Street is not as good as the one at Fifty-seventh and Park Avenue.

Many a correspondent has snickered over getting half a column printed in his metropolitan paper, when he knew full well in his heart that it wasn't worth the space.

The correspondent has other competition, however. The unknown voice. The local district attorney doesn't like to be awakened at three o'clock in the morning, even if the newspaper desk in the city does think that what it wants is important. The local district attorney is just as likely to bawl the correspondent out and hang up on him as not. But—the unknown voice! The voice of the paper that has no correspondent in the territory. Let that unknown voice call up at three o'clock in the morning, with all the majesty of the *New York Daily Blat* behind it, and the local district attorney rubs his eyes and tries to remember just what did happen and to answer, as best he can, all the questions asked. Such situations invariably lead to the correspondent's casting lengthy slurs on anyone from the city, and warning his local office holders and local big people that they are not to trust those outsiders who telephone or who occasionally appear on the scene in person.

Then, we have the Big Newspaper People who come out on big

stories, lord it over the correspondent, try to put over an exclusive angle, and, usually, take a terrific beating because of it.

On a recent murder case, one of the New York evening newspapers sent a young woman into Nassau County, with instructions to interview a grieviously wounded girl, sole witness to a big-name murder case.

That young woman dressed herself up as a nurse, actually got into the hospital, and was on her way to the wounded girl's room when a correspondent learned of the scheme. Of course, that correspondent telephoned to the hospital, where, equally of course, he knew the superintendent, and told of the scheme. He couldn't masquerade as a nurse, why let that gal from New York put over an exclusive? She didn't.

Once in a while, the man—or woman—from town, so plays on the sympathy of the correspondent that the correspondent forgets that the reporter from the city is a deadly enemy. Not always, but sometimes.

There was the instance of a well-known woman writer from a New York tabloid who set out to make the correspondent feel that he was the most important person on earth. She so far succeeded that the correspondent used every contact he had, pulled every string he knew how, and even held out on his fellow correspondents, those he ordinarily worked with, in order to produce exclusive news for this tabloid writer.

He succeeded. For four successive days, the woman writer had an exclusive by-line story. It was a year later that the correspondent learned that the woman writer received a bonus when she got back to the office—that she never mentioned his name at all in connection with her exploits. She has never been in Nassau County on a story since and this correspondent is only hoping that she will live long enough to be sent out again to cover a yarn. She'll get no bonus.

But with all of this, the correspondent is the happiest of newspaper men. He doesn't have to be in the office at a certain hour every morning or every evening. He seldom goes to the office at all. Once a year is considered too often by most correspondents.

He may know the entire staff by telephone voice, but he seldom knows more than two or three by sight. When he does go in, there are those introductions, those "Good work, old chap" remarks, that are sandpaper to the correspondent's soul. He knows he's good. Just let a dozen of those fellows lolling behind desks come out to Nassau and try to cover a story—without his help, that is.

Then, when the man on the desk, or occasionally the city editor himself, calls up, there is always an air of respect in the voice, for the man in the city knows that he depends on his correspondents. That he can't replace them like he can his district men, or other members of his staff in the city. Where would he get another man to cover Nassau without that new man spending six months or more taking daily beatings at the hands of the correspondents of the rival papers before he learned the ins and out of the territory? Or, perhaps I'm wrong.

There was a city editor who fired a correspondent once. He accused the correspondent of sending in a story of a train hitting a pie wagon and scattering pies over the right of way for a mile. The correspondent insisted that he has never heard of such a story, and he hadn't. But he was fired nevertheless and for six months watched his old paper take beatings. Now, that correspondent is back on his old sheet. The old city editor is gone, so the correspondent will probably never learn where that pie story came from. It didn't happen in Nassau County.

There have been murders in Nassau County that made the front pages of the nation. When they happen, then the correspondent is in his glory. His are the first bulletins that arrive in the news rooms of the city's papers over the wires.

He greets the incoming staffers when they arrive, totes them around in his car, and brings them up to date on the yarn. If there is a man from one of his own sheets in the group, the correspondent is polite but seldom friendly unless he knows the man personally or has that special kind of respect that one newspaperman can have for another.

But the correspondent is happiest when he is left alone with the story. His paper has the best chance of getting the best story. Then is when the correspondent is willing to work the clock around, work till his feet drop off, while his unionized colleagues knock off when their forty-hour week is over, or else gloat over the overtime they will get. The correspondent remembers his forty-hour days and wonders what a forty-hour week is like. It's then that his telephone rings. It's the office on the wire. "Here's a little obit, Johnnie. Will you get us a paragraph? The guy's name is. . . ."

[19] THE OBITUARY

by Richard G. West

PROFESSOR Charles Townsend Copeland, of Harvard, whose salty comments on life and letters stuck in the heads of generations of students in his English courses, used to remark, in his later years in the lecture room, on the number of his contemporaries who were departing this life.

"They die daily in *The Transcript,*" he would observe lugubriously. Yet his audience, knowing Professor Copeland, was sure that he never would skip *The Transcript's* obituary page because he dreaded the news he might find there. That was one page he read thoroughly, if only for the occasional satisfaction of thinking, "Well, that's one I beat."

There is no doubt that the obituary page is one of the best read by thoughtful people who know how to read a newspaper properly. For the death of any person is news: "Any mans death diminishes me, because I am involved in Mankinde," John Donne wrote. It is obviously news of the first order when a man dies who has made his mark on his time, whose passing at a critical moment may affect the lives of millions and the destiny of nations. Such were Abraham Lincoln and Franklin D. Roosevelt. Not so spectacular but still important are the deaths of a teacher like George Washington Carver, a physician like Sir Frederick G. Banting, a musician like Sergei Rachmaninov, a sculptor like Daniel Chester French, a poet like Stephen Vincent Benét, an actress like Mrs. Minnie Maddern Fiske.

The passing of a baseball player, a prize-fight manager, or a circus clown will sadden thousands who never heard of Justice Benjamin N. Cardozo. To a discriminating few, who never knew the man except by name, the death of someone who writes letters to the editor about gardening or the stars will bring a sense of loss. And every day some reader will find a paragraph about a hardware merchant or a small-town high-school teacher whom he knew and say to himself, "Why, I saw him only last week!"

On the obituary page may be found the summing up of the glories, the achievements, the mediocrities, and the failures of a life which the rest of the paper chronicled day by day. A few columns on one morning may tell the last of a physician whose researches saved the lives of thousands, of a woman who fought to end the sweatshops, a statesman who sold the Spanish Loyalists down the river, a banker whose one step outside the law was remembered when his years of honor were forgotten, a vaudeville juggler, a missionary in China, an anticigarette crusader, a writer of immortal tales for children, a grower of prize pumpkins, and a conductor who traveled two million miles on the Erie Railroad. In the democracy of the obituary page they lie side by side; the disparate headline sizes do not alter the lead paragraphs of each story. They all died.

This rich content of the stuff of human experience is a challenge to any writer. It should command for the obituary page the best attention of editors and reporters. Yet it is commonly neglected by both. Writing obituaries is regarded too often as a melancholy but necessary chore, to be discharged with a fraction of the effort that would be lavished on a murder. Many editors delegate this chore to the freshmen or the drudges of the staff and squeeze the fruits of their labors into an odd corner of the paper, perhaps around a three-quarter page advertisement or next to some honest reading matter. The most important thing that can happen to a man is to die, but that event often receives more perfunctory newspaper treatment than much duller matters that involved him years before.

Preparing an obituary is a delicate and exacting task, demanding the utmost diligence, insight, and imagination. His obituary should be, as far as human judgment and ability may create it in the limits of newspaper space, a man's monument. It should be a "Let's look at the record" of a life. Usually an intelligent reporter can assemble the basic facts from several sources and put them on paper without much trouble. But he must go deeper. He must try to appraise the color of mind and character, to determine what made the man tick, and write his story so honestly that it will appear not as a dreary recital of dates and names, but as a portrait of the man as he lived, with lights and shadows.

To accomplish this, the writer need not and should not indulge in amateur psychoanalysis. Neither should he be a critic or defender of his subject. Let him leave that to the editorial writers. But he may achieve his effect by acute synthesis of facts which illuminate character and such judicious appraisal of those facts as might occur to any thoughtful person.

The easiest subject to handle in this fashion is the great world figure, whose life was rich in known or accessible detail. Also, because such a subject's career was familiar to everyone, the writer may be permitted more license—and more space in the paper—for the personal writing which in lesser instances might be ruled out as editorializing. An historic moment deserves more than a chronicle. This is how *The New York Herald Tribune's* writer began his obituary of Adolf Hitler:

"Adolf Hitler sought to enslave the world and almost succeeded in destroying the civilization which it had taken Europe 2,000 years to achieve.

"History can hardly deny him a place alongside Genghis Khan, Attila the Hun, and the other great conquerors and scourges of human freedom, but in all the annals of mankind a stranger or more unsavory figure was never enthroned in their questionable Valhalla.

"He combined the appearance of a low comedian of the music halls with the savagery of a South Sea Island head hunter. Womanish hysteria was as much a part of his character as the ferocity which drove him to start the worst war in history. He could simper over the prettiness of a flaxen-haired Bavarian child in one breath and in the next gloat over the bombing of a hundred British children of equally Aryan blondness.

"His was a character of tortuous complexities and astonishing contradictions. The sufferings of his victims left him unmoved, except by childish glee, but Wagner's music made him weep. . . .

"Hitler restored tyranny to history. He hung chains on a civilization that thought it was finished with slavery. He understood the basest impulses of the human heart and gambled that they governed other men as they governed him. But his bet was wrong—he underestimated, because he could not comprehend, the force of the spirit of men of good will. This spirit baffled him in the small countries which he conquered and defeated him when he met it in the three nations which compassed his downfall."

This obituary ran more than eight columns. About half of it was devoted to a study of Hitler's character as written in the facts of his career and the remainder to a detailed, chronological account of that career. Few obituaries are so long, and few devote such a proportion of their space to generalizations. But Hitler's death was an event which justified—or demanded—treatment in the news columns which actually constituted a biographical essay. And if ever a critical judgment of a man was justified in the news columns, it was in this case. In his closing paragraphs the *Herald Tribune's* writer supplied it, but not in his own words:

" 'My whole life from now on belongs to the German people,'

he [Hitler] said. 'I now do not want to be anything but the first soldier of the German Reich.'

"From his point of view his words would have made an excellent epitaph for his gravestone. From the world's point of view Winston Churchill enunciated a better one:

" 'This evil man,' said Churchill. 'This monstrous abortion of hatred and deceit.' "

The man's monument was constructed in eight thousand words of newspaper type; the superscription in the last sentence.

Another example of swift summing up of a different character, one well known and certainly more affectionately regarded than Hitler, was the *Herald Tribune's* lead on the obituary of James J. Walker, the former mayor of New York:

"James J. Walker, dapper, debonair Jimmy, was late for everything but always had a wisecrack to make the wait worth while. In his slight, laughing person, the sharp crease of his trousers and the sharp flick of his tongue, he symbolized better than any one else the New York of the 1920's, with its dazzle, its Prohibition speakeasies, its Wall Street boom and its old time Tammany Hall. . . .

"When standing in breadlines and selling apples on street corners took the place of big-time speculation, the people's mind turned to serious things. No one ever pictured Jimmy as an ideal companion for a serious chat."

But of the hundreds of obituaries which a newspaper will carry in a year, not many lend themselves to this semieditorial treatment. Few run more than five hundred words; most of them much less. But an anecdote or a sympathetic description of a personal idiosyncrasy may highlight a character. The late George Lyman Kittredge of Harvard was one of the greatest Shakespearean scholars and teachers of his time. In his recital of his academic achievements, the writer of the *Herald Tribune's* obituary could say:

"His sense of academic etiquette was rigid and his manner was that of a top sergeant. Anybody who coughed during his lectures was banished. He told his classes: 'Before the lecture I cough. After the lecture I cough. But during the lecture I do not cough and neither shall you. . . .' He believed that hats should be worn only out of doors and used to lurk behind a pillar in the lobby of Widener Library with his stick and knock them from the heads of the thoughtless.

"In dealing with the world outside the university he was as imperious as in the classroom. When he crossed the street, ignoring traffic lights, the drivers had to beware, not he. He simply raised his hand and walked on, to a chorus of squealing brakes."

Even in a short obituary, such vivid flashes are possible. A brief story in *The New York Times* of the death of a wealthy retired business executive who lived on a Long Island estate included this in a factual account:

"He was known to the village folk as few of the estate colony residents are known. He knew the butcher, the baker, the news dealer, and it was significant that he died in a moving-picture theater surrounded by a fireman, a policeman, and the head usherette."

No platitudes could have rung so true.

Now as a practical matter it is often impossible to obtain such telling material, or the writer can find nothing that is not trite. It is better to say nothing about a man rather than to say something dull. To say that a man was friendly or witty or eccentric is not enough; if a sharp illustration is lacking the facts of his life will be sufficient.

What the writer can say about any man's life is limited by two things: what he can find out and how much space is available in the paper for the story. The first of these depends on the fruitfulness of the sources and the diligence of the writer; the second upon the judgment of the editor—how much an obituary is "worth" in type, in relation to others and to the rest of the day's news.

On most newspapers the obituary news is handled by the city editor and his assistants or, in a few cases, by a special editor. The word of a death may come to the editor's desk in a number of ways. A telephone call or telegram from a friend or member of the family is a common source. Another is the duplicate copies of paid death notices for the classified advertising columns, which the advertising department supplies to the editor. From distant points the news-service wires or the paper's own correspondents will bring the news. The editor will give each obituary, from whatever source, to a reporter or rewrite man, who is expected to discover in the paper's library all available information on the dead person in clippings or reference books, and to verify and expand that information by a check with the family, friends, or business associates. If there is no record of the dead person in the library, the reporter must assemble his information as he can. He reports his findings to the editor and is told how much to write.

The editor, in judging the proper length of an obituary, and the writer, in preparing it, must consider how much information there is and how reliable it may be. Assembling facts for such stories is exacting and often trying work. The reporter must be accurate and painstaking in the face of scanty records or no records at all, of faulty memories, indifference, and occasional spite or hostility. And he must always remember that, more than in most news stories, his topic touches profound human experience and requires all his tact and patience.

Speaking to a reporter, a bereaved family may be too shocked and grief-stricken to recall exact facts and even less able to supply the side lights which might lift the story above the mediocre. Sometimes they are reluctant to talk at all, and sometimes they declare that they wish no obituary to be printed. In this last event, it is courteous to defer to their wishes, but if the death is important news the reporter must explain tactfully that the paper has no choice but to print it and that he is interested only in the accuracy of his facts.

Information in a newspaper library about a dead person may be more tantalizing than helpful. Reference books rarely offer more than a framework of names and dates. A file of clippings may be meager or full of inconsistencies, contradictions, and obvious errors. Sometimes a press agent or a secretary has contributed an "approved" version of a man's life, but these are of doubtful value.

From these diverse sources, this welter of fact, half fact, and gossip, the reporter must prepare his obituary simply, honestly, and truly. The lead, the first paragraph, should present no difficulty. The straightforward statement of fact is the only one possible. It should begin with the dead person's name, his age, an identifying phrase, say that he died and when and where. There is no place for purple prose. You cannot dramatize death beyond the fact.

Beyond this, there are no rigid rules for organizing an obituary. Clear, orderly thinking, simple writing, accuracy and honesty will create a good obituary as they will any news story. The problem concerns as much what to leave out as what to put in. The first rule is: If you are not certain of a fact, leave it out. Don't jump at a conclusion. Another rule is: Leave out the dull stuff. A great many obituaries are inflated by lists of clubs and associations and by forgotten facts long out of date, better unremembered. No one cares what minor encounters a man may have had forty years ago. If he ever amounted to anything, he had done much more important things since.

What about omitting the scandal in a man's life? Pressure is often brought on the writer to do so. In this, above all, the writer must be honest, but he must obey the promptings of good taste and common sense.

Obviously, if a man was involved in a gigantic fraud and did little else in his life, the story of the fraud will be the story of the obituary. But many men who have led useful lives have gone wrong once. If the misstep was important news when it occurred, known generally to the public, it cannot be overlooked and should be mentioned but not dwelt upon. But there is no justice in raking up the record of a disorderly-conduct arrest or a breach-of-promise suit which was thrown out of court.

The complaint is heard frequently that newspapers do not give the cause of death. Very often this is difficult for a reporter to learn. Members of the family do not know or prefer not to say. Reporters are reluctant to press the question. The only certain source is the attending physician, and if he is available he is apt to refuse to answer or to say simply, "Heart disease." He knows that the phrase covers many forms of disease, but he hesitates to be specific, because ill-informed reporters often misquote physicians and make them appear absurd.

For some reason, many people regard cancer as a disgraceful disease to die of. Sometimes a reporter is told that a person died of cancer and is requested not to mention it. The family's wishes are usually respected in this matter. Lacking an exact diagnosis of the cause, a reporter may write that a person died of "heart failure." This means nothing, because the immediate cause of any death is failure of the heart.

Also, it is commonly written that a person dies "suddenly." Of course he does. Any death is sudden. The man is alive one second and dead the next. In an immeasurable fraction of time the clock has ceased to tick, the machine has ceased to function, and the man is physically dead. Nothing can be more sudden. It does not matter if he has been ill for months or is struck down by angina pectoris.

What the writer usually means by "suddenly" is that the death was unexpected—a surprise. After a long illness no death, perhaps, is unexpected. But a fatal stroke or complications in an apparently trivial illness might be so described.

How long should an obituary be? Each must be judged by the values which any news story must meet—importance, timeliness, and space available in the paper. The question of importance must remain debatable; one man's importance is another's indifference, but editors and newspaper readers know intuitively who is worth reading most about. A man who dies at the peak of his powers will be worth more space than one who lingers.

Likewise it is a tragic truth that news values change with the volume of news and the size of the paper. A fascinating game which newspaper men occasionally indulge in is to guess how much space their own obituaries will be worth. Most editors and reporters are pretty objective. They have handled too many obituaries; they know that on a dull Sunday night their death might rate thirty lines, on a busy Wednesday, ten. The same shifting scale is valid for anyone.

It is curious how obituaries date. Most newspapers keep in their files copies of prepared obituaries—"wait obits" they are called sometimes. These are biographies of prominent persons which are prepared perhaps when there is no prospect of the subject dying. This may appear a gruesome practice, but editors must remember that if the President of the United States or any public figure should die late at night, it would be impossible to write an adequate obituary in a hurry. They will have these obituaries written and brought up to date from time to time, so that in an emergency a competent story will be ready.

Often these prepared stories, because they are written without the pressure of time and space, are fairer and finer reading than what appears in the paper. But such a prepared story goes bad after lying in the files. Time diminishes its values; the subject grows older, and so do the readers. In 1935 the *Herald Tribune* had ready almost ten columns on the Kaiser—Emperor William II of Germany, the villain of World War I. When he died, on June 4, 1941, another world war was raging, and the Kaiser was worth less than half of that.

A man needn't be the Kaiser to live too long or die on the wrong day. Elmer Davis once wrote a piece of fiction about a smalltime citizen who became obit-conscious after he was erroneously reported dead. The obituary which was printed repeated a ridiculous quotation which he had thoughtlessly given an inquiring reporter years before. From then on, the resurrected gentleman made it his business to amass a stack of newspaper clippings by delivering sage remarks to reporters at the proper time, and after years of endeavor he was sure that he had accumulated a backlog of wisdom from which any rewrite man could make something. And he had; but the night he died an ex-President of the United States and a glamor girl of the movies died, too; there was no space in the paper and he got a paragraph.

No obituary can do justice to a man. Closing an account is a solemn business, and the best newspapermen will be thoughtful when that account is of a life. They may remember the judgment of one of the finest editors, who knew that pride of achievement dwindled to nothing before a fact. He was Charles A. Dana, editor of *The Sun* of New York for thirty years. He died on October 17, 1897. In those days newspapers were intensely personal organs. Everyone knew Dana and *The Sun*. He had made it. *The Sun,* its staff, and its readers were as proud of him as he was of the paper. If ever there was a chance and an excuse for a fulsome obit, here it was.

Dana had played the game of guessing obituaries, too. Once he told one of his editorial writers, "For you, two sticks; for me, two lines."

And that is what he got. The day after he died every newspaper in New York carried columns on Dana's life and achievements. *The Sun* printed ten words at the head of the first column on the editorial page, without a heading:

"Charles Anderson Dana, editor of *The Sun,* died yesterday afternoon."

No more can be said truly about anyone.

[20] COPY DESK

by Allan Holcomb

HEAD OF THE COPY DESK OF

THE NEW YORK HERALD TRIBUNE

A GROUP of visitors on their way through the editorial rooms of *The New York Herald Tribune* paused briefly one night off the starboard bow of the big horseshoe copy desk. Their escort, apparently a volunteer and not sure of his own way around, hesitated, and then remarked: "This is where they write headlines—and fix things." That was a fair description of what a newspaper copy desk does, or should do.

How well it succeeds depends on its workmen and the way it is geared with the rest of the office. Much of the day's news comes through its slot on the way to the printers. It is where the copyreader, the mechanic of the editorial room, takes over the reporter's story, the Washington bureau's special, and the foreign correspondent's piece. His job is to see that they have all the necessary Who's, What's, Where's, When's, Why's, and How's, that names and facts are correct, and that their diction, spelling, grammar, and punctuation are working smoothly. Also that the brakes are in good condition against libel. He eliminates fancy trimmings, keeps stories inside their assigned space, and writes the headlines.

This paradoxical paragon has his days. He may produce a world-shaking atomic headline: "BASIC FORCE OF UNIVERSE IS UNLEASHED." Or a pun: "SLUMP MAY CATCH CITIES WITH THEIR PLANS DOWN."

Then he will fall flat on his face and absent-mindedly pass a piece about the weather: "MOSTLY SUNNY TODAY AND TONIGHT."

Most offices refer to him as a copyreader. He is also a desk man, rim man, the gentleman in the green eyeshade, and the butcher. On English papers he is a subeditor.

His pay has increased in recent years. In New York it is about double what it was before the war. Here the minimum in contracts with the Newspaper Guild is $100 a week. Most are paid well over this on the rim. This is for a five-day deek of 37½ hours. Time and a half for overtime, for he's mostly a union man now. At least two weeks vacation after a year, six holidays, and sick leave based on length of service. There are death benefits, some pension systems, and hospital insurance. Personnel departments, office doctors and nurses, and office cafeterias help. He does not go out to meet all the interesting people, gets no by-lines, and his work is anonymous. He does, however, keep regular hours, he works sitting down, and the copy desk is a recruiting ground for office executives. His lot is not an unhappy one.

The old time copyreader was a wandering character, not any too dependable, and addicted to small financial and alcoholic shenanigans. Younger men are being attracted now. They are keener, more accurate, and concise, and eager to get ahead in the business. Most of them saw war service. They include former air force captains and colonels, Navy commanders, electronic experts, Office of War Information men, and State Department aides. They can make sense out of the involved science story and the technical aviation piece. Trouble in Trieste, riots in Greece, civil war in China, occupation mixups in Germany, and Moscow Peace Conference wrangles are just their dish. It was only yesterday that they were there. Their health and habits are improved.

Veterans of the craft continue on the job. The head of *The New York Times* telegraph desk for many years was William D. Fairbanks who was well in his eighties when he retired in the summer of 1946. He handled the *Times* telegraph news throughout the New Deal and war years with vigor and alert intelligence. "Judge" William D. Evans, also in his eighties, heads the *Times* obituary desk. He is the second oldest living graduate of Yale. He keeps the obit of the oldest living graduate in his drawer and periodically polishes it up with fond attention.

With women starring all over the newspaper lot, the copy desk remains one of the few male strongholds. Some good women copyreaders are operating in various parts of the country, but not many. Their talents and inclinations, apparently, lie in other directions. Few efforts have been made to train them.

The copy-desk setup is flexible. It varies from office to office. There are two general types, the universal desk and the separate desk system. A universal desk edits and writes heads for most of the spot news, with the exception of sports, financial, and departmental matter. The independent desk system operates under the different editors, each with his own crew of copy readers. This is the system at the *Times* which has probably the biggest staff of copyreaders of any paper in the world—seventy to eighty men. Seven desks handle its daily news. These are the cable desk, telegraph, city, obits-amusements-society, finance-business, sports, and reserve news. The last named handles C.G.O. stories—Can Go Over. They have no time element and run as needed to fill early editions. "Filler" and "punk" are the words in some offices.

At the top of the *Times* copyreading hierarchy is a group of assistant managing editors, elegantly referred to as the bull pen. Three usually are on the job every night. They are in charge of the first page and the split page (or the "second front"), after the managing editor has gone home. They write the banner and big display heads and put the paper to bed.

Special stories to the *Times* from abroad, from its Washington bureau, and from all points not in the jurisdiction of the city desk are mimeographed—fifty to sixty copies of each. At least six copies go to the desk handling the story. Others go to the bull pen; to the library; to the reference file that is kept for a week; to the editorial writers; to WQXR, the *Times* radio station; to the *Times* syndicate; to Arthur Hays Sulzberger, the editor—and perhaps even to the Library of Congress.

Foreign stories are booked by the assistant head of the cable desk. One book may include stuff from three or four *Times* correspondents, together with Associated Press, United Press, and Reuters stories. The books go to the cable-desk head, who is the foreign editor. He decides whether they are to be spreads, and how much space to give them. The copyreader then gets the book with the slug, or name of the story, on the outside. "Greece," for instance, or "Trieste," or "Stalin." The job of putting the story together and writing the head is his from there on. He may pick the AP story or the *Times'* own special. He may lead with United Press and tack on some AP. He can move the last paragraph up to the top if he thinks that is the news. On page-one spreads the bull pen sends the heads over to the men who are handling the story on the desk for a check on facts. They may dispute them—usually they don't. Many page-one heads on foreign news are written by the cable-desk chief. The system on the city copy desk is not so elaborate. Here there is usually only one story, as put together by the reporter, no piecing together from the various services. Some editing and cutting will be done by the night city editor.

On stories such as the death of President Roosevelt, an election, a national convention, or a big disaster, a special desk may be set up under a member of the bull pen as editor in charge.

The *Herald Tribune's* general copy desk is a smaller and faster working outfit that is fitted into an assembly line, mass production system. In its old Park Row days the *Tribune* operated a true universal desk with the telegraph and cable editors working on one end and the night city desk directly back of it. Following the purchase of the *Herald* and the increase in size and news volume that followed the merger, changes were necessary. The telegraph and cable editor split off and set up shop for themselves. Today much of the copy desk's work is done in advance by these editors and their assistants and by the night city editor and his assistants. News is selected on these desks, put together and given a fair amount of editing. The desired head is marked.

When a story arrives on the copy desk the slot man in the center of the horseshoe is able to go through it quickly and determine its news value almost at a glance. He picks his copyreader for the job, suggests what the head should say and any changes that seem desirable in copy. He may write the head or part of it himself, correct the copyreader's head or turn it back to him for another try. He knows the strong points and blind spots of his crew. He does not ask one of his political or Washington experts to handle a piece and write a head about a new jet plane when he has an aviation man available for the job. It is not possible, of course, to give the desk specialist his own kind of news exclusively. Some nights most of the news will be from Washington. Again it may be foreign—or local may have a lot of big stories. The deskman has to be an all-around fellow. He can not fall into a news rut.

From the copy desk, stories and heads go to the night desk, the last stop in the editorial room. This desk, operating under the night editor and his assistants, make-up men and picture caption writers, is an approximation of the *Times* bull pen. Suggestions are made here for revisions in page-one heads. Some spreads and banner lines are written by the night news editor. The managing editor and assistant managing editors may take a hand on big stories. Late changes on the first page are made here and orders sent to the copy desk for new heads.

Following the early news conference a dummy of page one comes to the copy desk. It carries the slugs of all the stories with their position on the page and the heads they will require. It is from this dummy that the desk head divides his work on the rim and organizes his evening's campaign. A dozen important stories may appear on the page-one dummy. The slot man knows in advance what many of them will be. "Peace" was the continuing slug for the Moscow Peace Conference story. "Council" designates the story of the United Nations Security Council proceedings. "Tax," "Housing," "Truman," "Atom," "France," "Storm," "Wreck," "Plane," "Murder" are usually self explanatory. A strange slug for which the late afternoon editions and the early night news schedules give no clew calls for prompt inquiry. The night editor will keep the slot man informed of new stories that are coming and changes that are being made on page one.

The ideal arrangement, from the desk head's point of view, would be to have all his big stories on hand at the start of the night's work. He would have time for a good look at the news, could deal his copy out evenly, and get his heads away early. But that isn't the way news comes. Small stories trickle along early in the evening while the other desks are checking and putting together their bigger ones. An hour or so before the deadline the dam busts, and the flood starts from all directions. The copyreader who has been loafing finds himself up to his ears in last-minute news and the desk head is all but drowned with a dozen incoming and outgoing pieces, running a page or so at a time. It is a job calling for practice, speed, judgment—and a strong back. It is a good spot to get stomach ulcers.

With the first edition of the paper up from the pressroom, all desks go to work correcting mistakes. The copyreader polishes up his job. Short heads and long ones are fixed. Clumsy ones are rewritten. Long stories are cut down for late news. New leads and inserts call for new heads. The office brass orders changes.

The morning-paper copy desk is no bed of roses but it does, at least, have all night to get its stories fixed up. The real, one-armedpaperhanger-with-the-hives job is the desk on the afternoon paper. Here the copyreader operates while the news changes every hour, and edition follows edition all day. The President has a 10 A.M. press conference. This makes a couple of eight-column banners. A hurricane heads for town. Down goes "President" and up comes "Storm." A good murder story breaks and leads the paper for an edition. An airplane crashes into a skyscraper. "Storm," "Murder," and "President" are shoved over abruptly and up goes "Crash." Fast editing, head writing, and acrobatic make-up men do the afternoon job.

Date lines cause frequent mixups. Some papers have tried omitting them and saying that the President spoke yesterday in Washington or will address Congress tomorrow. The confusion persists. On a morning paper a story runs under the previous day's date, but the head writer says "today" in his head instead of the story's "tomorrow." An afternoon paper may print the next day's news from Tokyo in today's paper. All this must be kept straight in the head. Strikes will be called for 12:01 A.M. The paper's first edition is going to press several hours before the men strike, if they do, but will be read several hours afterward. The participle headline helps, "STRIKERS GOING OUT" or "CITY FACING TIE-UP."

Many stories or parts of stories are handled in advance, as a President's address to Congress, or texts of speeches. The copyreader may have his head written, too, but he must be sure when the lead comes along that his head fits it. Al Smith was famous for straying away from the prepared text of his address and "looking at the record." A pathetic deadline sight is the copyreader waiting for a story on which he has already sent advance matter to the composing room, and who is compelled at the last minute to produce a head without any real news.

Copyreaders are at work around the clock. Lobster-trick men may be on their way to the office around midnight as others are leaving for, among other places, home. There is no standard for a day's work. A *Times* copyreader may handle no more than one or two stories all night, while the member of a four- or five-man desk on a small daily will schedule enough to fill a mail-order catalogue. Five to ten columns a night on a big desk is average, and much of this may be waste effort that never gets into the paper.

A newspaper may be judged pretty accurately by its headlines. If its aim is to amuse and shock its readers first, and inform them afterward, its heads will display an extensive repertory of shockers and thrillers. When a balanced news perspective is the idea, the head writer will endeavor to get the picture in focus, use just the right word and avoid the bromide, the shopworn phrase, and the wisecrack. The headline to some copyreaders is just doing what comes naturally. They have an essential grasp of news, the orderly mind to arrange it properly, and a vocabulary of short, vigorous words to compel the reader's attention. To others it is a matter of blood, sweat, toil, and tears. Many erudite editors stand completely baffled by space limitations and technical rules. A good news head tells what a story is about, clearly and without any ambiguity. The top presents the main idea and the details are told in the banks, the secondary parts of the head. Action is emphasized by the use of the present tense.

"ONE KILLED IN CRASH," with variations, in an old desk stand-by. It is a bit vague. More facts are required. A crash at Forty Second and Broadway interests more people than one at Hickory Hollow. And what crashed? An air liner, a school bus, two racing automobiles, a ship in the harbor? When Mrs. Roosevelt collided with two other motorists, the fact that she was nodding at the wheel belonged in the head almost as much as her name.

Names are what make nearly all headlines. The most startling of statements means little if the person who said it was of no consequence. Some names are short and fit in easily. Others are a nightmare to the head writer. The head will take just so many letters and spaces. The printers have no rubber type. The bigger the head the less room there is to say it. And letters are not the same size. The *m* and *w* are fat. The *i* and *l* are thin. Others vary, too, and the head writer is forced to proceed in fractions on a unit count of his own devising.

Identifying the various Roosevelts, Rockefellers, and Vanderbilts calls for ingenuity—and frequently a two-column head. The full names of the New Deal and war agencies were completely hopeless. Hence the rash of initials from the NRA to the OPA. Many head writers took a dim view of the United Nations Organization at its birth. "League" and "Geneva" had done for the old League of Nations. The situation worked out nicely when U.N. was accepted for the newcomer. Taft was the favorite president of all head writers. Schicklgruber was smart, at least in becoming Hitler. Mr. Dzugashvili does much better as Stalin. Mussolini appeared oftener as Duce, and Eisenhower is often Ike or Gen. Ike. GI for the American army enlisted man is a life saver.

The flush-left head expedites the job and makes life easier on many papers. No effort is made at balance or filling out lines. The head writer says what he has room for and the printer sets it all flush to the left of the column. It looks a bit ragged and untidy —if the reader ever stops to notice.

Members of the craft on the more conservative sheets watch with horrified delight, and possibly some envy, the antics of their brethren on the tabloid and breezier side. It is here that Churchill becomes "Winnie," former Mayor La Guardia is "Butch" and all sorts and conditions of notables are referred to familiarly by their first names or worse. If President Truman isn't mentioned casually as Harry he is lucky. It was always FDR and Eleanor. Slang, puns, and double talk run wild. Anything at all is abbreviated. A gay life, but hardly enhancing the prestige of the press as a great medium of public enlightenment and a standard of good taste.

Trade papers have their own vernacular. An example is *Variety*, the old diary of Broadway and the bible of show biz. It originated *S.A.* for sex appeal, *B.O.* for box office, *turkey* and *floperoo* for unfortunate theatrical ventures. It is credited with *scram, panicked, palooka, clicked, push-over* and *high-hat*. A famous headline during the 1929 market crash read: "WALL STREET LAYS AN EGG." Its style marches on with the gossip columnist and café-society reporter.

Clarity in the restricted space of the head is not easy to achieve. What the writer means to say and what he writes are not always the same. For instance: "KIWANIS CLUB TO HEAR TREE TALK"—an unusual tree, to say the least. Or: "CHICK SALES PLAN LOSES IN SENATE," and you may think of something else besides baby chickens. Many nice words have unfortunate double meanings. When President Truman repudiated the Madison Square Garden speech of Henry Wallace, a *Herald Tribune* copy reader wrote: "TRUMAN DENIES WALLACE VOICES A NEW U. S. POLICY." That seemed clear enough and appeared in the first edition. Closer thought, however, raised doubt as to whether it might not mean that the Wallace "Two World" speech was old American policy—which was far from the case. The rewritten head said "TRUMAN DENIES WALLACE VOICES AMERICAN POLICY"—and nobody could misunderstand that.

Heads on feature stories can be fun to write. They can be very hard work, too. The copyreader may feel as though he were taking the baby's candy if he gives the point away in his head. All of the holidays bring a story slugged "Day." The deskman who struggles year after year with the Easter and St. Patrick parades, New Year's Eve revelry, the arrival of the first spring robin, the ground hog seeing his shadow or vice versa, the Thanksgiving bird, and a lot of April Fool jokes begins in time to take a very unfestive view of the calendar. One March chronicler did a neat job with: "WANT TO GAMBOL? IT CAME IN LIKE A LAMB." Punning on a person's name has to be very good to get by. A Hollywood columnist turned the tables and interviewed the reporters at a cocktail party. The headline said: "HEDDA PUTS REPORTERS THROUGH THE HOPPER."

Racial issues cause trouble both in heads and copy. The rule on many papers—and it should be the rule on all—is that persons involved in crimes and trouble are not to be identified in heads and the leads of stories as Negroes, Jews, Italians, Chinese, Irish, and so on. They are not identified as whites or as Baptists, or Catholics, or Christian Scientists. On the other hand when a Negro has accomplished something of note the identification may be made as a matter of news. It is no news that there are crooks and miscellaneous heels of all colors, races, creeds, and professions. Riots and big stories involving racial minorities must be handled frankly, however, to make sense. But the headwriter can try to be fair. The Golden Rule is as good as anything else to go by.

Libel is the ghost that sits on every copy desk. The story may say that a person has been arrested on a charge of murder. If the head says "MURDERER ARRESTED," that's libel. "HELD IN MURDER" is correct and is not libelous.

Most dangerous stories carry their own warning and the copyreader should be on the alert instantly. In doubtful cases stories are checked back with the office lawyer. Changes may be made, deletions and additions directed. He may advise throwing it in the wastebasket. He will certainly ask to see the headline if he passes the story. A person against whom serious charges are made should be offered the chance to give his side. And this should be included in the head, if only to the extent of saying that the accused person denied it. Many small mistakes and libelous statements can be remedied with a promptly printed correction. Plain facts do not need to be messed up with a lot of needless "allegeds" and "allegedly's" and the timid copyreader who does it makes a fool of himself and his paper.

Always available in checking names, facts, and previous stories is the office library or "morgue," an invaluable reference point and a welcome aid in time of stress and doubt. Here, for the asking, the copyreader may obtain at once a folder containing all the available clippings on a person or story in the day's news. These run into the hundreds of thousands. He has on call all the dictionaries, atlases, encyclopedias, almanacs, directories, Who's Who's, the back files of his own and other papers, and a thousand and one reference books. The real McCoy of the desk is the office style book with its rules on spelling, titles, capitalization, punctuation, grammatical usage, and so on. It may contain the office blacklist, or words and expressions to be avoided. In some shops the blacklist is an unofficial set of legends concerning what various editors, past and present, have liked or have not liked.

A notable contribution to uniformity was made early in the war by The National Geographic Society with a completely revised gazetteer. Its spelling for place names all over the world was accepted generally by newspapers and press associations. Some exceptions were made, Rome, for instance, instead of Roma, and Dublin in place of the Geographic's Baile Atha Cliath.

When the Nazis invaded Norway the *Herald Tribune* was fortunate in having on its copy desk Ted Olson, Wyoming-born, but of Norwegian stock. He knew the country intimately, and he served as the gazetteer and headline specialist of the Norwegian campaign. On D-Day the desk's specialist was Bob Stern, an American newspaperman who had worked in Paris, passed his vacations along the Breton coast and had a summer home near Saint-Malo. Deskmen come from all over the country—the world, in fact. On one of the *Times* desks is a former Swedish diplomat who took part in the Versailles Peace Conference. Many read and speak several languages. Their personal interests range from horse racing and baseball to geopolitics and Egyptology, with poetry and crossword puzzles on the side.

A great copyreader who corrected astronomers, understood Einstein's theory of relativity, and knew who was leading the National League in batting was the late Carr V. Van Anda, for many years the managing editor of the *Times*. He had curiosity, imagination, a methodical mind, an eye for detail, and the technical skill to stand at the forms in his composing room early in the morning and dictate the banner lines and main head for a national election extra.

Changes, no doubt, are ahead for the gentlemen in the green eyeshade. Some already have jumped to the "Mexican League" and are now radio news writers and broadcasters. Facsimile newspapers may be around the corner—a receiving set in every home and the late city edition a matter of dials and push buttons. But no matter how tomorrow's news is collected and distributed, somewhere in the middle of the proceedings—to "fix things"—there'll always be a copyreader.

[21] LIBEL

by E. Douglas Hamilton

[Newspapermen know many things but they often are weak in their knowledge of the law of libel. Newspapers therefore need libel lawyers, as a guard against publication of unfair and damaging statements about any individual or any group. Editors are required to submit such possibly libelous copy to a lawyer. When such questions arise on *The New York Herald Tribune* they are submitted to Mr. Hamilton, member of the firm of Brown, Cross, & Hamilton, and it is a tribute to him that reporters and editors consider him as good a newspaperman as he is a lawyer.]

SOCIETY has an interest in protecting reputations. It also has an interest in the wide dissemination of news and the individual's freedom of expression. These interests conflict. When the interest of protecting reputations outweighs the other interests, the law considers a publication defamatory. Oral defamation is slander. Written defamation is libel. Publishers normally are interested only in libel and the following discussion is limited to that.*

To determine whether a publication is libelous one must weigh the conflicting interests, the individual's interest in his reputation against the public's interest in news and the writer's interest in expression. These interests are not constant and change from time to time.

Hence, what is libelous depends somewhat on time and place.

* Because of limitations of space this chapter deals primarily with the law in New York. Occasionally, where there is a pronounced difference between the law of New York and other jurisdictions, these differences are noted.

In the South it has been held libelous to state of a white person that he has Negro blood. This is not so in New Hampshire, New York, and other Northern states. When public opinion was aroused against the Mormons in the nineteenth century, it was held libelous to say that one was a Mormon. This is no longer true now that the bitterness has been forgotten.

Every word in an article must be considered to determine whether or not the article is libelous, and at times some matter which may not appear in the article at all. Facts which do not appear in an article may make that which appears innocent libelous. To write of a married woman that she was divorced by her husband in New York would be libelous because it would charge her with adultery. Since standards in a community differ, that which may seem damaging to the reputation of one person will not be so to another. Where it is a question of degree, the test is the effect of the publication on a substantial number of the readers of the publication.

Before considering definitions of libelous publications, two further observations must be made. The publication must identify the person who asserts he has been defamed. Here an objective test is applied. The writer may not have intended to identify the victim but if the words used identify him to any third party, that is sufficient. The use of a person's name identifies that person but one may be identified in many additional ways, such as by the use of an address, or by an identifying description, or even as a member of a group. The name of a person in a libelous article may identify two or more persons of the same name. Unless properly qualified, the writer may discover that someone not intended to be referred to or not even known to him has been objectively identified and may be able to recover.

Liability for defamation, unlike most unintentional torts, attaches irrespective of negligence. The victim of an automobile accident may recover only when the other party has been negligent. The publisher of defamation is liable irrespective of negligence. His is a case of absolute liability irrespective of fault.

LIBELOUS MATTER

Generally speaking, any charge which exposes a person to contempt, hatred, scorn, ridicule, or exposes him to disgrace or obloquy, or tends to cause him to be shunned or avoided is libelous. More briefly, that which naturally tends to cause readers to think worse of a person is libelous. For convenience in classification, libelous matter may be grouped under four heads.

1. A charge of crime, fraud, dishonesty, immorality, vice, dishonorable conduct, or lack of chastity in a woman.

Not only is it libelous to charge that one is guilty of a crime; it is libelous to say that one is suspected of or arrested for a crime; or even to say that a witness would be welcome before a grand jury if he would waive immunity, as imputing a crime. Similarly, to impute unchastity to a woman, directly or indirectly, is libelous. Thus, to say that a woman is the "lady love" of a man not her husband is to impute unchastity and is libelous. Charging a person with fraud, that one sold goat's meat as leg of lamb, or with dishonesty, that an unmarried woman in a beauty contest open only to single girls had been secretly married two years before, are both libelous. A charge of vice or dishonorable conduct is also libelous. Ordinarily, it is not defamatory to charge a person with doing that which he has a legal right to do unless that act is extremely unpopular at the time. It has been held not libelous to say of an employer that he refused to employ union labor because he had a right to select his employees. One has a right to defend an action on an old debt by pleading the Statute of Limitations, hence it is not libelous to say that one evaded a just debt this way. Ordinarily it would not be libelous to call a man a profiteer since one normally has a right to charge whatever he wishes for his wares but, in time of war, such a charge is libelous because under wartime conditions it imputes dishonorable conduct. So long as the Communist party was a regularly recognized legal party in New York and entitled to a place on the ballot, it was not libelous to call a man a Communist. Recently, since the Communists have lost a place on the ballot and have incurred greater public disfavor, it is now libelous to call a man a Communist, and in 1941 was so held.

2. *A charge which holds a person up to public ridicule or scorn, the effect of which is to degrade him or otherwise interfere with his normal intercourse in society.*

A charge which holds a person up to public ridicule is libelous because it interferes with a man's right to enjoy social relations. Mere ridicule, however, is not libelous unless it is of an injurious nature and has a natural tendency to hurt the victim. Thus it is not libelous to write that a man is dead even though it may expose him to jest and banter. But it is libelous to say of a married man that he is being sued for breach of promise, to compare a person to an animal whose habits and characteristics are revolting, such as a snake or a swine, to publish of a young woman that she competed with another in an unusual way (rowing race) for a handsome beau, or to write that a young lady was left at the altar by her prospective groom, with provisions for a wedding feast including twenty chickens and twenty geese. Damaging ridicule is libelous.

3. *A charge which imputes that one is the victim of mental defectiveness or illness or a loathsome or contagious disease.*

It is libelous to charge that one is insane or an idiot or a mental defective or that one is suffering from a loathsome disease such as leprosy, smallpox, or a venereal disease. Such a charge is libelous because it is likely to deprive a person of the social intercourse he is entitled to enjoy and cause him to be shunned or avoided. But it is not libelous to charge that one is suffering from diphtheria or measles or other mildly contagious diseases. More liberal views on social and mental diseases may in time be reflected in the law.

4. A charge that has a tendency to hurt or is calculated to prejudice one in his business.

To charge a business or professional man with bankruptcy, insolvency, or lack of responsibility is libelous. It is also libelous to charge a businessman with a business fraud or dishonor a professional man with breach of professional ethics, a business or professional man with general incapacity or unfitness, or to publish anything which tends to impair one's means of livelihood. Thus it has been held libelous to charge a minister with the use of profanity, to write of a lawyer that he is incapable of defending negligence suits, or to accuse a physician of being a quack, or to publish of an architect that a public building he designed was in a dangerous condition, or to say of a businessman that his extravagance got his company into trouble.

Ordinarily it is not libelous to charge a professional or a businessman with making a single mistake or of acting unsuccessfully or unskillfully in a single instance, for everyone is prone to make mistakes and everyone is likely to depart from high standards in particular instances. But such an accusation may amount to a charge of general lack of capacity or general incompetency in which case it is libelous. It has been held not libelous to say of a dentist that he performed unsuccessful work on one patient whose jaw became infected thereby, or of an artist that he performed badly on one painting.

Included in those who may successfully sue on statements calculated to prejudice one's business are business corporations if the publication adversely affects the credit or the management of the business or tends to deter third persons from dealing with the corporation. Also included are nonprofit corporations provided the publication tends to prejudice it in public esteem and interfere with its ability to obtain financial support from the public. Municipal corporations, however, may not sue for libel.

FALSE NONLIBELOUS LANGUAGE

An individual suing on a libelous publication does not have to prove damage. Damage is presumed. An individual may, in addition, however, recover on a false publication which is not libelous if he can show that the publication caused him special damage. He must prove that the publication directly caused the particular damage claimed. Such damages are difficult to prove and, as a practical matter, this kind of suit is relatively unimportant.

DEFENSES

The law does not allow a recovery on every defamatory publication. The victim of a libel may not recover when, because of the public's overwhelming interest in the truth or of other considerations, the publisher of the libel has a defense.

Defenses need be considered only if one is satisfied that the publication is libelous for, if it is not libelous, no defense is required under any circumstance. For the purposes of newspaper men there are three important defenses.

1. Truth.

Society's interest in truth outweighs any interest it has in protecting reputations, and truth is therefore a complete defense.

A common error of inexperienced writers is to assume that a charge made by a speaker or writer concerning some third party, if accurately reported by a publisher, is justified by proof that the statement was actually made. This is not so. The defense of truth is available only if the charge made by the third person can be proved true. Proof that one accurately repeated libelous matter is no defense.

Truth is a defense only if the writer can prove the truth of the particular charge which has been made. It will not do to prove the truth of another and similar charge, or even a more disgraceful charge. The writer's proof must be as broad as the charge. Thus one cannot justify a charge that a woman is guilty of adultery by proof that a jury's verdict, absolving the woman of guilt of adultery, was set aside by the court as being against the weight of evidence. To justify the charge the writer must prove the woman committed adultery. Yet, in proving truth, one need not prove the literal accuracy of every statement contained in the article; it is sufficient that the substance, gist, or sting of the charge is true. The test is whether the matter as published would have a different effect on the mind of the reader from that which the truth would have produced. A charge that a professional football player was a "rough gent who's discreet enough to slug under cover" was justified by allegations that he had struck opposing players in scrimmages with his closed fist.

While truth is a bold and courageous defense, it should be used with caution unless the writer is confident he can fully support the charge lest in failing the writer run the risk of punitive damages based on malice.

2. *Fair and true report of a proceeding.*

The interest of the public in its courts, legislatures, and official bodies in a democracy is so great that it outweighs the interest of an individual in his reputation. Hence one is privileged to publish "a fair and true report of any judicial, legislative or other public and official proceeding" even if it contains libelous matter. In New York this privilege is absolute. In some other states it is qualified and may be lost by proof of actual malice. Whether absolute or qualified, it is the most important defense that a writer has available.

Legislative proceedings, reports of which are privileged, include sessions of Congress, the state legislatures and municipal governing bodies. Legislative proceedings also include the hearings before committees of national, state, or municipal legislatures and the proceedings and reports of such committees.

Judicial proceedings include trials, decisions, and arguments in open court, all of which may be reported within the protection of the privilege. In addition, in New York and some other states, the privilege is extended to the contents of legal papers which have been served and filed but upon which no judicial action has been taken. In other states the contents of preliminary pleadings before any judicial action has been taken thereon are not privileged.

But in addition to legislative and judicial proceedings, the statute extends privilege to fair and true reports of "other public and official proceedings." It was once urged that "public" as used in the statute limits the privilege to official proceedings which are open to the public. This view has been rejected. It is now generally conceded that "public" as used in the statute means any proceedings in which the public is concerned. There is included under the protection of privilege official action of executive and administrative officials and bodies of the federal government, state and municipal governments, and quasi-public bodies such as bar associations and medical societies when engaged in official action with which they are charged. The report of an investigation of the administrator of the federal Civil Works Administration, an account of an official investigation of a municipal water board, and the report of an arrest of a person charged with crime, are examples of official proceedings within the broad scope of the privilege.

Reports of the actions of legislative, judicial, and official bodies are protected even though they are illegal, as for example, the proceedings in a city magistrate's court, though it later develops that the magistrate had no jurisdiction, or an arrest which later turns out to have been illegally made.

There are limitations to the privilege and they may be summarized as follows: (1) the privilege extends only to reports of a proceeding or proceedings and the writer must make it clear that he is not making a direct charge but only reporting and the article must appear on its face to be a report; (2) the report must be a fair and true report; both sides must be presented fairly; if damaging testimony is offset by favorable testimony, that favorable testimony should be reported if the report is to be fair; (3) the headlines must not go beyond the body of the article and must be a fair index thereof; (4) the privilege does not extend to matter and comment extraneous to the proceeding which may be added by the writer; (5) events which are not a part of the proceeding are not privileged. Thus libelous matter in a speech of a convict about to be executed is not privileged since there is no public sanction for such a speech and it was not a part of the proceeding. Statements of prosecuting attorneys after arrests and before trial, and statements of judges while not trying the case, are examples of matter not privileged because they are not parts of the proceedings.

3. Fair comment or criticism.

Lord Ellenborough observed in the early days of the nineteenth century, "Liberty of criticism must be allowed." The prevailing opinion of one generation often becomes an absurdity in the next. Without freedom of expression, thought, science, and literature would be hopelessly fettered. Hence we find that the law recognizes the defense of fair comment or criticism to a defamatory publication. This defense is limited to expressions of opinion as distinguished from statements of fact and, so far as newspapers are concerned, is largely limited to editorials, critical articles, and book reviews.

There are four requirements to the defense:

(1) The subject of comment must be a matter inviting public attention such as the acts of public officials, candidates for public

office, judicial officers, public and semipublic institutions such as hospitals, churches, colleges, and those who appeal for public patronage such as authors, painters, singers, actors, and football coaches.

(2) The matter must be an expression of opinion and not an assertion of fact and the underlying facts commented upon must be truly stated or privileged.

(3) The comment must be free from imputations of dishonorable motives unless warranted by the stated facts. The motive of the person whose conduct is criticized must not be aspersed unless his acts warrant criticism of motive.

(4) The criticism must be made without actual malice. If the comment represents an honest expression of the writer's real opinion or belief, this satisfies the test of malice.

Subject to these limitations, the writer may express his honest opinion no matter how absurd, erroneous, caustic, or devastating it may be, and he will have a complete defense. He may, as the late Heywood Broun once did, describe a performance as "ludicrously inadequate" and the "worst" ever seen, and describe an actor as resembling Simon Legree "attending a masquerade in the character of Little Boy Blue."

MISCELLANEOUS DEFENSES

There are several other complete defenses. One of growing importance is consent. Frequently, someone who has been charged with dishonorable conduct will issue a statement to the newspaper and will directly or inferentially consent to the publication of the libelous matter in order to get his denials and his side of the controversy published. Consent is a complete defense.

Other defenses include the privilege of a reply to a libelous charge and numerous partial defenses such as a belief in the truth of the published matter, the publication of a correction, or any set of facts which tends to rebut malice and show good faith.

RIGHT OF PRIVACY AND CONTEMPT OF COURT

Shortly after the turn of the century a limited right of privacy was recognized by statute in New York. The use of a person's name, portrait or picture, without consent, for advertising purposes, or for purposes of trade is now a misdemeanor. The aggrieved person may also enjoin further use and recover damages.

The statute does not apply to current news articles, to motion picture newsreels, or to educational articles. The growth of opinion advertising during and since World War II has created lively speculation on the limitation of the statute. It is not uncommon now for an advertiser to publish his views on controversial problems of a national or international nature. The use of names of individuals can scarcely be avoided. The statute was directed at the unwarranted use of a name or picture for the sale of commercial wares. The statute probably does not cover the use of names to propagate ideas.

A publication may be a contempt of court. Such publications fall into two classes. Publications in violation of a court order such as the taking of forbidden pictures in a court room or the publication of obscene testimony which the court has forbidden. The second class of contemptuous publications are publications which interfere with the administration of justice such as the premature disclosure of judicial action or grossly inaccurate reports of judicial proceedings. Criticism of judicial action after finality has been reached is not a contempt.

[22] MAKE-UP AND PICTURES

by Al E. Davies

MAKE-UP

MAKE-UP is one of the backbreaking jobs in the newspaper business, but to a man with the right temperament one of the most pleasant. The good make-up man is part printer, part reporter, part editor, and part alarm clock. He proceeds with the complexities of his duties always mindful of his basic responsibility—the press start is never late; the paper must always come out ON TIME.

Like a good many jobs around a newspaper, it is learned best by performance. The reporter or desk man who wants to know what make-up is all about can read all the books in the world, and never learn as much as he will by knocking about for a week or two down in the composing room. There he will learn the confusing vocabulary of the trade, with its forms, bancs, widows, chases, lifts, and closings; * he will learn how to read type; and most important of all, he will make friends with the printers.

* Banc (or bank): A table or bench set up in the composing room where completed type matter is assembled and slugs are taken out.
Chase (or form): The steel or iron frame into which pages or columns are placed, then locked up tightly, so that mats or plates can be made.
Lift: The changing of one or several pages quickly, as in the case of an extra, not a complete edition.
Closing: The time that a completed page is locked up and made ready for the stereotypers. Closing time is the time set for the last editorial or advertising copy to reach the composing room.
Justification: Making the columns solid, so that when the page is locked up in the chase the type will not fall out. This is done by the insertion of metal strips called "leads" between the paragraphs and in the first paragraph of the story.
Widow: The turning of less than one full line of type from the bottom of one column to the top of the next column.

These are the boys who can make or break you. If they like you, it is surprising what good editors and copyreaders they are. If they don't, it doesn't matter how much ability you have. You might just as well go back to some dull job in the recesses of the city room, and give your job to a man who doesn't know half as much as you do about making up a paper but who can recite the batting averages of the Dodgers while the printers help him get out a good paper.

The work of getting out a paper begins, from the make-up man's point of view, with the decision about the size of the paper. On some newspapers he is in on the decision himself, working with the advertising layout man.

But on most newspapers this chore has been done before the make-up man comes to work, either by the managing editor, the night editor, or (God forbid!) the business office. Let us assume that the powers-that-be have decreed a forty-page paper, and see how the make-up man fits it together. To begin with, we must get it into terms a make-up man understands—forty pages of a full-size paper, at 8 columns a page, makes 320 columns.

As an ordinary thing, this means about 120 columns of advertising matter, leaving a "hole" of 200 columns to be filled by reading matter. Certain departments can be depended upon to fill the same proportion of space day after day—sports, society, columns, drama, financial and business, marine, real estate, cartoons, amusements, news pictures, and the like. In the paper we are dummying they might leave a net of sixty columns for the general news of the day.

The three editors who are responsible for city news, foreign news, and telegraph (or national) news advise the editor-in-charge of their requirements, and he divides the sixty columns among them. These days local news wins the lion's share, but during the war it was foreign news, and in times of national stress the Washington bureau will balloon national news into first place. The editors are supposed to stay in their allotted space, but it is a rare day when they do. More often, it's the make-up editor's job to squeeze seventy or eighty columns of type into sixty columns of space.

His first step is a tour of the city room. The editors have prepared a schedule of the stories they plan to send along to him, and he must familiarize himself with it. Each story is identified with a brief one-word "slug," and the editors estimate the space it will fill. The make-up editor dutifully notes this information down.

Usually there are a number of stories that tie in. The telegraph desk, for example, may have a story from Washington about a soft-coal strike. This would be slugged "Coal." But the city desk, if it is on its toes, will have a story on local effects of the coal strike, and the two stories must be reasonably close together in the finished paper. To insure this, the make-up man sees to it that the local story is slugged "City and Coal." Here the first word of the slug identifies the story, and the second word ties it to the principal member of that family of stories. Similarly, the foreign desk would slug any overseas reaction "Abroad and Coal." And in this way, without ever seeing the stories, the make-up man has no trouble assembling them when they come in.

Next, the make-up editor lists the sizes and names of the pictures which are available for the day's paper. Those that illustrate specific stories share the stories' slugs. Others will "run wild."

By this time, the advertising department has left the advertising dummies on the make-up editor's desk. There is a dummy for each page, and the exact area to be taken up by advertising matter has been marked. Most papers use variations of pyramidal make-up for advertisements, with larger advertisements on the right-hand side of the page, and smaller ones stepping down according to size to the lower left-hand corner. The space that's left—two hundred columns of it—belongs to the make-up man.

One more problem remains before the paper is ready to be made-up. Someone—publisher, managing editor, night editor—or a news conference is deciding what news will go on page one. When the make-up man gets his copy of the page-one dummy, he is ready to go.

Let's see what problems lie before him as he shucks his coat and gets to work. First of all, the paper must be easy to read. A volume could be written on this subject alone. For example, if two headlines of the same type face are permitted to run side by side, the eye will read them together, and the result will be a vague confusion. The make-up man must see that such things never happen. He must break up his page attractively with type faces, type sizes, and pictures.

If his is a well-run paper, he must classify his news. Stories covering the same general field should be on the same page or the facing page. Pictures must be with the right stories, and on those pages where, for mechanical reasons, they will print best.

Finally, he must turn his dummies into a newspaper. So far, you will notice, he has been dealing exclusively with programs and schedules. All these stories have yet to be set in type, and the pictures have yet to be engraved. As the night wears on, they are not going to come downstairs in a placid, steady stream. Type will come all at once, scrambled and confused. It must be assembled and fitted into the proper "forms." The story that the telegraph editor confidently scheduled for half a column turns out to be a column long. It must be cut in the composing room, or another story scheduled for the same page must be cut, or perhaps left out of the paper for the time being.

The forms are filled and go to the stereotypers, one at a time. The stereotypers need so much time for each page, and they cannot take them in bunches. If a story is overdue, the page goes without it for that edition, perhaps with "reprint" stories, left over from the previous day's late run, filling the empty space. All papers have such stories in type, called "punk," "deferred," or "hold" copy. The make-up editor always has them within reach.

Naturally, the least important pages go to the stereotypers first, while page one and the "jump" pages—the pages where the page-one stories are continued—go last. These are the pages on which last-minute changes are made. They are the make-up man's most serious responsibility, for if anything goes wrong he must fix it on his own. If a headline doesn't fit or copy doesn't make sense, there is no time to send it back for correction—the make-up man writes a new head or edits the copy on the scene.

Now the paper goes to press. It is the first edition, and the make-up man has a little time in which to ready the second edition. He will dress up his paper, restore stories that were left out by pressure of time, make corrections, and fit in new stories. He must be ready for a tremendous story, which may mean tearing much of his beautiful paper apart. But he is ready for it, for in his mind's eye he has the position and size of every important story in the paper, and most of the unimportant ones. Page dummy or no page dummy, if anything needs redoing he can stand at the forms and see that it is done.

Meanwhile, the presses are rolling. The first paper comes off the first press just in time to be wrapped, addressed, rushed across town, and loaded safely aboard the only train that will take it to a news dealer far upstate for the morning trade. A few minutes delay, and it would never get there in time. That is what all the rush is about. A make-up man works by train and (these days) plane schedules. When he dies, he wants his tombstone to say, "He got them in on time."

PICTURES

If you must use the cliché that "a picture is worth a thousand words," use it with reservations. It's worth a thousand words only if it's handled right. And if it's handled wrong, it's only a blur on a page.

There is something peculiar in the way most newspapers use pictures. When the half tone was invented in 1890, it became possible for the first time to print news pictures with some degree of success, and in the years that have passed papers have given over more and more of their space to "art." In some papers, there is more picture space than text space.

But on those same papers the picture editors insist on printing a four-column picture in two columns of space, either by "cropping" the print and leaving out a major portion of the material that makes the picture newsworthy, or reproducing it so stingily that no detail comes up on the newsprint.

With that off my chest, I can get on to a description of how a picture desk should work. The picture editor, on today's major newspapers, has as his raw material about two hundred pictures a day from which to choose. Of these, he will select twenty-five or thirty that will find their way to the finished page. To place these pictures on his desk has involved a great deal of organization, planning, leg work, human endeavor, and in some cases the risk of human life.

To a large extent, the cameraman remains the madcap of the newspaper business. He is one of the most single-minded persons in the world. All he wants is his picture, and his picture he will have. It may mean setting up shop in the middle of a fire, wading into the turbulence of a flood, climbing to where squirrels get dizzy or (in wartime) dodging bullets. But he gets his picture, every time, and then goes after another.

The picture editor (on newspapers that enjoy such a luxury) works in close accord with the city editor. Sometimes he has as many as twenty staff men at his command, and he knows exactly what each man can do. One may be a great photographer when it comes to getting a picture of a mother whose five children have burned to death in a fire, but he would come up with nothing at all if he was sent to cover a meeting of the chamber of commerce. The picture editor must frame his assignments accordingly.

In addition to the staff, most papers subscribe to at least one of the three great picture services, Associated Press Pictures, Acme Newsphotos, or International News Service. These cover the same spot-news assignments and in addition keep a steady stream of pictures rolling in to their clients from out-of-the-way places as well as world capitals.

And now, with all the pictures from staff men, associations, free-lance photographers, volunteer amateurs, publicity agents, and the paper's own files, the picture editor is ready to sort the wheat from the chaff. His pictures fall into five major categories:

Spot News: a picture that is of immediate news value, a great disaster, the crowning of a king, a leading diplomat making a statement of world import, a murder that has "lace on it."

Human Interest: mother and son reunited after forty years, a boy weeping at the grave of his dog.

Dated Pictures: not news at the moment, but covering some event of a few days previous, on which a picture was unavailable at the moment. Or perhaps there was a wirephoto or radio photo available that couldn't be used—yes, even in these days of ultrascience, pictures come in so bad that the best retouchers in the world throw up their hands in despair.

Obituaries: pictures of men and women who are of some note. Here the trick is to dig up a picture that will show some celebrity of the past—an actor or athlete, perhaps—in the costume or uniform in which he attained his greatest success.

"Musts": pictures the editor cannot miss, if he likes his job. For the most part, they are handouts from advertising or publicity men, that have passed through the front office and come down marked "Please use." The "please" could have been edited out.

His selection made, the editor must decide how he wants each picture played—one column, two columns, up to eight columns.

Perhaps only the center of the print has news value—he crops it by marking the portion he wishes to appear in the paper. He may have a picture with three men in it, when he only wants two. The retoucher's airbrush takes out the unwanted character, thus bringing the other two into prominence. A good retoucher can do wonders with a picture, painting out one detail, painting in another.

Now that the pictures are on their way to the engravers, the editor writes captions to run above the picture, and the more detailed underlines to run below them. Most papers have a specific style for these, and too many papers encourage the use of plays on words or dubious humor. They should conform to the same standards as any copy in the paper. They should be even more concise. If it takes six lines of eight-point type, four columns wide, to tell what the picture is about, either the picture or the caption writer should be disposed of.

Each caption carries the slug, which is also on the picture and, if it runs with a story, on the story. If the picture is to "run wild," the editor makes up his own slug for it. About this time the engraving department sends along its own schedule, telling how many columns wide, and how many inches deep the day's batch of pictures will total. This is checked by the picture editor and goes to the make-up man, who is told which pictures need a good printing page, which can be left out if need be, and which must remain in.

Then the picture editor can relax, start on any new pictures he would like to see in the next edition, and nurture his ulcers by worrying about how many pictures will come out upside down, and how many transposed captions will result in libel suits. The ulcers undisturbed by these considerations are slowly corroding in anticipation of the opposition paper. The best picture of the day, by definition, is the one that reposes in the wastebasket, and later turns up, five columns wide, in the opposition. At any rate, it's the one the boss thinks was the best.

[23] PUTTING THE NEWSPAPER TOGETHER

by Henley Hill

ASSISTANT MANAGING EDITOR OF

THE NEW YORK HERALD TRIBUNE

IT is a few spare minutes before press time in the composing room of a great metropolitan newspaper. A telephone perched beside the type form of the front page jingles with certainty. A waiting editor answers. Here is the story for which a city or a nation has been waiting—the execution of a Hauptmann, the result of a bitter election, the decision to make a war.

At a nearby typesetting machine a few lines of the story are set. At a type case, which hasn't changed much in the five centuries since Gutenberg, a screaming headline is contrived. The news is put into the waiting page and a newspaper goes to press.

Newspapers do not always go to press with a melodramatic rush, but sometimes they can do it if the story is big enough and doesn't need too many words to tell. Also, they can do it only after the 99,000 hours of work that go to make a great daily have been all but finished and one small space remains. The rush story may not be complete or perfectly written, but it will carry a selling headline and tell people what they want to know.

Speed, accuracy, and the terseness which comes from judicious editing are the ingredients of newspaper making. Complex, expensive, mechanical devices in the modern publishing plant make possible the frequent editions, the huge circulations, the carefully timed deliveries.

Telephones, telegraph, teletypes, electric typewriters, telephoto transmitters, facsimile reproducers, telephone recording and radio listening devices, linotypes, intertypes, monotypes, telautographs, high-pressure mat rollers, automatic casters for press plates, high-speed presses that change paper rolls without stopping, mechanical collators that assemble sections of a Sunday paper, automatic wrapping and stamping devices—these are some of the useful machines that promote speed and accuracy.

A newspaper is produced in five stages which can be visualized in their media of paper or metal: (1) the copy on which the news is written or pictures are produced, (2) the type set from the copy, or the metal photoengraving, (3) the papier-maché matrix impressed from the assembled type page, and used (4) to cast a half-cylinder plate of lead alloy to be locked on the presses, and (5) the printed and folded paper.

The metal steps, the second and fourth, naturally are backward so that the ordinary person might require a mirror to read them. Stereotyping (processes numbers three and four) is not necessary on smaller publications which usually print direct from type.

THE COMPOSING ROOM

As the perfected copy from the editorial department reaches the composing room—the first stage in printing—it may come paragraph by paragraph, piece by piece, or all together. The thread that holds it together is the "slug"—the name which the editor has given it.

"Slug" has several meanings to the newspaper. To the editor it is the arbitrary descriptive title of a story which follows it from reporter to printer. To the printer it also may be a solid line of type or a strip of metal. The editor's slug is supposed to be apposite, terse, and easily understood by voice. If, for example, a story about an election is called "Elect" everybody understands what is meant.

An active, spot-news story with a constantly changing situation can have enough new introductory paragraphs, inserted matter, and additions, with banner headlines, subsidiary heads, tabulations, photographs and captions to match, to keep a hundred men busy. "Straight Add Insert X New Lead Elect" might sound a little complex, but in a running story it could denote a particular place for a particular sentence on which a banner head might be scratched.

If it is true that ten men can build a fence in one-tenth the time it takes one, then the same is true of typesetting in a hurry. The first man to receive copy in the composing room is the copy cutter whose job is to apportion it two or three paragraphs at a time and shepherd it to the compositors. Various sizes of type go to separate typesetting machines, all copy tagged with the editor's slug.

The pieces of a separate story are numbered in sequence by various systems designed to get it together in type. The numbers and other special directions to the compositor usually are marked in blue, so that blue-penciling has ceased to be a perquisite of the editor, who uses black to correct his copy and red or some other color to attract attention to his instructions. The compositors take sections of the copy from the copy cutter's stand in rotation and thus the pieces are universally known as "takes."

From the time Johannes Gutenberg thought up movable type, about 1450, until Ottmar Mergenthaler perfected the linotype in the 1880's, all printing was put into lines by hand. The letters were picked from a case—an oblong wooden tray partitioned into small compartments for each letter, figure, or other character. Compositors could set the lines deftly but the spacing was laborious and all the type had to be redistributed into the case after use and until worn out.

Then came the linotype, offering composition at least six times as fast as hand work, with type in slug or bar form for easier handling, and a new face for each new job, the metal being simply remelted after use. Whitelaw Reid, then editor of *The New-York Tribune,* dubbed the machine "linotype" when it was first demonstrated to him.

Mergenthaler's invention is founded on an alphabetical collection of small brass matrices, with a set of long, thin steel wedges, called spacebands, to space the lines evenly and automatically, and a potful of molten lead alloyed with antimony and tin to cast the lines.

All this is arranged in a complex machine which takes up less room than a baby grand piano with its top up and costs more than most limousines. Large, oddly shaped wheels—eccentric cams—are the heart of the machine, causing its many parts to function in exact rotation as the matrices are set in a line, the line is cast, and the matrices are redistributed into the top of the machine.

The compositor's case is reborn here in the flat, keystone-shaped magazine containing the matrices in slots ready to drop into lines when released from the keyboard.

The matrices are approximately one inch wide and half again as high, but vary in thickness according to the particular letter they cast. In this they differ from the standard typewriter, whose letters are all the same width.

The keyboard at which the operator sits is more than twice the size of the typewriter board. The copy is held at a convenient angle in front of the operator in a flat tray slightly larger than a sheet of 8 x 11 paper folded in half. Thus the dimensions of this copyholder control the size of all newspaper copy, either full sheet or half sheet. The standard newspaper practice of folding copy with the written side out is in part designed to let the operator turn his copy from the top half to the bottom without unfolding it.

At the operator's lightest touch of the keys the matrices will drop in front of him in an assembly which can be set to any specified width of column up to five inches. The mold part of the individual matrix is away from the operator and usually has two molds of one character, one light or roman and the other bold face or italic, one above the other. On the rear edge the matrices are marked for identification so that the operator can read them for mistakes. The top of the matrix has a V-shaped notch with two rows of teeth in an individual combination, so that when it is carried back into the machine it drops off into the slot from which it came. The slots, likewise the keyboard, are arranged in the general order of frequency of letters in the English language, *etaoinshrdlucmfwypvbgkqjxz,* followed by their capitals and a variety of punctuation and other marks. Above the assembly are the spacebands which are keyed into place between each word.

When the line of type is ready for casting, the operator sends it into the machine, whose cams do the rest electrically. The mold for the slugs is set in a wheel which is in position between the matrices and the molten metal pot. The hot metal is forced in against the matrices and fills the cut letter form, cools, expands, and a line of type is deposited in a tray—the galley—at the front of the machine. The spacebands go back into place above the assembly and the matrices are carried to the top of the machine for redistribution.

During this operation the operator will have set another line, and the average skilled man or woman will work just as fast as the machine allows. If a word is too long to go at the end of the line, it must be broken on the next by the accepted rules of syl-lab-i-ca-tion. If the word is a long monosyllable such as "strength" the line must either be thin-spaced with special narrow matrices to get it at the end of one line or wide-spaced to force it to the next. The usual space is the width of one letter and is called a letter space.

As the compositor's takes of type are completed, they are returned to an assembly banc—the spelling goes back to antiquity. Let us say that the story was cut apart and marked as B19, B21, and B22. The operator with the first take of the story will have set the slug which denominates it, the operator with the last take supplies the dash which closes it. The others have set isolated takes, possibly with little meaning or interest to them without context.

Where separate machines set the headlines there is generally a machine and man for each size of type. The banner headlines—the type sometimes two inches high—are usually set by hand from the old case, however, because it is not economical to stock a machine with a font of type which may set only one line a day. Before copyreaders were ever heard of, it was the printer's chore and prerogative to devise the headline and put it into type that would fit the column.

On many English newspapers, which usually are published by contract printers rather than in paper-owned plants, the top line of headlines is set by hand for no reason except to satisfy the printer. In France and the Latin countries, headlines will appear in almost as many varieties of type as there are stories. The type fits the headline rather than the reverse, which is the not entirely logical American method.

Many of the sensational American newspapers keep scarehead type of various thinnesses of letter which are indexed according to the number of letters that can be put into a certain number of columns. Thus, if a head is best told startlingly in, say, twenty-nine letters and spaces, the biggest type that is known to count that many units across the page is employed. The type fits the head.

When the headlines and the takes of the story are regrouped in type metal, the galley proofs are taken on proof presses and go with the copy to the proof room to be read and corrected and to the editors for reference. The type goes to the make-up section of the plant where it is to be put into type forms.

On larger newspapers, make-up in its quieter branches, when there is plenty of time, may start with the careful preparation of layout sheets for the printer. Generally there are two matching sets—one made by the advertising department, which has its special requirements, and one by the editorial department. The make-up editor's latitude varies widely with the individual paper. On some he receives the layout which the editor in charge has made for the first page and designs the rest in accordance with the requirements of the various departments, the style of the paper, the thoroughness with which the paper wants its news grouped and the urgency of overset—the news that the paper has no room for.

The pages are made up in a rectangular iron frame—in the chase, which is an etymological cousin of the chassis and the sash of a window, as a type of box. Steel wedges lock type in the page and the columns are made of uniform length by the use of strips of lead inserted between the lines and around the headings where the reader is least likely to notice them.

The printers place the advertisements, illustrations, and news matter in the pages at the direction of the make-up editors. As rapidly as the galley proofs are read, and corrected by the setting of new lines (a whole line must be reset to insert a needed comma), the printers also correct the type stories.

A common practice in America is that of "railroading" or sending the paper to press without fully correcting it. This is done on the theory that getting the news to the reader is paramount and that he will forgive unavoidable imperfections which can be corrected in subsequent editions. By contrast the English newspapers are corrected painstakingly to the last detail before any are printed, because of the severity of the British libel laws.

It is the despair of thoughtful and conscientious editors when a reader is heard casually to say, "Where do they scrape up all the uninteresting stuff to fill this paper?" On the contrary, in a paper of any size, there is always more news than there is room for it. After a corps of trained men have condensed, shortened, and edited the news of the day into what always seems to them to be too little space, there is that scourge of the newspaper trade, the mountains of news that ought to be in but isn't, those gems that the reader of the edition just printed will not see—the overset.

With each edition more piles up. Imagine yourself as the controlling editor of a newspaper who has one hundred columns of news space at his disposal for the day. Stretched end to end that is about as far as from here to the corner drugstore. But there are two hundred or three hundred columns of news waiting to get in from the staff, the press associations, the feature syndicates.

As each succeeding edition rolls by, the overset may dwindle or it may magnify as more and better news happens. In the editorial rooms the editor must treat the news—in or out of the paper—as a whole and do the best he can. Figuratively, with arms two hundred columns long, he must compress the cream of the type into the space he has; there is no more. In the composing room the problem is one of moving vast amounts of metal to create a complete newspaper with the aid of a trained force of craftsmen in one of the oldest of the trades.

Printing is an art which has a tongue and custom all its own. The rule with which a printer measures his work is marked, not by the inch but by the pica, which is one-sixth of an inch; the nonpareil, which is half a pica; or the agate line, one-fourteenth of an inch, for advertising matter.

All the measures are based on what is called the point system, a point being one seventy-second of an inch. 24-point type, possibly the commonest in use for newspaper headings, is therefore one-third of an inch high. Newspapers are commonly set in 7- 7½- or 8-point; books in ten, eleven, twelve, or larger. (This book is set in 11-point.) The agate type of the classified advertisements which is 5½-point is fractionally not quite the same as the agate line of display advertising.

The standard newspaper column of today, which is two inches wide—it may appear slightly less because of the shrinking of the matrices in stereotyping—is rather referred to as being twelve picas wide. The "em" of the crossword puzzles is a square of any size type and is most easily noticed as the indention at the beginning of a paragraph.

All type must be of the same height to print evenly. On all printing surfaces the "height to paper," as it is phrased in the United States, is .918 of an inch. In Europe and other parts of the world it varies, just as the spacing of railroad tracks varies between France and Spain and elsewhere.

PROOFREADING

The newspaper proofreader, like the copyreader, is usually versatile and widely informed, and is charged with a similar duty of keeping the newspaper accurate. Style rules vary in magnitude with every newspaper, and it is the proofreader's task to be strict or lenient as the case may be. There is an old rule that the proofreader must follow copy "even if it flies out of the window," but he queries or sometimes changes obvious inaccuracies or inconsistencies.

Proofreaders usually work in pairs for useful reasons. On careful work one reads the proof aloud and corrects spelling and punctuation, while the other holds and watches the copy and calls out factual mistakes. This is the reverse of the mechanical and mental order in which the compositor has set the type, so that errors are not compounded.

Proofreaders' marks are now well standardized and may be found in many dictionaries and other reference works. Many newspapers have more or less complicated style books which contain special rules for capitalization, punctuation, abbreviation, spelling, the formation of compounds, the choice of variants, and even grammar and syntax.

ENGRAVING

While the typesetting is proceeding, a most important adjunct of modern printing—photoengraving—is produced in another department of the newspaper. News photographs are made in half tone; cartoons, advertising drawings, maps, and the like are reproduced in line cuts.

The half tone is a mass of heavy and light dots in tiny rows; the line cut is in continuous lines. Both are made by various chemical processes which employ acid to etch away the parts of a metal plate not wanted for reproduction. The plate is usually of zinc, although copper is preferred for magazine work.

Part of the success of the half tone began on so simple a chemical fact as that ordinary white of egg, or albumen, when mixed properly with potassium bichromate, will remain soluble on the surface of a metal plate so long as it is not exposed to light. Simpler and more satisfactory chemical solutions have perfected this process in modern photoengraving.

From the photograph or drawing a camera produces a negative somewhat like the one the Sunday camera devotee takes to be developed Monday morning. The camera, however, contains a screen of fine inked squares which breaks up the negative into tiny sections. When the screened negative is placed against a sensitized metal plate, light penetrating through it lets part of the coated surface of the plate be made soluble, so that the etching acid can get at the metal, and leaves the rest hard so that it resists the acid. Thus the ensemble of dots in their many gradations produces the lights and shadows of the half tone and shows a facsimile of the original copy. The finer the screen the finer the work, but too fine a screen requires paper of much better texture than that in the ordinary newspaper. Any picture in a newspaper or magazine is worth studying under a reading glass where it will be seen how myriad rows of dots of all sizes combine for an optical effect of light or shadow.

To produce the line cut from a line drawing no screen is required. The etched part of the plate is further cleared by routing with a fine drill so that smudges will not appear in the white paper surfaces in printing.

As a rule the engraving is no thicker than the cover of a book and the rest of the "height to paper" is supplied by a metal base. Wood bases are used in printing direct from type, but not where they might swell from heat.

STEREOTYPING AND PRESSROOM

Stereotyping converts the face of type into a cylindrical shell of metal which can be attached to a high-speed rotary printing press. The earliest presses printed direct from type a sheet at a time. Various forms of the screw were used, as in the familiar hand press of Franklin's day, to impress paper on inked type set by hand.

Then came the simple cylinder press in which a sheet of paper was revolved on a blanketed cylinder and pressed against a type form on a movable flat bed below. Cylinder and bed were synchronized by gears, which disengaged when the bed jumped back at each revolution of the cylinder. Much of the finest printing of today is produced from a perfection of this mechanism.

Among newspapers, however, the desire was for speed and volume, even in the middle of the last century. So the rotary press which would print from a continuous roll of paper was devised. Basically, this press consists of companion pairs of cylinders, each having a diameter equal to the length of two newspaper pages and a length usually equal to the width of four pages. At first, type was locked ingeniously into one cylinder and inked from an independent set of soft rollers which spread ink into a thin film. A resilient blanket covered the other cylinder and pressed the paper against the type. One pair of cylinders would print one side of the page and another pair the other.

Then came stereotyping which made a hardened paper matrix and then a metal cylinder or half-cylinder duplicating type in one piece of metal. When this began to be used on the printing cylinder and paper makers perfected newsprint in huge rolls, then great newspaper circulations became possible.

The type form which the stereotyping department receives from the composing room is generally on a truck resembling a high table on casters. Having made certain that the face of the page is exactly level, the stereotyper places the form on the bed of a simple but powerful matrix roller not unlike the cylinder press.

In one common standard process the matrix, of pliable and usually damp papier-maché of Bristol-board thickness, is placed on the type form and covered with a soft blanket, often of pressed cork, and a hard blanket, generally of thin, highly tempered steel.

The function of the mat roller is to press the matrix into every tiny crevice and open space of the type and engravings without injuring the printing face. As bed and cylinder roll together in gear an enormous pressure, exerted uniformly for a tiny fraction of an inch, converts the underside of the matrix into an embossed card which can be read like the printed page.

Since the next step is to mold a thin half-cylindrical slab of metal from this matrix and since the weight of the molten lead will push in the paper in its opener areas, the back of the matrix is filled with strips of thick paper pasted by hand. This prevents smudges in large white spaces in the finished paper, where the weight of the metal would tend to force the matrix back to the level of the type face. Before the matrix is ready for casting it is placed briefly in a semicylindrical roaster which bakes it, almost to the point of scorching, into a hard curve, whose arc runs with the long way of the page.

Next the matrix is placed erect on its curved edge in a casting box which is merely a steel mold the size of a printed page. Automatically, from a reservoir of molten type metal—again lead, antimony and tin—the curved plate is cast so quickly as to scorch the paper only slightly. When the edges of the plate are trimmed and beveled, the plate is ready for the press.

Normally, the plates for eight pages are locked together on one cylinder of an ordinary press. Angular strips of steel, held by machine screws, grip the beveled edges of the plates so they will not twist nor fly off when revolving at high speed. Two full sets of cylinders, would, of course, produce sixteen printed pages, the paper passing first through one set and then the other. A modern rotary press, with units for printing sixty-four pages, is quite a gigantic machine, with its printing cylinders, its inking devices, and its mechanism for assembling and folding the papers.

Since cylinders and paper usually are four pages wide, the simplest device for cutting the continuous paper to two pages in width is a circular knife under which the middle of the roll passes. Sets of rollers and bars at angles place one set of pages against another in proper order. Combinations of half-plated cylinders and paper in rolls one, two, or three pages wide can be arranged to make almost any size of newspaper at will.

The creases or folds of a paper are likewise produced by rollers and dull knives. A single paper is cut off the stream of paper at each revolution of a knife set crosswise in a cylinder which revolves against the roll. A knife slightly saw-toothed works better and stays sharper longer than a straightedge. Constant adjustments of the "pull" on the paper rolls is necessary to keep the printed page centered on the paper page. The paper inherently strong must be pulled along evenly by the press to avoid breaks in the roll. You could pull yourself up on a sheet of your newspaper, which otherwise tears so easily, if you could achieve absolutely equal strain on the top and bottom edges.

The inking rollers, which operate against the metal plates, are fed by compressed air. There are screws which adjust the amount of ink roughly to every column. Most newspaper ink contains a considerable quick-drying element to prevent smudges at high speed.

If colors are to be used, separate cylinders are given over to each color and separate inks are used. A sheet of a Sunday comic section will run through four double sets of cylinders and appear in all the primary colors. Separate plates made from one drawing produce a yellow printing, a red printing, a blue, and a black. Their combinations produce orange, green, and a variety of violet-indigo, with many other shades thrown in.

As the folded papers speed out of the presses on conveyors—an effect often utilized in the movies—an automatic trip can be adjusted to give a slight tilt to every fiftieth or some other number of paper. As the papers reach the mailing room or delivery department this makes for a quick count of quantities.

In the delivery room the newspaper gets its final preparation for sale. Automatic stenciling and wrapping machines bundle mail copies one or more at a time. Bulk packages are wrapped by hand or tied by wire by a machine which works like an old-fashioned hay baler. An automatic collating machine will put together the many sections of a Sunday newspaper by dropping one into another from piles fed into it. The wrappers and stickers which designate quantities, transportation routing, and addresses are prepared well in advance each day. In mail bags or on conveyors newspapers by the thousands pour out of these manifold mechanical contrivances to the waiting reader wherever he may be.

[24] MANAGING EDITOR

by George Cornish

MANAGING EDITOR OF

THE NEW YORK HERALD TRIBUNE

A MANAGING editor I know well could never persuade his young son that his job was a hard one.

"All you ever do," the boy would say on the basis of several visits to the office, "is talk to people."

Whether talking to people is hard work is perhaps debatable; but it is not debatable that managing editors of large newspapers spend most of their time doing just that. Few of them write many stories or even edit much copy. Their contribution to their newspapers is almost entirely through other people. Whether they succeed or fail depends largely upon their ability to blend the varied talents of a large and occasionally temperamental staff. They must be prepared within any given hour to listen sympathetically to problems as diverse as those of a music critic, an irate news editor, a returned foreign correspondent, a fashion editor, a Washington bureau chief, a bridge expert, a librarian, a financial writer, an office boy eager-to-be-a-reporter, a reporter eager-to-be-a-correspondent, and a copyreader eager-to-work-anywhere-except-on-the-copy-desk.

Between interviews such as these, the managing editor finds time to write to a few readers, to consider budget problems (no matter how much the paper is prepared to spend on its editorial content, there is always a temptation to spend just a bit more), to decide whether to use or not to use the four-column text of a French statesman's speech, to see an occasional press agent, to serve as a referee in the never-ending battle for space among the various departments, to look at a few new comics, to see about the size of the Sunday paper, to talk to the foreign editor about sending another man to the Far East, to the city editor about employing another political writer, to the news editor about covering a meeting on the Pacific coast. If he is lucky, there may be a day when he has a few moments to think up an idea of his own.

It will be noticed that no mention has been made of any discussion of one of every newspaper's key pages—the editorial page. The meaning of newspaper titles varies greatly; but it is the general custom in the larger cities for all the pages of the paper to come under the managing editor's jurisdiction except the editorial page. This custom has come about perhaps partly because of the necessities of newspaper organization: there are only a limited number of hours in the day and directing a news staff or directing an editorial page is each a full-time job. It may also be the result of the sound practice of divorcing the news from the editorial columns of the newspaper. With the best intentions in the world, a man who writes strong editorials in favor of a certain policy might find some difficulty in presenting the news on this subject with complete objectivity.

The executive in charge of the editorial page is in some cases called the "editor" even though his authority is limited to that page; on other papers he may be called the "chief editorial writer." In cases where the same person does direct both the news and the editorial policies he may be called the "editor" or, in rare instances, "executive editor." In such cases there may be both a chief editorial writer and a managing editor working under him. Usually, however, the managing editor is responsible directly to the ownership of the paper.

Since, as has been pointed out, he has almost no firsthand role in the production of the paper, the managing editor's chief job is to get and to keep an able staff. Until accurate devices are invented for peering into the human mind and psyche, this problem will continue to fascinate and to plague executives in all fields. Certainly in journalism there is no fixed method by which you can talk to four hopeful young people and decide conclusively that one will become a brilliant reporter, another an able editor, and that the other two, whatever their talents in other fields, have no business on newspapers. One's mistakes in choosing beginners can at times be nerve-racking; but not so much so as the failure of some one of your own staff to do a bigger job as well as you thought he could.

Fortunately in most cases the managing editor has the benefit of the judgment of his associates in selecting new members of the staff or in making promotions. He would be most ill-advised not to seek the recommendations of the department editor for whom the new man would be working. Aside from the fact that each of these editors knows best his immediate requirements, the managing editor realizes that few things disrupt the news room more than for some division head to feel that a new member of his staff is being forced upon him. Whatever the ability of the new man, the editor will have difficulty finding it.

If there are no set rules for making decisions, there are certain clews which usually are reliable. The man who has done one writing or editing job well will in most cases do another well. There is an important qualification: he must be *interested* in the new job. Given a short time to learn a few technicalities and to find out the proper news sources, a good reporter can switch from police news to financial news and be as competent at one as at the other—provided he can maintain the same interest. If he is not interested, no matter how hard he tries, the result will be disappointing.

The first step in choosing new members of the staff or in making promotions is, of course, to study the record of the man under consideration. If he comes from another paper it is wise to try to get an honest estimate of him from some of the people with whom and for whom he has worked. These estimates are not always easy to obtain. Despite their reputations for being hard-boiled most editors are so softhearted that they are likely to speak all too kindly of former members of their staffs—even of those they have discharged. Frequently it is necessary to weigh degrees of enthusiasm and to decide that "excellent" means "good," "good" means "fair," and "fair" means "touch-at-your-own-risk." One also can check facts against opinions. If the man in question got top assignments, either writing or editing, over a fairly long period, one can be fairly certain that the other paper thought well of him.

Many applicants come loaded down with clippings. These are not too trustworthy clews. In the first place, the value of newspaper stories after they are old is as hard to judge as the quality of the ice cream after it is melted. The editor looking them over is not really interested in a Des Moines civic campaign which took place six months ago; he does not know how accurate the account shown him is; he does not know whether the reporter worked at top speed or wrote at leisure; he does not know how much polishing the copy desk gave the stories; and he has not seen the opposition paper's account, which may have been so much better as to constitute a news beat. Furthermore, he assumes that any even fairly competent reporter would have written a few good stories over a long period and that therefore a carefully selected sample does not mean too much. The sample, however, may mean something; and he scans it hopefully.

Seeing people who want jobs is time-consuming, frequently boring, and only rarely productive. News executives are inclined to shun doing so when they can. Yet nothing they do is more important. Every staff needs new blood or, at the least, frequent transfusions from one department to another. The quality of the paper over a long period will hinge upon the effectiveness of these operations.

In watching newspaper staffs one learns to appreciate both brilliance and steady competence. A few people are capable of both, but they are as rare in the newspaper field as in any other. It is impossible to say which is the more important. Certainly the paper would be dull if it were written and edited merely on a level of competence. But those papers which have in effect tried the all-star cast plan have been as little successful as are most theatrical productions based on the same scheme. Stars are wonderful as stars, but are not so good as butlers. A scintillating newspaper writer is a great asset to a staff; but one needs also the men and women who day in and day out produce a high standard of straight news writing.

Like other news executives, managing editors usually work in complete anonymity so far as the readers of the paper are concerned. Normally their names appear only twice a year when, by law, they must be printed in the statement of the ownership and management of each daily paper. Yet they get a tremendous vicarious satisfaction when someone they have had a hand in picking for a job makes a distinguished record. For Bert Andrews, *The New York Herald Tribune's* Washington bureau chief, to win the Raymond Clapper award for the best coverage from the capital for the year, and for Homer Bigart, a month later, to win the Pulitzer prize for foreign reporting is little less satisfying than winning such honors oneself. There are dozens of less spectacular cases. To see a young man without previous newspaper experience who has been picked partly on his educational and war records—but largely on just a hunch—develop into a first-rate foreign correspondent within a year, also brightens dark days.

No problem is more continuous for the managing editor than the battle among all the department heads for space. The only appetites more insatiable for clean white paper than those of the writers are those of the editors. This clamor for more columns, if it is a fault, is at least an understandable one. Indeed one would not want a sports editor who did not think that the rest of the newspaper existed chiefly as a binding for his own sports pages and who did not see why you shouldn't leave out the entire financial section in order to get in ten thousand more words about the Saturday football games. (How deep this feeling is I once discovered when I made room on the front page for one of our sports editor's stories. "It's all right with me," he said with the nearest equivalent of a sports editor's sigh, "if you just have to *bury* me on page one.")

These admirable departmental enthusiasms make for a few tense moments in the managing editor's office. He knows that the telegraph, financial, fashion, foreign, dramatic, city, and food editors are each telling only the simple truth when they point to the tremendous interest among the readers in every one of these fields. Yet he knows that there should be a common-sense limit to the size of newspapers even if there were no business considerations at all. He is convinced that if every department over a six-month period were given every inch of space it wanted the paper would become intolerably dull. Stories would soon get so long that the whole enterprise might sink in a sea of words.

There are, of course, also business considerations regarding space. The trend of newsprint prices continues upward and there are limits to the amount of space which may be used if the enterprise is to be solvent. Editorial people usually are bored by the financial facts of life, and it is to be hoped that they may continue to be spared most of them. Their job is to put out a good paper, not to spend time worrying about money matters. Yet their professional interests are tied closely to newspaper economics. Unless the paper for which they are working is successful *as a business,* their chances of turning out a first-rate editorial product for more than a brief time are slight. A newspaper must be a financial success or it must be subsidized. It can hardly become a great newspaper if it is dependent upon the whims of some wealthy man or the political or economic interest of some corporation or party or union.

No decent paper would decide its space requirements for a single day's issue on the basis of newsprint costs. If a tremendous story breaks the editors take whatever number of columns they may need. If a sixteen-column document of great interest is made public, two pages are added to the paper without thought of expense. During political campaigns when the texts of speeches must be printed, the paper may use more than its normal news allotment for several weeks. But these exceptions do not change the basic fact that there is an economic limit to the size of papers.

More important than this is the evidence that the readers themselves welcome shorter, more tightly written stories. Certainly the newspaper writer or editor who learns the technique of putting information in tight packages without spoiling its flavor or leaving out essential ingredients will be more and more valued on staffs.

Much of the managing editor's time is given over to direct contacts with the newspaper's public. These contacts may vary from attending a public luncheon to writing to a critical reader. It may perhaps be said that most of the luncheons are boring and most of the letters are dull. Yet hours spent away from immediate news problems serve a double purpose: they give the editor at least a few notions as to what the paper's public is interested in, and equally important, they give him a chance to answer questions concerning the paper's news policies. It is frequently said that newspapers do excellent public relations jobs for all businesses and organizations except themselves. Even those editors who tend to shy away from the whole public relations mumbo jumbo may feel that they owe something to the readers who are enough interested to write their opinions of the handling of some story or to ask why they did not see a certain item in the paper. A few letters come from people who are quickly classified as "nuts"; others come as thick as autumn leaves not from readers of the paper but from outsiders who have been prompted by some organization to write for propaganda purposes. Frequently the latter variety complain of stories which did not appear in the paper to which they are addressed or to ask the paper to adopt some policy which it has long followed.

The bulk of the paper's mail, however, contains honest expressions of opinion. Occasionally there are suggestions so pertinent that the editor wonders why he did not think of them himself. Sometimes an old reader friend feels that the paper has badly let him down by something it has printed, or again a loyal follower merely wants a bet decided. A polite answer, even when the letter is most critical, may bind each of these readers closer to the paper.

When readers telephone their opinions or call in person to express them, the problem of being courteous is more difficult. Nothing is more maddening than to be trapped on a busy day by a reader-with-a-Cause. This sometimes happens regardless of how good your outer defences may be. The Cause is, to the visitor, all important, and he ignores your squirming or your secretary's insistence that ten other people are waiting.

The managing editor also sees a large number of people with something to sell: a new feature, a comic, a news story, a column—especially, one might say, a column, for one does not remain a newspaper executive long before learning that everyone in America over fourteen regards himself as either a Lippmann or a Winchell. Not one such interview in a hundred leads to anything whatever; but no newspaper can afford not to be receptive to new ideas.

The working day of the managing editor of a morning newspaper—which usually begins about two o'clock—is likely to be divided into two parts. His afternoons are devoted largely to broader editorial problems having no direct bearing upon the production of the next day's paper. After dinner he joins his associates in working on immediate news problems.

In the case of the *Herald Tribune* the size of the next day's paper is determined at 6:00 P. M., and the space allotments for the night are given to each departmental head. This is the work of the night desk, but frequently the managing editor is brought into the discussion by some divisional editor who is certain that the night editor is a completely ignorant so-and-so because he granted only fifteen of the twenty columns the department had requested. The managing editor considers himself lucky if he keeps the battle merely verbal.

At 7:00 P. M. the managing editor, the assistant managing editor, the night editor, the city editor and the foreign editor hold a news conference. In turn the night city editor, the telegraph editor, the cable editor and the picture editor come into the meeting to report the major developments in their fields—not all stories but only those which might be candidates for the front page.

After mentioning the slug of each main story, the night city, telegraph, and cable editors summarize each story. Here again the human factors which make newspaper editing both fascinating and maddening come into play. Some editors tend to "sell" each news event; others can describe the execution of war criminals in as calm and unconcerned a voice as though they were relating the passage of the dullest and least important bill ever to go through Congress. There is no correlation between such temperamental differences and ability: the excited and the calm editors may be equally good at their jobs. But those responsible for deciding later which stories to "play" and which to put inside must weigh these human factors.

The cable and telegraph editors not only summarize their stories, but tell their sources. The large newspapers usually have three or four versions of every out-of-town news story—one from their own correspondent and one each from two or three news services. The divisional editors themselves usually decide which version to use, but in a few cases, where there is great variation among the stories, they may ask the advice of the members of the news conference.

Each member of the conference has a copy of the schedule summarizing stories being covered by the Washington bureau. This schedule is always an interesting example of the way in which barriers both inside and outside the United States are being broken down. Some of the Washington stories are so closely related to New York that they become in effect local stories and are turned over to the city desk. Others, although dated Washington, are in reality foreign stories (a note to Romania, for example) and are given to the cable editor.

The picture editor is able to show, not just describe, his wares. He brings to the conference the three or four photographs most likely to prove suitable for the front page, and their merits as to newsworthiness and possibilities for reproduction are discussed.

With thirty or forty slugs on pads in front of them, the five "permanent" members of the conference (as distinct from the four "visiting" editors) begin selecting the ten or twelve stories which are to go on the front page. The bigger the story, usually the less argument about its "play": no one doubts that a crippling strike is worth banner headlines. On three nights out of five some event is so obviously the major one of the day that everyone agrees promptly that it should have the lead position. Even in these cases, however, there can be discussion as to whether the headline should be one, two, or three columns; and sometimes the debate becomes lively.

It is impossible for any editor to explain exactly why he rejected two stories for the front page and chose a third. Yet the factors which influence his decision may be summarized by listing the following questions which—consciously or unconsciously—he asks about any single story:

Is it important? If the event is likely to affect vitally the lives of most of the people in the city, the state, the nation or—as so often happens nowadays—the world, then there need be no further consideration.

Is it interesting? The most interesting things are by no means always the most important, or vice versa. If the story is human enough or humorous enough it may be worth a spot on page one even though it affects only a small boy and an alley cat. (Possibly one could argue that such stories are important as well as interesting, for in an age where each person finds himself listed as one statistic among thousands or millions of other statistics, it may be a fine notion to stress occasionally the fact that people are people.)

Is it new? All news would seem, by definition, to be new; but a story which the afternoon papers have been "playing" all day and the radio all evening will not make fresh breakfast reading unless the paper has been lucky enough to find some new angles.

Does it describe a distant or a near-by event? We may believe in One World and yet recognize the fact that an event taking place five hundred miles away has far less interest for the reader than the same kind of event happening in his immediate vicinity.

Does it fit well with the other stories you have chosen? Even if there were five "big" murders in one day, an editor—unless his paper were extremely sensational—might feel that all of them on page one would be too heavy a diet of crime. The same principle would hold regarding more serious events. A front page should have variety.

Is it true? Not all news consists of definite, indisputable statements of fact; sometimes news may consist of reports or even rumors of happenings. There is no objection to a newspaper's printing such news *so long as it makes clear to the reader the nature of the story.* It misleads the reader inexcusably if it gives page one prominence to improbable reports without underscoring their unreliable sources. During World War II some papers slipped into the habit of putting the rumor in eight-column banner lines and the fact that it was merely a rumor in body type.

Is it exclusive? A story is especially appealing if the editors are reasonably certain that the opposition does not have it. To the joy of bringing their own readers the news are added pleasant thoughts of the consternation in the enemy's camp when the first edition arrives there.

While final responsibility for the selection and "play" of front-page news rests with the managing editor, the choices at the news conference are more likely to be made on the basis of at least majority agreement among the editors present after careful though rapid discussion. As the talk goes on the night editor "dummies" the page, indicating the size and position of each headline and of the pictures. Sometimes he has to make erasures when the decision goes against some story which has been tentatively scheduled. On rare occasions he may tear up the sheet on which he has been working—a miniature page with eight blank columns—and start over again.

As is true of most newspaper operations, the news conference has to be conducted with speed. Usually only forty minutes elapse from the time the editors assemble until the page is laid out. There are no further meetings during the night of all the editors, but there are frequent informal consultations, and sometimes the page is completely changed as the evening advances. New stories break which may be better than those scheduled; a story may not develop as was expected and may be taken off the page; another story may turn out to be considerably more newsworthy than was anticipated. The night editor is directly responsible for watching these developments.

This chapter on the functions of a managing editor should perhaps not close without some mention of the often debated subject of newspaper "policy." The better the paper, one is tempted to say, the less frequently will this word be heard in its news room. "Policy stories" are almost invariably stories intended not so much to report the news as to further some cause the paper has indorsed on its editorial page. The editorial-page position may have been inspired by the best of motives. Yet the paper is hardly playing fair with its readers if it prints under news heads articles which are not news but disguised opinion.

It is easy for the critics of the press to point out some powerful papers which flagrantly pursue this method of influencing their publics. Almost all editors and reporters share the critics' distaste for such practices. Yet there can be no dispute that American newspapers, on the whole, have become more objective in their news coverage. The best papers of the last century were little more careful about keeping their opinions out of the news columns than are the worst papers today. The trend now, despite the exceptions, is toward greater objectivity.

Those of us who are engaged in getting out objective newspapers are occasionally discouraged by the tendency on the part of a few readers to regard every news story as an expression of opinion. If there is an article about some public official on page one—or especially if his picture appears there—these readers are certain that the paper has lost its collective mind and has endorsed him. One falls back on the ancient saying that a paper does not endorse crime simply because it prints stories of murders. On the other hand, there are the hero-worshiping readers who believe that the paper has sold out to Wall Street (or Moscow, as the case may be) if it fails to carry the full text of every word their particular hero utters.

Yet these discouragements are more than compensated for when the paper gets letters from candidates whom its editorial page has opposed saying that they received completely fair treatment in the news columns. The staff of one of the country's leading Republican papers was for many years frequently made happy by being told that theirs was the favorite paper of the Democratic President.

The paper which wins the respect of its readers by being in its news columns neither Republican nor Democratic, neither prolabor nor antilabor, neither for nor against Russia, will win, one likes to think, respect also for its opinions, however vigorously it may express them on its editorial page.

There is a field between the editorial page and the spot-news columns which the newspapers are only timidly beginning to cultivate, and which is likely to gain increasing importance. As the world becomes more and more complicated, the reader gets less and less real understanding from an account of a single happening in a series of related events. For example, it is not always sufficient for him to know merely what the British delegate said yesterday at a United Nations session. He should know also whether the speech represents a change in British policy. If there has been a change, he should have an explanation of the probable reasons for it. Further, he should be told the effect the change is likely to have on the positions of other countries. The interpretation, in other words, may be more important news than the text of the speech itself.

In other cases, a subject may have been in the news for weeks, with various facts gradually being made public. There comes a time when even the most diligent reader is more aware of the individual strands than of the pattern as a whole. An article pulling together these isolated facts and explaining their significance, may mean more to him than a dozen separate pieces.

Newspapers have tried various methods of printing this kind of interpretation. Sometimes a few lines written into a news story will be sufficient. At others, a separate article written by a reporter who has been following the situation will be printed. The better columnists often serve this function.

No paper has as yet found the perfect technique, for interpretation can be a dangerous as well as an effective device. The difficulty, of course, is the fact that in many cases there is no sharp line between interpretation and the expression of opinion. Give a staff unreined liberty to interpret and you run the risk of no longer having news columns but merely hundreds of editorials. There are, however, a few sound principles to guide the editor who wishes to be completely fair to the reader. The first and most important is that such interpretation should not be tied to the newspaper's editorial-page opinions. The second is that the reader should always know whether a story is intended as interpretation or as a straight account of a news event. (Sometimes different headline treatment will indicate that an article is not "spot news": type not generally used in news headlines may be employed, or the wording of the headline may show that the article is a general discussion.) The third principle is that only those writers who are thoroughly familiar with a situation should be trusted to interpret it. The fourth principle is that interpretation should be used sparingly, with the realization that only a comparatively few stories need this kind of treatment.

There are of course *news* policies which have nothing to do with *editorial-page* policies. Each paper must decide what kind of paper it is to be. Will it make its appeal chiefly on news coverage or will it seek circulation primarily with columnists and comics? Will its news coverage be directed chiefly towards important events or chiefly towards crimes and scandal? Will it build a great foreign staff and stress international coverage or will it play down such news? Will it feature Washington news or chiefly local news? Will it seek a national audience or a state-wide audience, or will it be content with blanketing its own city?

The answers it gives to these questions in most cases have nothing to do with its political or economic views. It is sometimes forgotten that a sensational paper may be conservative politically, while a paper which is conservative in its news treatment may be liberal or even radical on its editorial page.

Established newspapers frequently seem to have personalities of their own, entirely apart from the personalities of the men and women who produce them. The best of them are welcomed into homes as old friends—old friends who are frequently perverse, full of faults, but old friends just the same.

It is not always easy to point to exactly the traits which make Paper A so different from Paper B. Yet the faithful reader of one will tell you flatly that he simply can find nothing in the other. In each case, the appearance, the style of writing, the kind of news emphasized, the features, have evolved slowly over the years. Hundreds of editors and writers have built something of themselves into the institution. Their work, plus that of the present staff, has produced a paper with a character and a flavor of its own.

The importance of this kind of evolution can be seen each time a new paper is started from scratch. However able its staff, whatever expensive features it may have bought, the paper as a whole is likely to seem a flavorless hodgepodge. Only time gives it a personality. On the other hand, one sees old papers which apparently have decided that their evolution is complete and that they have reached that perfect state where no further change is required. Slowly but inevitably they find that they lose a sale whenever the undertaker calls at a subscriber's house and that they are gaining no new friends to replace him.

Like all human activities the work of managing editors is in turn fascinating and dull, inspiring and routine, satisfying and disappointing. There are days on which each of them has wondered why he did not become an electrician, a professor, a lawyer, a writer (especially a writer), a doctor, or, in fact, anything except what he is. Yet in his heart he knows he would not swap jobs with anyone else.

[25] THE EDITORIAL PAGE

by Geoffrey Parsons

CHIEF EDITORIAL WRITER OF

THE NEW YORK HERALD TRIBUNE

THERE is no one way to produce a good editorial page, any more than there is only one way to be a good city editor. The individual is the center of effective journalism and that system is the best system which yields the maximum product of which a staff is capable. Horace Greeley let himself go in his own intensely individual, earnest way, and so did Charles A. Dana, leading his band of brilliant satirists. The product—in *The New York Tribune* and in *The Sun*—was the best of their respective times. As for city editors, there was Herbert Swope whose stentorian tones came over the telephone to a cub reporter like the command of a top sergeant to a rookie. However insignificant the assignment, the directive was likely to end with: "Never forget, young man; the motto of the *World* is 'Service.' " When the city editor who taught me all I know about news, Tommy Dieuaide of the old *Evening Sun,* had an important assignment to give he would wander over to a reporter in the city room and say gently, quickly: "Want to do a little work?" If in what follows you can discover any influence of this early example I shall be happy, for my debt to Tommy Dieuaide is great.

Therefore all I shall attempt to do here is to describe one way of getting out an editorial page. It happens to be the method used on *The New York Herald Tribune,* and it seems to me a sound way of organizing such a page—that is to say, the mouthpiece of a large metropolitan daily in the world of today. But there are many others, as many as there are types of audiences and styles of thinking and writing.

Let me begin with the question of audience for it involves a basic point, the first essential quality of an editorial in contrast with, let us say, an essay or an article in an encyclopedia. I feel strongly that an editorial which is true to its mission must be addressed to a particular assemblage—the readers of the newspaper in which it appears—a definite group living in a particular time and place. There is obviously a close correlation between this attempted definition and the nature of news. Precisely as a sound conception of news would include in its subject matter everything of current interest in a community—from a bank robbery to a sick elephant, from a new motion picture to the atomic bomb—such a definition by no means narrows the scope of a page to politics and spot news. There is nothing in which more people are concerned than the seasons of the year, the current weather, the latest quirk of humor. Nothing human is alien to an editorial page. All I am insisting upon is the necessity, if you would have an editorial read, of aiming its speech at your readers in the frame of mind and with the mental equipment with which they will open to your page on a particular morning or afternoon.

It can be helpful to think of an individual reader when you write but there is obvious danger in attempting to guess what an imaginary average reader will or will not understand or like. The analyzers of this problem, like the newspaper promoters, fancy the word "field" to suggest an available newspaper public. They spend much time on the economic facts of a community, its industries, its income levels, and so on. Obviously if yours is an audience whose environment includes orchards, or mines, or a great river, you will wish to understand the peculiar problems of your local activities and write about them with firsthand knowledge and such foresight as you can muster. But it is possible to overstress parochial matters at the expense of topics of broader appeal. Let it be noted that a field has but two dimensions. If an editorial page is worth the doing, it should certainly practice the art of flight. It is in appealing to the imagination of its readers that it can perform its best service. An editorial writer must be familiar with the pages of books of reference, and not less with the poets and novelists. Well, the theater and music, too—why not? The richer a writer's background, the larger his ability to stimulate thought about anything. A good editorial writer addresses the largest classes ever reached by a teacher, philosopher, or critic. He must know as much as possible about his audiences, their likes and dislikes, their knowledge and interests. He cannot know too much if he is to hold their attention. Perhaps some day our pollsters will devise methods of rating tastes and intelligences that will be helpful to these great lecturers. In the meantime the old-fashioned rule-of-thumb approximation must prevail. Do they listen? Do they buy the paper? Do they write letters? Do they talk about your stuff? You add it all up and make a guess. The wider one's acquaintance among all sorts of people, the shrewder that estimate can be. A wide list of friends and a broad background are equally important.

Two specific examples out of my own experience may help suggest the type of estimate one can form. Obviously the clearer and simpler a style can be, the more chance there is of a wide appeal. On the other hand, I am certain that writing down to the level of a supposed greatest common divisor of intelligence in respect to vocabulary is a thoroughly wrong approach. Readers like to learn, to progress. Therein is one reason why they read. If occasionally you send a reader to the dictionary, so much the better. Long-winded sentences and polysyllabic words are far more of a hindrance to the reader than an unusual word that is accurately and significantly used.

My other estimate has resulted in a don't. From sad experience I can testify to the peril that lies in satire. Nothing is more tempting—or more fitting—in commenting upon, let us say, the humorless politician. Alas, the solemn reader in a hurry will not only miss the point of your delicate attack but assume quite wholeheartedly that you are a vicious and contemptible oaf. I have no percentages concerning the quantity of these sobersides. I can only say that their letters arrive with disconcerting certainty whenever the editorial writer attempts a Swiftian approach. Be as funny as you can in the accepted American method; leave the satiric touch to more spacious media.

Even more important than the composition of your audience is the timing of your utterance. Space may be more significant than time in the eyes of the philosophers. In journalism, time is of the essence. The best editorial, written either ahead of its time or belatedly, is sound and fury. To state the rule with more precision, the effort should be to write and print an editorial on the day when by reason of public interest and emotion, it will have the maximum number of readers and the maximum amount of appeal. Timing is undoubtedly the first and most essential talent of the gifted politician. Al Smith preferred to bide his time in a campaign until the moment arrived. So did Franklin Roosevelt. It takes courage and self-restraint and great instinctive skill to postpone and delay in this fashion. The gain in effectiveness is beyond estimating.

To give one obvious example of the principle as applied to editorial writing, let me cite the Willkie editorial which appeared on the front page of the *Herald Tribune* in the closing days of the Philadelphia convention of 1940. The race among the several leading contenders went through several stages. Toward the end it became clear that Mr. Taft had passed Mr. Dewey and that it was to be a Willkie-Taft finish. My newspaper had long been friendly to Willkie and the temptation to shoot the works in his behalf continued for days. At the cost of much nerve-racking restraint, the *Herald Tribune* held its fire till the last possible moment, the morning of June 27th, before the voting on the 28th. The issue was then sharply drawn between the two leading candidates, the final shifting of delegates was under way and emotional tension was at its peak. I think it was generally felt at the time that the *Herald Tribune* editorial, thus timed, was a considerable factor in gaining the day for Willkie.

That is a dramatic illustration of a principle that exists with respect to most editorials. There are plenty of media for the slow, pioneering creation of sentiment. The appeal to a handful of radicals, wherefrom may grow a cause and an issue, can be made through a Fabian Society which over the years, by personal contact, through meetings, in pamphlets, in essays, in books, exerts its influence. The point at which a newspaper editorial can begin to help may come late or soon. A long, hard editorial campaign can give vital help to an uphill fight. The point to be made is no plea for waiting until a jump on the band wagon is all that remains. Neither is it an assertion that a newspaper cannot lead an unpopular cause to victory. It is simply that whether a cause is popular or unpopular, the moment to strike needs to be studied and the manner of appeal closely related to the state of public interest. Many a political campaign is started too soon, with the net effect of boring readers instead of converting them. It is a particular audience at a particular moment that the editorial writer is addressing, not the world in general, nor yet posterity; if he is to interest and persuade its members he must be acutely mindful of its moods and tenses.

This is, perhaps, the point at which to note some of the more obvious mechanical devices by which a reader's attention can be gained and held. He must be thought of as anything but a docile student who will read an editorial as a task or from a sense of duty. Your appeal is a single voice among many that beset him in the midst of a busy day. It must compete not only with all the rest of the newspaper—front-page news, comics, sports, columns, critiques, obituaries—but with such rivals as bacon and eggs, plans for the day, advice to junior, and, for the commuter, a game of bridge.

A fresh look for each day's familiar page comes first on the list. That is why editors try to avoid repetition in planning their pages. If a subject is of overwhelming interest by all means lead with an editorial upon it for as many days as it is at the top of every reader's mind. Ordinarily it is a good practical rule after a leader on a foreign topic to shift to one on the city or nation or whatever is of major concern. By the same test, it is wise to alternate a long, solid leader with a short and lively one. Inertia and habit tend to cast a page in a mold. Only constant effort can save it from monotony.

I place great emphasis on a title and a first sentence. You must think of your potential reader as a shy and elusive trout, perpetually occupied with a score of midges and worms, to say nothing of a fellow fish and glints of sunshine. Your task is to cast a fly so vivid and appealing that forgetting all else he will leap at your bait. To put the principle the other way round, unless you can hook your fish, you have no possible chance of landing him, however vital your statistics or eloquent your peroration.

It is fatal to pursue a metaphor too long and I am not much of a fisherman, so I am probably committing some egregious errors of phraseology or technique. But surely the landing of a fish takes as much skill as hooking him. If the title and the first sentence must catch the eye and the mind, the pull of thought must be strong and constant. There can be no sound objection to any style that remains in close touch with its subject. Words can be short or long—provided they are the right words. Sentences can assume any form. The sole question is whether the attention of the reader is held by a steady tug of argument or emotion. There can be moments of shock and surprise; there must be no break in the continuity of your case. And a final sentence or paragraph, swift, accurate, and decisive, that leaves your reader completely conquered, is second in importance only to your initial cast.

If such are the general theories, how do you apply them to a staff? How should an editor train his writers to live up to these principles? It is my conviction that the same general procedure serves all these ends. If you are picking a writer, by all means take him from your news staff if you can. For then he will know your community and understand what its members are up to. He will have a shrewd knowledge of the great and the small, the crooks and the saints. And he will never make the mistake of writing an essay addressed to no one in particular—his news training will prevent that error. Of course you will try to find a man with a good all-round knowledge—as well as an expert's acquaintance with his specialty, if he is to be a specialist. One of the best writers on economics I ever knew was an ardent baseball fan—to his great advantage in his awareness of how the bleachers think. Perhaps I should stress the ability to write above all else—to write, that is, in the general style that you seek to maintain on your page. But I have seen too many writers develop with experience and under cautious, gentle training to insist that you look for style first.

We come to the point of training, which to me seems the heart of the matter. I have insisted upon the importance of the individual and surely here is the key to our method. The editor who boxes the ears of his staff and rewrites their work incessantly does not deserve and will never produce a distinguished page. He will lose the zest of his aides; why should they think or write as best as they can if their efforts are altered daily and made to conform to the personal technique of another man? A considerable measure of variety in style gives life to a page, in my view. At any rate, you cannot possibly get the best out of a group of really able writers upon any basis of strict conformity to a single sense of style.

Yes, there must be an editor—to set an example, to catch errors of taste and fact. But he should change as sparingly as possible and never to suit his own prejudices of vocabulary or structure. Have all the "don'ts" you are interested in; cast out the split infinitive and the double negative if they enrage you. Nobody minds conforming to such minor regulations. The spirit of a man's writing—the color of his vocabulary, his preference for Anglo-Saxon or Latin derivatives, the intensely personal idiosyncrasies which give salt to any writing, are another matter. They are to him sacred, and any interference with them is a sin and an insult. Fire a man if he remains too much out of step with your page. But don't hobble him with infinite corrections. It will be perceived that writing, in this theory, is not a body of learning that can be taught, like Euclid or the French irregular verbs, but the habit of a mind and heart functioning together in that little understood realm of expression which has given birth to all the masterpieces of prose and poetry, major and minor, and which we correctly if somewhat vaguely term creative.

What is said here bears an obvious relation to the problem of monotony which has been discussed. A group of varied writers, with independent minds and personal touches of style is the best protection against that sameness which is the bane of the editorial page. Perhaps I carry my prejudice here, too far. I doubt the value of a stated editorial conference for fear that it will discourage individual thinking. It is better, in my judgment, to save your group debates for particular issues as they arise and present a new problem for your page. My own custom is to ask each writer in turn daily what he has found to write about, and to discuss the news with him individually. Of course, there are each day certain obvious topics that naturally fall to specialists to handle. They assign themselves. But every time that you stimulate a writer to find his own topic, to think about it and defend it if necessary, you are halfway to securing a living article. If after the give and take of a personal discussion you can say, "Well, anyhow, write it as you feel it," you have set free the most precious forces at your command. Such is the natural road to any really creative words.

I have used the words *cautious* and *gentle* of training. They are implicit in the whole process I have sought to describe. If you have a proper respect for a good style—even though it differs from your own—you cannot possibly meddle with it arbitrarily. You realize instinctively that that way lies murder. The compliment I cherish most came from an experienced editorial writer trained under many bosses, who remarked that I rarely changed a word in his copy but that when I did, the change was necessary and the new word the right one. By all means get angry with a man because he fails you at a pinch, or for any other good practical reason—but never because he is himself and writes as God made him. If you do, you will be destroying the only thing that can make your page come alive.

[26] THE BUSINESS OFFICE

by William E. Robinson

BUSINESS MANAGER OF

THE NEW YORK HERALD TRIBUNE

THE business office of a newspaper is the prosaic side of a fascinating business. To some it is the villain of the piece. In this connection it has always been a matter of astonishment to those of us who have spent our lives on the business end of newspapers that so many people believe that advertisers control the news content of American newspapers.

It may be true that thirty or forty years ago there were major newspapers in the country whose news and editorial columns were within the control of the advertisers. I know that even today there may be a few obscure newspapers which succumb to such pressure . . . but not for long—because the character of such newspapers is not sufficiently strong to enable them to survive the highly competitive nature of the business.

The charges of "advertisers' pressure" on a metropolitan newspaper are preposterous because in any large list of advertisers there is represented every complexion of political, religious, and social philosophy. Any newspaper which set out to cater to any one group would soon find itself in trouble with the others. True, they may have one common economic conviction. But even here, the advertiser who might conceivably be successful in exerting pressure on a newspaper would soon lose confidence in that publication, knowing by experience that weak newspapers are bad advertising media. The advertiser is usually too smart to contir spending his money in any publication with a doubtful futur

I recall one amusing but clumsy incident where a group of advertisers banded together to withdraw their advertising from a certain newspaper because one of its critics wrote a severe indictment of a certain enterprise within that field. The group notified the advertising manager in question that, unless the critic were fired at once, all the advertising in that category would be withdrawn from the paper. The advertising manager suggested immediately that the group hold a press conference, with reporters from all newspapers, and make a statement as to their intentions and their reasons. The complainants were a little abashed at this, turned the offer down, but persisted in their declarations. Whereupon the advertising manager pointed out that, while they were guilty of collusion, he was willing to let that pass because the withdrawal of their advertising would mean excellent publicity for the paper and especially for the new critic who, being unknown, was in need of exploitation. He also pointed out that the increased circulation and enhanced prestige of the paper in that particular field would be well worth the loss of the advertising revenue.

Entirely aside from the character and morals involved, it is better business to resist such pressure, and bad business to succumb to it.

In approaching a study of the function of the business office of a newspaper, it might be easier to understand if we analyze it as we would the management of any manufacturing enterprise. Its essential responsibility is the daily manufacture of the product—the newspaper. This differs from the manufacture of refrigerators, or automobiles, or washing machines in that the product varies every day as to size and content. The news and editorial departments supply their respective ingredients, and the advertising department supplies the rest. Contrary to the popular notion, the volume of news and feature content is fairly constant in most newspapers. The factor that determines the variation in size of newspapers from day to day is the quantity of the advertising.

The two major revenue arms of the business office are the advertising and circulation departments.

Circulation departments of newspapers vary in their organization and function according to customs of newspaper buying and reading habits of cities in which the papers are published. In New York City, for instance, the operation of the circulation department is quite different from its counterpart in Rochester, Cleveland, St. Louis, or even Philadelphia, or Chicago. With the exception of New York, the great bulk of the papers is distributed through the home-delivery method. While the circulation of a given newspaper is dependent upon the breadth or kind of appeal in its news and editorial columns, the ultimate total of its sale is affected, substantially, by the efficiency of the circulation operation, and the soundness of its sales and promotion methods. In cities where offices and factories are close to residential areas, and where much of the travel to and from work is done by automobile, the newsstand sale is light on both morning and afternoon papers, the great bulk being delivered usually by boy carriers. The intelligence with which these carrier forces are organized and operated determines the extent of penetration of a given newspaper circulation, granting always that the paper is intelligently edited and provides adequate local, national, and international news coverage, with the proper balance of newspaper features.

In New York City the problems of newspaper distribution are different and more complex. Here the sale results from the voluntary day-to-day selection by the reader from the most convenient newsstand. In the case of afternoon papers, this process accounts for well over 90 per cent of the sale. For some years before World War II, however, certain morning newspapers had been successful in cultivating an ever-growing percentage of home-delivered circulation, and it is evident that this trend will be resumed and continued in the postwar years.

The organization of a large city circulation department is remarkably similar to the setup of a sales department of a manufacturing enterprise in which the product is sold in a large number of outlets having a rapid turnover. Under the circulation manager this comparable setup would call for two major assistants; one of these, who might be designated as sales manager, has the authority and responsibility for the business of getting the paper into the hands of the ultimate reader, from the time it leaves the "mailroom" at the point of publication. Working under him are department heads responsible for various territories which, in the case of New York City newspapers for example, naturally break down into three major areas; first, the five boroughs of the city itself; second, the suburbs within a radius of fifty miles; and third, the so-called "country" territory which would mean everything beyond the fifty-mile limit. Crews of men in each of these divisions call on wholesalers and dealers for the primary purpose of seeing to it that the paper is being properly distributed in the proper areas in relation to the opportunity for sale. Beyond the actual function of this type of daily check-up is the work of developing means of local promotion in the territories for which each of the men is responsible.

Back of this operation is the work of another assistant of the circulation manager who is responsible for the internal operation of the circulation department and its inside personnel engaged in subscription work, record keeping, and the co-ordination of functions which make for assembly of the distribution operations from the time the paper leaves the presses until it is dispatched to trucks at the loading platforms in the plant. In most cities outside of New York the wholesale distribution of the paper to dealers and to route men and boys is operated directly by the circulation department. This is also true of some New York newspapers, but in other cases the distribution is in the hands of wholesalers who operate their own trucks for delivery to newsdealers in the city, suburban, and country areas.

In every modern circulation department today there is also a promotion and research department whose business it is to develop new avenues of sale. Besides the use of general media, such as newspapers, radio, direct mail, this branch of the deparment is engaged in the cultivation of sale to various groups where wholesale personal solicitation is possible.

The revenue obtained from circulation on virtually all American newspapers is woefully insufficient to carry on the enterprise. Indeed, the price paid by the public today for newspapers in America is barely enough to cover the actual cost of the paper, the ink, and the distribution.

That the United States is the best-informed nation in the world today is due in large measure to the fact that the American public each weekday buys 48,384,188 copies of newspapers, and 39,860,036 on Sundays (1945 figures). Counting duplicate readership in those instances where several members of a family read the same newspaper, it is probably safe to hazard the estimate that more than 1,000,000 men, women, and children regularly read newspapers. This tremendous readership is, in turn, kept at its high level by reason of the fact that the daily newspaper is one product which is within the economic power-to-buy of virtually every man and woman in the country. Without the revenue from advertising, the price of newspapers would be more than doubled; circulation would decline; and public information would suffer accordingly.

It seems fair to state, in view of this, that the contribution of advertising revenue to the education and information of the American public is a major contribution to this basic element in a sound democracy.

The advertising side of the business office operation is onc of its most interesting phases. The physical structure of the department is generally the same on all newspapers in the country. Working under the supervision of the advertising director is a group of departmental advertising managers in charge of specific categories of business.

The retail advertising department is responsible for the largest single segment of the linage volume. Its major divisions include department stores, women's specialty stores, men's wear stores, shoe stores, grocery, and drugstores, etc.

The national advertising department is generally responsible for products sold in one or several of the retail channels described above. This advertising falls into such categories as foods, books, automobiles, and aircraft, drugs, drug products, beers, wines and liquors, cosmetics, etc.

Then there is the classified-display department responsible for a miscellaneous group of categories, such as theaters, movies, hotels, restaurants, resorts, travel, garden, etc.

The classified department, in point of personnel often the largest division of the advertising department, serves and sells the small classified advertisements which come to newspapers from thousands of sources every day. This organization is made up of trained people who service the thousands of advertisements that flow into a newspaper office over the busines-office counter and by telephone and by mail. In addition, there are the outside salesmen who are in daily contact with those who have occasion to use classified advertising regularly. This work is augmented by a staff of telephone saleswomen who, besides receiving advertisements over the telephone, daily call thousands of persons who may have occasion to use classified advertising.

In the easy-going years in the long-distant past, advertising salesmen of newspapers were pretty much in the class of the old-time drummer—slightly exalted. He was usually the best-dressed man in town, with the greatest fund of stories, and the kind of personality to which no one was indifferent or immune. Before the days of careful circulation measurement as to kind and exact amount, when advertising was created on hunch, caprice, and more often for the glory rather than the good of the business, this kind of salesman had a field day. In those days the highest-paid member of the staff was usually the fellow who could call the greatest number of advertising agents and advertising managers by their first names. And this fellow was no weakling because, to arrive at his particular distinction, he had to engage in feats of table fellowship which required the sturdiest of constitutions. What he failed to contribute in intellectual depth he certainly made up in sacrifice of health, family, and span of life.

Today's outstanding advertising salesman is far different from his convivial predecessor. On the way up from his beginner's job in the classified department, he has learned much about the practical values of advertising. The top-flight men in this side of the newspaper are all-around competent businessmen. They are analysts rather than salesmen. They are serious students of practical economics who can interpret the day-to-day trend of business and its effect on their customers or advertisers. In recent years these men have specialized in particular fields of business.

A good department-store advertising salesman, who is expected to do a thorough job, confines his work to four or five such stores. He seeks (through study, research, and his business friendships) to become expert in the professional technique of retailing. That includes analysis of the volume, sales, expense, and profit of each store. Beyond this, he undertakes to inform himself on the operation and merchandising method of each major department. By diligent analysis and check up he learns from day to day the kind and price of merchandise most in popular demand and particularly for his type of circulation. He attempts to analyze the advertising of all stores and specifically those for which he is responsible—to determine the changes in the relative pulling power of different types of advertising technique and merchandise presentation.

So that he may intelligently co-ordinate or relate this to the values in his own newspaper, he is an assiduous student of the consumer market, with special reference to the buying habits of his own readers. For this purpose many newspapers maintain consumer-research divisions to determine, by continuing surveys, the buying power and buying habits of their readers, in terms of every important category of merchandise. Such a carefully trained and conscientious analyst can be as valuable to his client as he is to his newspaper; and the counsel of such a man is often sought by the retail merchant who knows that the efficiency of his advertising expenditure will have a substantial effect on the year's profits as well as on the volume.

While the department-store case was used here as an example, this modern method of newspaper-advertising selling is applied to other businesses, such as food, automobiles, publications, travel, gardens, and other major categories of advertising.

Beyond the important contribution of advertising revenue to the cost of operating the paper, the advertising itself is of great value in enhancing the reader interest in a given newspaper. On one hand, the day-to-day price competitive offers of retail stores tend to insure the kind of free competition that safeguards the public against profiteering, and helps to keep retail prices at the lowest possible level consistent with a fair, and often a meager, profit. On the other hand, newspaper advertising has kept the public informed daily as to new products and new labor-saving conveniences, all of which have contributed to the high standard of living of the nation.

The basic reason for the high degree of reader interest in retail newspaper advertising is to be found in the merchant's concept of what constitutes the most effective advertising. Out of the hundred of thousands of items in a great department store, the merchant must select (through his merchandise executives) a comparatively small number for presentation to the public. I can re-

it is a surprising truth that at least 50 per cent of those who get in to present an idea are intolerant of delay, and give indications that they are unwilling to leave their material in fear of plagiarism. It isn't at all likely that any syndicate ever purloined an idea instead of buying it from its originator. If the idea is good enough to go ahead with, it is much easier for the syndicate to engage the creator of the idea than to hire somebody else to do it.

What has been stated above has to do with comic pictures with text—strips; Sunday comic-section pages or portion of pages; panels in one, two, or three columns size such as Webster's or Clarke's daily cartoons. All other syndicated material should be placed in an entirely different category.

Syndicate and syndication are really unsatisfactory newspaper terms, suggesting as they do cartels and combines, the control of vast sums of money, and large-scale operations. Nothing could be less descriptive of the American newspaper syndicate, which is simply a distributing agency.

The newspaper syndicate is an American institution, not generally found in England, on the Continent, or in Latin America. It is particularly well suited to the United States, with its network of hundreds of good newspapers in cities all over the country. Most of the newspaper syndicates have a certain market in the one newspaper for which they operate (like the *Herald Tribune* Syndicate and *The Chicago Tribune* Syndicate) or in a chain (like United Features Syndicate which serves Scripps-Howard or King Features which serves the Hearst newspapers). There are privately owned syndicates that make a handsome profit for the keen fellows who pick a winner now and then, and there are men who have made a good living from one feature, never proving genius by finding or selling another.

With the assurance of publication in the home paper or chain of papers, the syndicate can make the material available to newspapers all over the country at a cost to suit each newspaper's capacity to pay. Thus a newspaper reader in a small Midwestern city is able to read Walter Lippmann, Walter Winchell, the top comics, and special news forecasters, at a cost to his publisher of a few dollars a week, while the same material made available to a reader of a metropolitan newspaper costs that publication one hundred times that amount or more.

The newspaper feature syndicates with offices in New York, Chicago, Des Moines, Philadelphia, and other American cities have become and inevitably will continue to be the creative feature departments of practically every daily and weekly newspaper in the United States. Indeed, they have reached into the newspapers of nearly every part of the world. All the South American countries, Canada, Australia, and New Zealand buy popular comics from American syndicates. The British newspapers published in London are big customers for both comics and columnists. The Scandinavian countries long have translated the balloons of our top comics. France and Germany had not done much about our comics, but they were customers before the war for the more serious columnists such as Lippmann. Hawaii is a good market, and just after the peace Tokyo started buying American columnists and comics. In the war years when the British newspapers were cut to four pages they were buying and paying high prices for American special writers such as Lippmann, Sumner Welles, and several others who seriously presented the American point of view.

During a newsprint shortage created by a trucking strike in New York in 1946, the newspapers were reduced to eight pages but they were careful to print every comic strip and the established columns of comment or news evaluation. A Philadelphia newspaper during a similar newsprint crisis canvassed its readers for their preference: features or more news. Features won by an overwhelming majority and every comic and established column was carried during the period of restricted issues.

The question as to whether the newspaper or the syndicate starts features is like the old question about the chicken or the egg. Feature material in text is almost never purchased by a syndicate unless the writer has established his ability to interest readers to an extraordinary degree in one newspaper or has established himself as a specialist to whom a syndicate naturally would look to handle a good job of writing—the need for which had become apparent.

For writers, the way into the newspaper feature syndicate is from the newspaper and not the reverse, as many writers seem to believe. Get yourself a reputation if you want to write for newspaper syndication. Do a good job on one newspaper, or write a book, or a magazine series. There are no syndicated columnists of any importance who did not first prove their value as writers in other fields. Will Rogers was the exception in this case. He had become a tremendously popular figure on the stage saying the kind of thing he later wrote for newspapers. But he had registered and was a known success in the theater for what he proposed to do for newspapers. It wasn't difficult for the syndicate to convince newspaper editors that Rogers was worth a try. The occasional spurt of a radio success hasn't meant much in newspapers; none has lasted.

It can be stated that the way into the syndicate for a writer is from the newspaper. It hasn't often happened that the syndicate first found the writer. They have "found" him after he has proved he can do it.

News cartoons, or political cartoons, have not been successfully syndicated in recent years. Those that have fairly wide distribution are part of a complete syndicate package, known in the trade as a "budget." The exception to this at present is the news cartoon service headed by "Ding"—Jay M. Darling. For thirty years "Ding" has been distributed to more than one hundred newspapers and strangely, has been purchased by quite a few Democratic newspapers, although he would be classified as a Republican cartoonist.

The good editors of such Democratic newspapers have been willing to take what "Ding" and his assistants will do in order to please farmers, and industry, and the general newspaper reader who enjoys his nonpolitical fun about current happenings. During national political campaigns they just toss "Ding" into the wastebasket.

Let us say then that the comic strip of panel, a new puzzle idea, fashion drawings, or any other feature built around drawings, should go to the syndicate first, while written opinion, analysis, forecasts, and criticism should go to a single newspaper and make a reputation before trying for the great market of newspaper syndication. Exceptions to these rules have been cited.

There is no sound way to estimate the number of new features offered by syndicates within any period of twelve months but it is safe to say that a ten-year period would not average six truly successful launchings in any one year. Many features are started and survive for several years because the artist is satisfied with a small financial reward, but they die out and disappear. Few survive mediocre success.

On the other hand the great successes of the past have shown a tenacity that is surprising. Some of the comic strips considered to be things of the past and old hat among the men who are handling the successes of recent origin, still can show a list of seventy-five to one hundred newspapers and produce a very good profit for the artist and the syndicate—"Mutt and Jeff," for instance.

They are not in the great big money, but there's still a good income in them. Some of the old-timers are doing very well indeed and can't be dislodged from preferred positions in some important newspapers. The rule is, however, that a new success in comic strips pushes out one of the old-timers. Few newspapers can afford more space for comics. The editors almost resent a new strip success and frequently wait until forced by proof of popularity in other cities and by surveys to make way for the newcomer.

No matter how outworn the old-time strip seems to be it will have some considerable following after ten or twenty years of daily appearance, and the followers of old comic strips are likely to be fixed in their comic habits and articulate in their opinions. They write letters and make demands. The editors don't like to face that kind of trouble.

Will facsimile (the radio process by which newspapers can be printed by a special device in the subscriber's home) affect syndication? It may modify it, but in spite of dire predictions to the contrary, most newspapers have gained readers in the face of improved radio news broadcasting. It is possible that facsimile will open new markets for the newspaper syndicate, in its role of distributing agency.

In the long list of syndicated newspaper features, comparatively few of even the well-known ones bring the artist and writer anything more than a very comfortable living. In other words, there is much more money talked about than is delivered. All things considered, the syndicate is a tough market and the surest way to get in is to do your stuff in some other spot and let the newspaper syndicates bid for you.

There lies the pot of gold—if any.

[28] FREEDOM OF NEWS

by Wilbur Forrest

ASSISTANT EDITOR OF

THE NEW YORK HERALD TRIBUNE *

WORLD freedom of information, the right of all peoples to know what their governments and others are doing, is not just a vague term describing an idealistic goal. The importance of honest, objective news and information conveyed by newspapers, radio, and any other means of communication in this postwar world cannot be exaggerated. It is a more potent agency for a permanent peace than is time-ridden international diplomacy because the latter carries the threat of force, while freedom of information bears the promise of international understanding.

World War II grew out of the disintegration of the League of Nations, out of the rise of Fascism in Italy and Nazism in Germany. Both Italy and Germany depended upon internal political control for power. Both stifled public thinking. Both, by brute force, led their peoples into blind alleys of hatred against other races, other nations. They were capable of this only because they were powerful enough to control all sources of intelligence which should normally flow to the people and, on the other hand, to use the press and radio almost exclusively as instruments of the venal policy of hatred and war.

* Mr. Forrest, elected president of the American Society of Newspaper Editors in 1946, was one of three members of the A. S. N. E. Committee which toured the world in 1945 to observe press conditions.

In Italy as in Germany, the forces of dictatorship took over the railways, the ports, the radio, and telegraph and, of course, the newspapers. The opposition was not only stifled thereby, but every shred of criticism from within and without was also stifled. The minds of the people were blacked out. Not only were the people deprived of information but they were held in a powerful vise while poisonous propaganda was pumped down their throats. The pattern of successful dictatorship was always the same: seizure of communications and of the press; poison propaganda fed to the people who stupidly swallowed it, or were imprisoned or exterminated if they did not. It stunted not only the people but the governments themselves. The Nuremberg trials have developed the fact that if Hitler and other Nazi chieftains had been informed accurately about the American situation, they never would have declared war against us. They were convinced that the American people were decadent, supine, and soft, and that our war potential was unimportant. Having controlled the German press and radio and having become masters of all information, they were hypnotized by the rhythmic beats of their own propaganda.

As a foreign correspondent in Europe almost a quarter of a century ago, I interviewed Mussolini in Rome two hours after the King had named him Italy's revolutionary Prime Minister. Mussolini painted a rosy future for his poor country. Italy was to embark on a foreign and domestic policy of peace and good will toward all. Time proved it to be merely an interim dose of soothing syrup, for which Mussolini was applauded throughout the world. Soon, in the press and radio, which were told what they could print and say, the drums of war began to beat. The peaceful, music-loving Italians, who knew how to laugh, were told that they were the inheritors of the Roman Empire. They were rounded up and drafted into the army and navy, and there was no medium of complaint or protest open to them. Mussolini began to build artillery, airplanes, and warships. The economy of Italy was rapidly geared to war. Here was the first bandit leader of World War II. We all know what happened. We saw Hitler follow Mussolini's example.

Japan, encouraged by German successes, followed the European pattern of totalitarian procedure. Here again the Japanese press was completely controlled and a single government source of information was established which through the press and radio fed the Japanese people such a multitude of lies as to defy imagination. In Tokyo, I talked with Japanese who believed that while Japanese cities had been leveled by American fire bombs, the score was equal because New York, Washington, Chicago, Detroit, San Francisco, and other American cities had been devastated by Japanese bombs. Almost up to the moment of the Emperor's rescript announcing Japanese defeat, 99 per cent of the Japanese population believed that Japan was winning the war. This held for Japanese editors as well, because the newspapers published only the news the government gave them. The government suppressed the news and dictated a constant stream of falsehood.

Despite these lessons, even today freedom of the press as we know it in the United States is not generally practiced in most of the nations. Some of the smaller states of Europe have press freedom written into their constitutions and liberally adhere to it. Great Britain and the Dominions protect freedom of the press, speech, and assembly. Other nations boast of laws guaranteeing these freedoms and then find means to circumvent them whenever necessary.

A survey this year of world press conditions by seventy correspondents of American press associations in fifty-four countries, dominions, or dependencies, indicated that only sixteen governments have press freedom comparable to that of the United States; twenty-one practice partial repression such as control of newsprint, licensing, subsidizing, or local laws prohibiting criticism of the government; eight support monopolistic, semiofficial news agencies; and nine make no pretense of permitting any measure of press freedom.

During 1946 there has been built up an infamous record of indirect censorship of the press in various parts of the world. Some governments have barred foreign correspondents from whom outright support in their articles could not be guaranteed. Others have suspended newspapers because of unpalatable articles. There have been police raids on newspapers by way of intimidation. At least one government forbade its newspapers to publish accounts of student riots which were taking place.

In all of these countries, millions of people daily are being deprived of news and information. In many of them the government controls all media of communication and information and uses this to spread propaganda designed to reflect a favorable view of government activities, whether in national or international fields. It was in this manner that Hitler, Mussolini, and the Japanese dictators led their people into World War II.

Freedom of the press has long been urged by the American Society of Newspaper Editors. Early in 1945, a committee representing the society toured the world to survey the thinking of fellow editors in many nations. The principle of a freer flow of news and information between peoples in the postwar world was supported warmly. Newspaper editors and newspaper workers in most nations were unanimous in their desire for freedom to gather, write, and edit the news without interference of government. Note, however, that we speak of principle. To some government officials, absolute freedom of the press appeared to be another matter. But to editors—with the exception of the Russians who are, in fact, government or party officials—freedom of the press was a long-sought goal.

During conferences between the A.S.N.E. committee and Russian editors and officials in Moscow, there were many good-natured debates on the relative merits of the different concepts of press freedom. We maintained that the American press was the freest in the world, but the Russian editors, who had never been to America, somehow had become convinced that American newspapers were for the most part controlled by wealthy owners who were fascist at heart and who otherwise used the power of the press to build up more wealth and power. Thus, they argued, the American people must absorb a constant dose of fascist doctrine along with the news, an unhealthy state of affairs. The Russian people, the Russian editors maintained, are more free, because fascist doctrine never reached them in the Russian press. It cannot be said that the Russians were not friendly, though it is true that we were speaking different languages and thinking different concepts of press freedom.

The Russian idea of press freedom made little sense to us.

A constant reader of the great Moscow dailies, or of any other publication in Russia for that matter, believes in all sincerity that the Western Allies played a minor role in the war against Germany (American crossing of the Rhine got six lines on the back page of *Pravda*) and that in the peace negotiations these Western Allies turned against Russia with designs of imperialism at Russia's expense.

While most news of the outside world is forbidden to Soviet citizens, high officials of the regime are adequately informed. Tass, the official Soviet news agency, brings in a heavy file of news daily. Tass is also the sole official agency for export of Russian news and opinion. Although the Soviet radio broadcasts sent by short wave to many parts of the world may be considered news by some, their function is principally propaganda. Foreign correspondents in Russia, mainly corralled in Moscow, may write only under heavy censorship. It is only natural that their dispatches are not illuminating.

So long as this policy is in force, there is little reason for American newspapers to maintain special correspondents in Russia. The press associations are able to provide ample routine coverage. It is true that occasionally some light is shed on the Russian scene by special correspondents who leave Russia with no intention of returning and spill all. But that is a one-time shot, and is not very effective. The facts are that the Soviet authorities do not consider most foreign correspondents reliable or capable of writing the truth. The question which I think most embarrassed our Russian hosts was that of why American correspondents were barred from covering the Red Army, whereas Russian correspondents were permitted full freedom in writing of Allied military developments on a par with any other correspondents. The reply was that the Soviet generals had ruled against this on the ground that the Russo-German battle line was in a constant flux and there could be no way of guaranteeing the safety of the foreign newspaper men.

As the conversation developed, it became evident that there is an abiding mistrust in Russia of the freedom-to-write and freedom-to-express system. It was incomprehensible to both Russian officials and editors that American columnists and commentators were permitted to write or speak anything uncomplimentary of the Russian war effort. Specific instances were cited. It was implied that our government should have protested this since Russia was an ally of the United States. The explanation that under the American system a writer is able to express personal opinions without speaking for the government did not satisfy the Russians.

It is perhaps natural that Revolutionary Russia, only recently emerged from isolation, should look at the new world with some suspicion. When this distrust is broken down then we will know more about the Russian people, and to know them better would be to like them. We are dealing at this moment, however, not with the Russian people but with the professional diplomat. With the people we have no contact because the Russian government policy dictates a rigorous control of every category of information.

The Russians enjoy the claim that we and the British are trying to enforce our will on them while holding the atomic bomb back as a threat; this at a time when the United States is offering in the United Nations the Baruch plan to denature the atomic bomb and give atomic energy over to international control. It is a good guess that the Russian people do not know Mr. Baruch from Adam—and know even less about his proposal.

It would be stretching all bounds of optimism to believe that press freedom will emerge as a universal working reality in any brief period of time. We are only at the beginning of an attempt to organize a system which we know is right and which eventually can bestow the blessings of international understanding. One of these attempts was begun this year in the United Nations by an eleven-member subcommission, which met in preparation for a full-dress, sixty-seven nation conference on freedom of information to be held in Europe early in 1948. At this international conference will be formulated, in accordance with the resolution adopted by the General Assembly, the "views concerning the rights, obligations and practices which should be included in the concept of freedom of information."

It is only fair to say that there will be opposition to the concept of press freedom at the conference, and that this will take the form of an attack from some quarters on the integrity and objectivity of the press. We will hear much about irresponsible journalism and the dangers of an uncontrolled press; and about the charge that there is no internal discipline in a profession which does not insist upon preliminary training or qualification and which, unlike the legal or the medical profession, supports no central disciplinary body to measure and detect unprofessional or unethical conduct. What this amounts to is the demand that world journalism raise its standards before freedom of the press is granted, or even the right to gather, write, and transmit news freely between nations.

Let us hope that this argument does not prevail. If it does, we may lose the cause of a freer flow of news throughout a large part of the world. It must be remembered that there are governments which will be reluctant to relinquish their control of the press—a control which is of long standing. Let us hope that the arguments raised against it by those governments which must show their hand before the United Nations, will do nothing more than advertise to the world that they have much to hide. Let these governments absorb the logic that a free press is, in the main, a responsible press.

Here in the United States where freedom of the press has been a bulwark of democratic liberty, the example stands for all to see. We have statutes which effectively curb libel, slander, obscenity, and treason. We have no copyright on such statutes. These may be enacted and enforced against press venality if it exists in any part of the world. What world journalism needs is self-censorship, not international censorship. Obviously the world press as a whole may never attain that sanctity which might seem desirable. But given the responsibility of freedom, it will be more alert and will more clearly approach standards of conduct which are so apparent today in nations where the press has long been free.

The means of raising press standards is first of all to free the press of government control, of government intimidation, thus permitting the free publication of news and comment. Of this any honest government should have no fear. That is the first and most essential step.

The American press and American editors are taking the lead today in an effort to spread press freedom throughout the world. It is their hope that other peoples who have never known the blessings and advantages of press freedom may one day be capable of contributing toward peace through international understanding, which in this atomic age is the greatest hope of civilization.

[29] WHAT NEXT?

by Fitzhugh Turner

THERE are those in this dawn of the Buck Rogers era who maintain that the newspaper is on the way to join such institutions as the bustle and the five-cent beer—that the printed page is doomed by the approach of television, facsimile broadcasting, and heaven only knows what else. Maybe so, but the day that Mr. John Citizen runs an antenna out of his collar, swallows a pill, and subconsciously absorbs the news is probably some time off. Nobody now in the newspaper business expects the profession to blow up in his face during his lifetime.

The prospect, rather, is that technological developments, while they will change newspapers, will stimulate, not supplant them. Evidence to support this outlook can be found in the industry's recent rather embarrassing experience with radio. As a preface to a discussion of the future, it might be well to give this experience brief examination.

Back in the 1920's, viewers-with-alarm, heeding the first broadcasts of news events, looked into the future, and cried gloomily that this new thing, radio, some day was going to put them out of work. With the news available first hand and early, they argued, who was going to bother to read it second hand and late?

Anxiety at first was confined largely to editorial departments, but with the depression years it moved into business offices. Hard-pressed publishers, accustomed to viewing the news as something much like personal property, began to give way to jealousy of the growing slice radio was cutting from the advertising dollar. As a result, many newspapers banned radio publicity, and some even refused to publish bare program listings, possibly on the theory that if they pretended radio wasn't there, it might go away. Unfriendliness grew into hostility, and in 1933, to forestall what it asserted was becoming "unfair competition," the newspaper industry took steps to reduce radio's access to news reports. This it accomplished by creating the short-lived, so-called Press Radio Bureau, which limited broadcasters to bulletins of "transcendent importance" plus the piddling allotment of two five-minute news digests daily.

The result was what might have been expected. Networks, forced to it, began to develop their own news facilities, and a newcomer, Transradio Press, entered the field of newsgathering. Surprised and scared, the established press associations began to falter within a year, then reversed themselves, and went actively into radio. International News Service and United Press were first to go into the selling of news reports for broadcast in a big way; Associated Press followed in 1940 through its subsidiary, Press Association Inc.

Meanwhile there was imminent bloodshed in Europe. *Anschluss* and Munich took the nation's attention, and radio rose to the occasion. As World War II brewed, broke out, and spread, broadcasters developed news and commentary programs to keep rapid pace with heightening public interest. One network, Columbia Broadcasting System, increased its news programs from a total of 581 hours in 1939 to 1,491 hours in 1944. Another, National Broadcasting Company, devoted less than 3 per cent of its total program hours to news in 1939, more than 20 per cent in 1944. By 1945, although total news time was reduced substantially with the end of combat, radio was claiming to have become the primary source of information for 61 per cent of the nation's radio-owning families.

In the light of its previous attitude, the newspaper industry should have been horrified by all this. Rather, with the years, while they watched broadcasting take its inevitable place in the news spectrum, publishers sensibly moved over and made room for radio as a natural companion to the newspaper. Individually, many of them helped the process along from the beginning. Thus, as of September, 1946, of the country's 943 radio stations 274 were newspaper controlled, many publishers hope to establish themselves in frequency-modulation broadcasting, and even those publishers without radio interests work hand in glove with broadcasters.

As an aside, it should be pointed out that this process is part of a whole which has occasioned distress in some quarters. Intramural competition, the depression and changing times have reduced the number of daily newspapers from possibly 2,000 in the 1920's to 1,763 at this writing, and have brought consolidations resulting commonly in the one-newspaper town, sometimes with the single publication also controlling a radio transmitter. Local monopoly of dissemination of the news is a subject in itself; suffice it to say here that the publisher or broadcaster willing to corner the market and peddle a second-rate product is assuring himself only of eventual demise. As for supposed dangers to the community, the argument appears to be based on the notion that newspapers can sway opinion as their whims direct. Actually, let them stray from their appointed field of information and the public rapidly gets wise. You don't have to look past William Randolph Hearst to see how little influence is exerted by lopsided, opinionated reporting, while President Roosevelt's three election victories point to a well-discussed moral: When newspaper editorial pages lose track of the public mind, the public simply ignores them.

To get back to radio, publishers have learned that in the job at hand, radio and the newspapers supplement each other, and that the combination of the two gives the public a more complete understanding of events as they occur. Oversimplified and translated broadly into terms of the individual, the theory is that the newspaper reader follows radio for new developments, the radio listener goes to his newspaper for more details and for the all-important summing up in print.

This two-fold titillation of the public attention unquestionably will extend to television when that service moves in on radio. Newspapers may notice it even more. It is an adage as old as the business that the reader who was there is the reader who turns first to the report of the event when he gets his morning edition. Radio's dramatic play-by-play accounts of football games, as an example, have interested more and more people in the sport, more and more have crowded into stadiums because of that interest, and more and more have followed that interest into the sports columns of their newspapers. Add to the man who was there in person the man who was there vicariously through television—all sides agree television will draw greater "listening crowds" than radio—and newspaper readership grows accordingly.

Television has a great future in presentation of sports contests, political conventions, celebrations, ceremonies, and all the other foreseeable events which make up a large proportion of the body of the news. Doubtless it also will go in for extensive spot news coverage. Along with newsreel and newspaper photographers, television cameramen will be on hand at the big fires of the future, will be at the pier to meet the survivors of the shipwreck, will be at the scene to report the aftermath of the plane crash. Television even may be set up to cover trials and deliberations of legislative bodies.

Already an existing medium, television is not too far away from its future in mass-audience coverage of news stories. Obviously, it will have to be reckoned with. Radio has reduced the urgency of the news; television should further emphasize the newspaper's job of adding background and significance, and this will require new and more exacting techniques of the newspaper reporter and editor. But newspapers will not be alone; there will be new considerations also in other fields, for instance, politics. Television offered a preview of one phase of its future at the first sessions of the United Nations Security Council at Hunter College, New York City, in the spring of 1946. To a few sets, television cameras sent visual coverage of the proceedings, and despite technical deficiencies did it so well that correspondents squeezed out of the crowded meeting chamber were able to follow the sessions intelligently by watching the flickering screen. But the camera, during one important speech, wandered from face to face along the council table, and focused on a key diplomat clearly seen to be fast asleep in his chair. The present generation of politicians has lived to see the importance of a good radio voice; future generations will see the additional importance of videogenic features and of acting ability, or at least presence of mind before the cameras.

Great news medium though it may come to be, television certainly is not going to confine itself to the field of news. Here comes worry over that advertising dollar again. Prophets of video foresee a a sort of golden age of advertising ahead, and if they can solve problems of terrific expense and proper presentation, they may be right. The prospect nevertheless fails to gray the hairs of newspaper business managers. Present indications seem to be that sponsored television will follow the pattern of sponsored radio: entertainment plus the interpolated commercial. Thus the real competition will be directed not against publications, but against such enterprises as the motion picture and the stage, with the wherewithal, or most of it, coming from the advertising funds now going to standard radio.

Remember that at this late date, if radio seems to be rolling in advertising money, newspapers, those which have met the challenge of the times and survived, are doing all right too. Radio advertising, confined by its own limitations largely to institutional copy, never was able to replace newspaper advertising. Television advertising seems destined to operate in another confined field, that of demonstration, a function not properly belonging to newspapers.

Besides, it faces tremendous problems of selling itself to its audience, once it has passed the novelty stage. Even if television does bring into the home a first-rate demonstration of, say, a vacuum cleaner in use, who is going to want to sit around the house watching a screen on which somebody is demonstrating a vacuum cleaner?

Finally, as with everything in the world of ideas, the spoken word plus mere transitory pictures cannot substitute for the written word any more than can the spoken word alone. Sounds and pictures can supplement, as we have noted, but there is nothing to show that they can replace. And not until the human mind can turn successfully elsewhere for retainable information and ideas will the printed page become obsolete.

Then how about facsimile broadcasting? Here is a combination of radio and the printed page, a mechanism which delivers a newspaper, or reasonable facsimile thereof, by radio impulse. Even in its primitive state, facsimile is an established accomplishment ready to be reckoned with. The receiving machine, certain to be refined in the future, already is a compact cabinet no higher than a small boy, no bulkier than a phonograph. It can produce in three and a half minutes a four-column page about a quarter the size of a standard newspaper page, duplicating art and advertising as well as type.

"Fax," as its familiars know it, certainly would seem at first glance to pose a serious threat to newspapers. But look at it more closely and it, too, turns into a supplementary rather than a primary activity. The day is not too distant, for instance, when passengers on a ship at sea or an airplane in flight will be able to unroll from a facsimile receiver a bantam copy of one of the great American newspapers, complete down to stock quotations and as recent as the edition then being sold on the street at home. The wealthy sportsman will have a facsimile receiver in his hunting lodge, the distant mining camp will be equipped with the machine. It seems clear that so far as newspapers are concerned, facsimile will be used to overcome difficulties of delivery to isolated readers, before it achieves more widespread use.

At future best, and this is a faint and hazardous eventuality laden with qualifications, facsimile may absorb one branch of the newspaper, the circulation department. When (and if) that happens, there will be a receiver in every home, and the roar of the presses will be stilled in newspaper offices. A master copy, after it has been written, set and made up, will be delivered to the radio transmitter instead.

This prospect is too dim for real discussion, but it does bring on a few obvious questions. The reader of *The New York Herald Tribune* now pays five cents for a newspaper containing two cents worth of raw newsprint alone; on Sundays, for fifteen cents, he gets seven to nine cents in newsprint. He doesn't begin to pay the cost of production, which is borne mostly by advertisers. Who and how much will the reader pay for the more expensive paper used by the facsimile machine? Who, indeed, will pay for the machine itself?

According to the facsimile people, it will all be worked out. One suggestion is that the advertiser will give away blank "fax" paper free, first imprinting a selling message on the reverse side. Another is that the transmitted copy will include coupons offering savings on merchandise, thus helping the set owner to defray costs. Be that as it may, it would seem that facsimile may be ruled out for mass newspaper distribution on other grounds. A modern newspaper can be produced with almost unbelievable speed. The glut of news events is not so heavy that the process of facsimile actually can hasten delivery of a daily news budget to city homes by much of a margin, particularly if the newspaper seeks to present more than the bald facts already being distributed by radio or television. Subtract expense and inconvenience, and there still remains little choice between the newspaper delivered in the parlor and the newspaper dropped on the front doorstep. Where metropolitan street sales are concerned there can be no choice at all, at least until some future genius invents a facsimile receiver which can be carried about in the vest pocket.

Meanwhile facsimile's backers grant that their immediate future lies outside the transmission of newspapers. They look for revenue not from this source, but from new advertising services to business and the home, with emphasis on their ability to provide a permanent record of matter transmitted by radio or wire. They speak of bombarding the set owner with dodgers and handbills, and, as a future possibility, of a radio program in which an announcer talks about preparation of dinner while the machine records the recipes in writing for the listening housewife. Without reference to home reception, and here they seem on surer ground, they promise important uses for facsimile in the field of communications. Point-to-point facsimile transmission of news copy—cheaper, faster, and more accurate than cable, radio, or even telephone, or teletype—is in the making. As wirephoto has revolutionized the distribution of news pictures among cities, so facsimile may revolutionize the distribution of news itself.

Other new things are in store for newspapers. Full color printing of advertisements and pictures seems inevitable, although it has far to go technically before it merits too much attention. *The Minneapolis Star-Journal, The Chicago Tribune, The New Orleans Times-Picayune* and *The Los Angeles Times* are papers which have done much in this direction, and United Feature Syndicate has followed recently by offering matted daily comic strips, notably "Li'l Abner," in color. Clearer pictures, more legible type faces, are coming. The stroboscopic flash gun for cameras opens new vistas in news photography. The walkie-talkie radio and mobile telephone should find a place in certain news assignments for reporters; the portable wirephoto transmitter undoubtedly will be used more widely. Faster and better stereotyping and press equipment will improve reproduction. Newspapers as never before are encouraging research in mechanical advancements expected to bear fruit all along the line.

The two newspapers more or less national in scope, the *Herald Tribune* and *The New York Times,* before long will be sold throughout the country on the morning of publication. The *Herald Tribune* already delivers its late city edition to Washington in time for the breakfast table and its city edition as far as Cleveland, Chicago, and Miami. No fancy electronic gadget makes this possible; it's done by so old-fashioned an invention as the airplane. When stratosphere freight flying becomes general, San Franciscans who want the New York newspapers, with their augmented national and foreign news, will find them available in the morning along with their own *Chronicle* and *Examiner,* for supplementary reading.

From the standpoint of content, newspapers have been undergoing a gradual change for years. Radio has brought new approaches to the news, the weekly news magazines have exerted influence, the nature of the news itself has changed. The old extra, which brought the first word of a world-shattering event, has all but disappeared; radio does the job better and faster. It is not enough any longer, if it ever was, to present the bare facts in print; the background and import of the story at hand have become essential too. Newspapers now attempt to combine in readable, concise, objective form the new facts which make the story timely, the allied facts which make it important or interesting, and, all together, to present an interpretive summing up of events during the twenty-four hours preceding publication—history, as it were, on a day-to-day basis, in print, directed to a public which already has had access to the fabric of the news through radio.

The last fifteen years, including the late depression and the recent war, have brought on an over-all improvement, believe it or not, in public intelligence and public taste. A companion phenomenon has been attraction to the newspaper business of a different kind of editorial employee, educated, serious, ambitious, and frequently competent. This is nothing new; by this time the stalwarts of the roaring twenties have all but disappeared from the trade. So scarce are they now that recently when the Ben Hecht-Charles MacArthur play, *The Front Page,* was revived in New York, young newspaper gentlemen in the audience, with unaccustomed irreverence, remarked that it was a shame and a lie to palm off on the public reporters like those inhabiting the play's Chicago criminal courts pressroom. Actually it was not so long ago that such characters dominated the business in newspaper towns like Chicago and San Francisco, and were part of it everywhere else.

The trend to more capable writers and editors is going to continue as newspapers cope with the job ahead. Partly because of the Newspaper Guild, partly because of higher standards, newspaper pay is going to continue upward. As many a city editor has observed, you can't cover diplomatic struggles, political revolutions, and economic convulsions with a flock of chronic police reporters.

The newspaper of the future, some authorities say, is going to be a vastly changed article in make-up and physical appearance. A monograph published in 1937 by the Columbia University Graduate School of Journalism predicted an eventual newspaper consisting of an outline of the news, boiled down to a summary on the front page and expanded inside the paper under stock heads like Labor, Business, Foreign News, and Crime. This was an extreme view, based on what was then the ascendancy of the weekly news magazine (another newspaper competitor which turned out to offer a supplementary service in a separate niche). But it noted the need for clarity of organization, and newspapers followed through by departmentalizing themselves. If they have retained headlines and left off the labels, it is a stupid reader who can't learn in a few days where to look for what. It seems doubtful that the basic newspaper format, or for that matter the fundamental newspaper treatment of the subject, is due to undergo real change. While there is considerable room for refinement and for improvement in all directions, it is difficult to look forward to a time when standards of bright make-up, imaginative editing, and accurate, well-handled reporting will have altered substantially the kind of newspaper which is the ideal, right now.

Mechanically, as we have seen, there are new things in store. The staff of the *Times-Picayune,* and occupants of buildings around that newspaper's plant on Lafayette Square in New Orleans, will never forget the edition of a few years ago which contained a whisky advertisement in full color, featuring a julep recipe, the green ink loaded with the pungent odor of mint to make the page smellable as well as readable. If sixty-four pages of that kind of thing ever pops into your living room from a facsimile set, there will be no question about it—the newspaper business will have arrived for sure.